Peninsular and
Waterloo General

Peninsular and Waterloo General

Sir Denis Pack and
the War against Napoleon

Marcus de la Poer Beresford

Foreword by
Rory Muir

Pen & Sword
MILITARY

AN IMPRINT OF PEN & SWORD BOOKS LTD
YORKSHIRE – PHILADELPHIA

First published in Great Britain in 2022 by
PEN & SWORD MILITARY
an imprint of Pen & Sword Books Ltd
Yorkshire – Philadelphia

ISBN 978-1-39908-320-1

Typeset by Concept, Huddersfield, West Yorkshire, HD4 5JL.
Printed and bound in England by CPI Group (UK) Ltd, Croydon CR0 4YY.

Pen & Sword Books Ltd incorporates the Imprints of Aviation, Atlas, Family History, Fiction, Maritime, Military, Discovery, Politics, History, Archaeology, Select, Wharncliffe Local History, Wharncliffe True Crime, Military Classics, Wharncliffe Transport, Leo Cooper, The Praetorian Press, Remember When, White Owl, Seaforth Publishing and Frontline Books.

For a complete list of Pen & Sword titles please contact
PEN & SWORD BOOKS LTD
47 Church Street, Barnsley, South Yorkshire, S70 2AS, England
E-mail: enquiries@pen-and-sword.co.uk
Website: www.pen-and-sword.co.uk
or
PEN & SWORD BOOKS
1950 Lawrence Rd, Havertown, PA 19083, USA
E-mail: uspen-and-sword@casematepublishers.com
Website: www.penandswordbooks.com

Contents

List of Plates

The City of Waterford Freedom Box.

The Duke of Wellington, by Thomas Lawrence.

Plan of the battle of Quatre Bras, 16 June 1815, by W. and A.K. Johnston.

Marshal William Carr Beresford by William Beechey.

Lady Elizabeth Louisa Pack née Beresford, artist unknown.

Denis Pack's octagonal pistol by Tathum & Egg, London; inscribed and with shoulder extension.

Lieutenant Colonel Noel Hill by George Dawe.

Monument to Denis Pack in St Canice's Cathedral, by Francis Chantrey.

List of maps

Acknowledgements

Thanks to all those who have encouraged me to undertake this project. Fortunately, much of the archival research was completed prior to the closure of archives due to coronavirus. I am grateful to the archivists and librarians who helped me along the way, including those in Ireland at the National Library of Ireland, Trinity College Dublin, and the Waterford County Library. The Public Records Office in Northern Ireland (PRONI) was helpful. In England I wish to acknowledge the assistance of the staff of the British Library, the National Archives in Kew, the National Army Museum, and the Hartley Library in Southampton. In Portugal I was kindly looked after by the personnel of the Torre do Tombo and the Arquivo Historico Militar in Lisbon.

I would also like to acknowledge the great debt I owe to the Hathi Trust for its reproduction of historic materials. The Napoleon Series is a mine of information. The versions of Wellington's Dispatches, The Supplementary Despatches and Memoranda of the Duke that I have relied on are from the Cambridge Library Collection and references are to those volumes.

Many individuals have generously given of their time, but I wish to recognize in particular General Rui Moura (retd), Pedro de Brito and Pedro de Avillez in Portugal; in Hawaii Bob Burnham, whose range of knowledge on the military of the period is extraordinary. In Argentina Maria Laura Maciel has once again been an enthusiastic rapporteur. She kindly introduced me to the well-respected Argentine historian Roberto Elissalde, with whom I conversed on the British invasions of the Rio de la Plata. In England Zack White, Mark Thompson, the late Richard (Dick) Tennant and many others have made my life easier and I really do appreciate it. Suzie Pack-Beresford in Northern Ireland and Moya Maclean (née Pack-Beresford) in Scotland have once again generously made available family paintings and memorabilia. To all those who have shared their knowledge at conferences, whether in person or online, I give my heartfelt thanks.

A special recognition and my gratitude must go to Jane Totterham, whose late husband Robert E. Tottenham was the great-great-grandson of Charles Synge, Denis Pack's aide de camp while Pack served in the Portuguese army. Jane kindly made available Synge's memorandum of his time in the Iberian Peninsula as well as other family papers.

My family have been most helpful, whether as sounding boards or otherwise. Edel, as always, has supported my endeavours. To Robert and David I owe my particular thanks as they have, respectively, produced a number of the photographs, maps and plans which are an integral part of a volume of this nature.

Dr Rory Muir and Dr David Murphy both read the draft of the script and made suggestions which were most helpful. I appreciate their setting aside valuable time to support a fellow historian. Dr Muir has kindly written the Foreword, for which I am most grateful.

It has been a pleasure to work with the team from Pen & Sword Books. The interest of and patience shown by Rupert Harding and Sarah Cook has been not only helpful but informative.

Any mistakes in the text are mine alone. I do hope that you, the reader, will enjoy this account of the life of a noteworthy and remarkable soldier.

Straffan, 2022

Foreword

Denis Pack had a remarkable career. He was only seventeen when the war with France broke out in 1793, a young army officer in trouble for assaulting his superior officer. But in the following year he redeemed himself, serving with distinction as a volunteer with the British army in Flanders in one of the first campaigns of the war. Over the next twenty-one years he fought in countless campaigns, seeing action on three continents (Europe, Africa and South America) and declining a command on a fourth (North America). He took part in some of the greatest British military disasters of the war (Quiberon Bay, Buenos Aires – where he was captured not once but twice – and Walcheren), and also in some of the army's proudest triumphs. He was an Irishman who made his name commanding a Scottish regiment (the 71st), who then commanded a Portuguese brigade for much of the Peninsular War, before being given command of the Highland brigade in 1813, and leading a mixed Scottish and English brigade at Quatre Bras and Waterloo. He was thanked by Parliament on five separate occasions, and awarded the Army Gold Cross with seven clasps, more than any British soldier of the Peninsular War other than Wellington and Beresford. He was in the Peninsula from the beginning at Roliça and Vimeiro; he took part in the retreat to La Coruña; missed Talavera, but was at Walcheren instead; and then was at Buçaco, Torres Vedras, Almeida, Ciudad Rodrigo, Badajoz, Salamanca, Burgos, Vitoria, the Pyrénées, Nivelle, the Nive, Orthez and Toulouse. It was a remarkable record which few men, even among the hardy veterans of the Light Division, could come near matching. And then, as if that had not been enough, he was in the thick of the fighting at Quatre Bras and at Waterloo.

No one ever doubted Pack's courage. He led his men into the hottest fire and was wounded at least six and possibly as many as nine times in his career, as well as suffering from Walcheren fever. But his luck and physical toughness ensured that neither wounds nor illness kept him out of action for long. Pack was not only brave, he was also cool and astute in action, realistic about what his men could accomplish, and also looked after them with great care off the battlefield, although there was little he could do to make up for the deficiencies of the Portuguese commissariat in the early years of the war.

Pack was only six years younger than Wellington, but those six years were crucial in determining his seniority in the army. Wellington became a lieutenant-colonel in September 1793, a major-general in 1802, and a lieutenant-general in 1808; while Pack was only a subaltern in 1793, and did not become a lieutenant-colonel until 1800, or a major-general until 1813. This meant that he was not only very much Wellington's junior, but also a clear step below officers such as Thomas Picton, Robert Craufurd and Lowry Cole, whose seniority entitled them to command a division in the Peninsular army. It was only by entering the Portuguese service that Pack gained the command of a brigade in 1810, at a time when he would have been limited to leading a regiment in the British army. As soon as he had enough seniority to be given a British brigade he switched back, and Wellington, who thoroughly recognized his value, appointed him to lead a brigade in the 6th division and almost immediately to take over the division temporarily while its regular commander, Henry Clinton, was absent. When he joined the Portuguese army in 1810 Benjamin D'Urban, the Quartermaster-General, remarked, 'This is a great acquisition – an Officer of tried service, sound judgement, and proved intrepidity.' And this reputation was only enhanced over the next five years of constant campaigning in which Pack's brigade was so often at the forefront of battle.

Despite his distinguished record, Pack's life has remained obscure. His early death in 1823 may have contributed to this, as may the fact that for much of the Peninsular War he commanded Portuguese troops – and many accounts of the war are based heavily on British memoirs and diaries, while few British historians feel confident tackling Portuguese sources. This gap has now been admirably filled by the current volume, which benefits greatly from Marcus Beresford's understanding of the problems faced and overcome by the Portuguese army during the war. That story has been told broadly in his earlier book – a biography of William Carr Beresford, the commander and reviver of the Portuguese army – while this biography of Denis Pack shows the process at work at a lower level, that of the most distinguished brigade in the Portuguese army. But there is as much here about the British as well as the Portuguese army, and everyone with an interest in Wellington's campaigns will be grateful that the life of Denis Pack, 'scarred with wounds and covered with glory', has at last been told. A junior officer who served under Pack at Toulouse gives us a glimpse of him in action, sitting 'on horseback in the middle of the road, showing an example of the most undaunted bravery to the troops. I think I see him now, as he then appeared, perfectly calm and unmoved; and with a placid smile upon his face amidst a perfect storm of shot and shells.' It was men like Denis Pack, commanding companies, regiments, brigades and divisions, who turned Wellington's plans into action, and who led his army to victory after victory from the coast of Portugal to the bloody slopes of Waterloo.

Rory Muir

Preface

Major General Sir Denis Pack was one of Wellington's more junior generals, many of whose stories remain untold. He was born in Ireland, where his family are understood to have moved from Northamptonshire at the close of the seventeenth century. Like so many officers in the British army at the time of the French revolutionary and Napoleonic wars, Pack was the son of a clergyman, though his maternal grandfather, Denis Sullivan, served with Bragg's regiment of foot, better known as the 28th (North Gloucestershire), a regiment which was to add to its fame in the wars that were to dominate Pack's military career.

Pack was one of a phalanx of brigade commanders from many nationalities who served under Wellington when he commanded the allied army battling Napoleon's France. They came from England, Scotland, Wales, Ireland, the German States, Portugal and Spain, and even further afield. Wellington was to complain periodically that he did not get to choose his own officers and, no doubt, left to his own devices he would on occasion have chosen otherwise. Where Wellington disliked or had reservations about an officer, he tried to prevent his appointment. Others he managed to get recalled, though he had to be mindful of the, sometimes powerful, political connections at home of general officers.[1] Pack had neither substantial wealth, nor strong political connections. He alludes to the latter fact from time to time. His correspondence reveals financial concern on occasions, though he, or his family, evidently had sufficient means to secure advancement through the purchase of a number of commissions.

A good number of his brigade commanders served Arthur Wellesley, ultimately Duke of Wellington, with distinction, others indifferently; some were cooperative, others less so. Pack deserves to be numbered in the first rank of those commanders, not only because he was trusted by Wellington, but also because, along with Lord Edward Somerset, he was one of the few brigade commanders to serve extensively in the Iberian Peninsula, at Waterloo and afterwards as part of the army of occupation in France from 1815 to 1818. Others such as John Keane and Colquhoun Grant did not serve to the same extent in the Peninsula, while Thomas Bradford and

Thomas Brisbane did not serve at Waterloo. Pack was one of the more junior generals, like Victor Alten, John Le Marchant and Colin Halkett, who were responsible for putting Wellington's orders into effect. Wellington was intolerant of perceived incompetence and was sometimes sarcastic of officers' talents, such as when he observed 'I only hope that when the enemy reads the list of their names he trembles as I do.'[2] It was not by chance that Wellington said of Pack 'no officer in the Service has been more zealous or more distinguished than himself upon all occasions'.[3]

From 1793 until 1814, with one short interlude in 1802–03, Great Britain and France were at war. In the spring and early summer of 1815 the conflict erupted again. Called by contemporaries 'The Great War', it was a truly global confrontation, involving competing powers as both allies and enemies as circumstances changed. Great Britain had already emerged from the Seven Years War (1756–63), perhaps the first global war, as the pre-eminent world power. Yet during the years when Napoleon ruled France, Great Britain faced another titanic challenge to its influence, and its very survival, as a leading power. France's military success during these years led it to become, for a time, the dominant European state. The achievements of French armies during the last decade of the eighteenth century and the first fifteen years of the nineteenth century instigated or assisted other developments which were to reshape the nineteenth-century world. These included the rise of Prussia in Europe, the expansion of the United States of America and the emergence of liberation movements in South America. Within thirty years of the loss of its American colonies, Great Britain augmented its power through the acquisition of territory and influence in Africa and Asia. Denis Pack was one of those who fought and led troops in southern Africa, South America and above all in Europe in the struggle to curtail France and its erstwhile allies. Only a quirk of fate meant that Pack did not go to fight in the United States in 1814, a development which meant he was present for the campaign of 1815 in the Low Countries and France.

Pack did not leave any known memoirs. While it is uncertain he would have done so, had he led a long life, his early demise at the age of forty-eight means that the researcher at times has to rely solely on the papers of others to glean the picture of Pack's actions. Luckily, he is mentioned by both Wellington and Marshal William Carr Beresford on a large number of occasions. In addition, as a Portuguese brigadier general he features in the Portuguese military archives. In 1946 Peter Carew, a neighbour of one of Denis Pack's descendants, published a short account of the General's life in *Blackwood's Magazine*. In this he refers to a journal of Denis Pack's which I have been unable to locate. In the article Mr Carew quotes from a number of letters I have not seen, and in which the text appears to vary on occasion from documents available to me. One can only hope this journal is still extant. From the sources currently available, it is clear that Denis Pack emerges as a courageous commander, not prone to give up in adversity. I have restricted my discussion on a number of battles in which Pack was involved, as these are the subject of extensive commentary elsewhere. In choosing this course I hope that I give sufficient flavour to enable the course of these engagements to be readily understood. To this end I have introduced a number of maps and diagrams.

In the text I have referred to Arthur Wellesley as Wellesley until the end of August 1809. Thereafter he is Wellington, following the announcement on 26 August of the granting to him of the titles of 'Baron Douro of Wellesley in the County of Somerset, and Viscount Wellington of Talavera, and of Wellington, in the said County.'[4]

Chapter 1

Early life

Denis Pack was born in Ireland on 7 October 1774, the youngest of Thomas and Mary Pack's four children.[1] Thomas was the Church of Ireland Dean of Ossory, a position attached to Kilkenny Cathedral in the city of Kilkenny. The Pack family had arrived in Ireland in the second half of the seventeenth century, establishing themselves initially in the area of Ballinakill, County Laois (at that time Queen's County). A successful and distinguished military career was terminated with Denis's death in 1823 at the relatively early age of forty-eight.

As a young boy Denis attended Kilkenny College. Founded in 1538 by Piers Butler, Earl of Ormonde, Ireland's oldest grammar school was situated in a seven bay Georgian building in the city built in the 1780s under the guidance of the then Master of the College, the Reverend Richard Pack, uncle of Denis.[2] On leaving Kilkenny College, Denis, aged fifteen, enrolled in Dublin University (Trinity College Dublin), but did not graduate, leaving a year later. Denis's mother, Mary Pack, was an heiress. She was the daughter of Denis Sullivan of Berehaven, County Cork. Denis Sullivan had been a captain in the British army and it was in his footsteps that the young Denis Pack followed when, aged sixteen, he was commissioned as a cornet on 30 November 1791 in the 14th light dragoons. He joined the regiment in Dublin in January 1792.[3] The regiment, while ostensibly English, was by the time Denis joined it known as an Irish one, for on being sent to Ireland in 1747 it spent the next forty-eight years in Ireland, frequently stationed in the city and county of Kilkenny. Denis's military career might have ended very quickly, for less than two years after obtaining his commission he was subject to a court martial held in the courthouse in Kilkenny. Some accounts reported young Pack as being cashiered for striking another officer, Captain Sir George Dunbar.[4] However, there is no note to this effect in his military record or the *London Gazette*, so he may have been suspended.[5] Much later, after his life had ended, Pack's misadventure was still being quoted, for in 1834 the *Naval and Military Gazette and Weekly Chronicle of the United Service* referred to him as 'having unfortunately fallen under the fangs of the law at the commencement of his military career'.[6] The reason for apparently striking Dunbar has been lost in the mists of time but by all accounts Sir George was a difficult person and a later argument with his fellow officers was to have a disastrous outcome when he took his own life in 1799.[7]

Unabashed, and perhaps because of the British government's thirst for soldiers, Denis reappears in the army as a gentleman volunteer in 1794.[8] Remarkably, he appears to have been able to rejoin or continue with the 14th light dragoons. This seems to give weight to the theory that he was suspended rather than cashiered. Almost immediately, he left Ireland to serve in Flanders as part of the force commanded by the Earl of Moira, designated to assist the army already there under HRH the Duke of York. Lord Moira's force disembarked at Ostend, but, while it managed to link up with that under the Duke of York, the campaign was a disastrous one, ending in a winter march across the Low Countries, finally reaching Bremen whence the army was evacuated back to Great Britain.[9] This campaign, however, gave young Denis Pack his first combat experience. Commended for carrying a dispatch to Nieuport, south of Ostend, he was later joined there by part of his regiment. The town was subsequently besieged and captured by the French in July 1794. On its surrender the Hanoverian and British troops were taken prisoner but many French emigrés were massacred. Immediately prior to the surrender Pack and some two hundred emigrés managed to escape by boat and after a sharp engagement he rejoined the Duke of York's army near Antwerp. Pack subsequently took part in the Battle of Boxtel in September 1794, which led to the precipitate withdrawal of the British and Hanoverian army to a new defensive line on the Meuse, only for that to be abandoned during the winter, beginning the long and severe retreat to Bremen.

Pack's promotion to lieutenant by purchase was gazetted on 24 March 1795.[10] In that capacity he served with a detachment of the 14th light dragoons on Britain's next foray in continental Europe. This involved an attempt to support French royalists in Brittany and the Vendée. A force made up of French emigrés and some British marines convoyed by a fleet under Sir John Borlase Warren landed at Quiberon in Brittany at the end of June.[11] This landing was to prove a further military failure, with French revolutionary forces driving them off the peninsula before the end of July.[12] The British government had determined prior to this withdrawal to send another force to support the royalists.[13] This body of three thousand men under the command of General Welbore Ellis Doyle arrived too late to take part at Quiberon.[14] Warren and Doyle then planned a landing to capture the island of Noirmoutiers, but this plan was abandoned before they finally seized Île d'Yeu just to the south of the Loire estuary on 30 September.[15] The island was fortified, but a decision was taken to pull out British forces in mid-October on the basis that the likely benefits did not warrant a force of this size being garrisoned on the island. Bad weather first delayed the arrival of these instructions and then postponed the evacuation until the end of November. During this time Pack served on the island.[16] Returning to England, Pack was made a captain in the 5th dragoon guards in January 1796.[17] Although in origin an English regiment raised in response to the Monmouth rebellion of 1685, the 5th dragoon guards had been placed on the Irish establishment at the close of the seventeenth century and was heavily populated by Irish soldiers. Shortly after Pack's appointment to the regiment it was sent to Ireland, where Pack was to serve for the next three years. In 1812, commanded by Major General William Ponsonby, the regiment was to win fame as part of Major General John Le Marchant's cavalry charge at Salamanca, but in the closing years of the eighteenth century it was closely involved with the suppression of dissent in Ireland.[18]

The island of Ireland in the final decade of the eighteenth century was a ferment of agitation. The victory of William III (William of Orange) over James II, culminating in the Treaty of Limerick in 1691, resulted in Ireland being ruled by a small minority professing the Anglican faith of the established church: a minority determined to maintain its position, but beset by both the Roman Catholic overall majority and the thoroughly disaffected Presbyterians making up the majority in the north of the island. Discontent and resentment led to the formation of armed bands. The Protestant Hearts of Oak and Steelboys operated predominantly in Ulster opposing tithes, tolls and agrarian inequality. They were countered by the Defenders, a Catholic organization, originally defensive in nature. In counties further south, where Catholics substantially outnumbered Protestants, the Whiteboys emerged to defend tenant rights and oppose tithe collection and eviction. Outrages were met with savage retribution by the establishment and those relying on the support of the establishment.

The position of the Irish Protestant ascendancy, which relied on backing by the British government, was made more difficult when that government realized that in Ireland there was an untapped reservoir of potential soldiers to meet the demands placed on Great Britain by virtue of its struggle for world dominance with France. From the time of the Seven Years War (1756–63), through the American War of Independence (1775–83) to the French revolution and Napoleonic wars (1789–1815), the British government increasingly ignored and then repealed the laws forbidding Catholics to bear arms. Over the same period Irish Protestants increasingly flexed their own muscles, achieving free trade and greater legislative independence from England during the American revolution. That revolution brought radical ideas to the fore in Ireland just as it did in continental Europe, but the fire was well and truly lit with the outbreak and success of the French revolution commencing in 1789. The philosophy of a democratic republic led to the rise of the United Irishmen, an organization including radical Protestants and Catholic Defenders. The suggestion of an independent republic based on universal suffrage (for men) proved a powerful clarion call. These developments presented considerable challenges for a Dublin-based administration endeavouring to promote British policies, but dependent upon an often-divided Anglo-Irish support base to do so. The stage was set for conflict.

France not unnaturally sought to take advantage of a situation involving substantial discontent with British rule in Ireland. In the winter of 1796 a naval force of over forty vessels carrying some fifteen thousand soldiers under the command of General Lazare Hoche sailed from Brest intending to invade Ireland. This expedition was no mere *chouannerie*, for the ships carried arms for forty thousand. The French managed to evade the Royal Navy squadrons responsible for surveillance off the west coast of France. However, the invasion fleet became separated by storms, and though a number of vessels carrying 6,500 troops entered Bantry Bay on the extreme southwest of Ireland on 21 December, bad weather prevented a landing. The fleet, suffering heavy losses, returned to France, but not before it had caused consternation in Ireland. The British government and the Irish administration had placed great reliance on the ability of the Royal Navy to intercept and destroy any invasion force before it effected a landing in Ireland. This factor, and demands elsewhere for military intervention, had led the British government to withdraw regular regiments from Ireland following the outbreak of war with France in 1793, replacing these with local militia and regiments sent from Britain either seeking to recruit or bringing with them untried recruits, or both. Expectations of the likely performance of yeomanry and fencibles were not high. In December 1796 General Dalrymple, who commanded at Cork, felt he could not defend the city but would have to engage in diversionary tactics, while Colonel Vallancey, in command of the Tyrone militia in Limerick, expressed a distinct lack of optimism about the defence of that city.[19] The failure of the French to effect a landing, while earning the administration a temporary reprieve, did not remove the threat of invasion. It did, however, enable those in charge to both improve military capacity and move to

50 km

30 mi

Killala

X Ballinamuck

Dublin

X Prosperous

○ Kilkenny

Waterford

○ Cork

○ Bantry

Ireland, 1796–98

violently suppress disaffection, primarily in Ulster. This turn of events was to prove disastrous for the United Irishmen and their supporters.

Denis Pack and the 5th dragoon guards, along with other troops, had undertaken a forced march to County Cork in late December 1796 to counter the threatened landings but in the event were not called into action. The regiment returned shortly afterwards to County Kildare, where it was based on the Curragh of Kildare throughout 1797. There it was reviewed by Lieutenant General David Dundas, who approved of what he saw. Dundas wrote the definitive texts for the regulation of both infantry and cavalry drill and in later life became commander-in-chief of the army. Increasing government apprehension at the prospect of a rising led to the regiment being moved to Dublin, where it was based when rebellion broke out in 1798. Part of the regiment was involved in the fighting in counties Wicklow and Wexford, but Pack led a detachment sent to County Kildare.[20] There he encountered several rebel forces, most notably at Prosperous on 19 June where, following the defeat of the rebels, Pack was mentioned in dispatches by Lord Cornwallis, the recently appointed lord lieutenant and commander-in-chief of the British forces in Ireland.[21] Pack was called into action again later in the summer. The rebellion had by then been defeated in Ulster and Leinster, when a small French force of some thousand men under General Jean Joseph Amable Humbert landed in Killalla in County Mayo on 22 August.[22] After initial success in the west of Ireland, that force was defeated at Ballinamuck on 8 September. The 5th dragoon guards were engaged there, and subsequently the recently promoted Major Pack was charged with conveying the French prisoners, including General Humbert, to Dublin.[23] Here the officers were treated with generous hospitality. Humbert and his second in command Jean Sarrazin, together with a number of other officers, were put up in the Mail Coach Hotel in Dawson Street, before being repatriated by way of exchange.[24]

On 16 September, unaware of Humbert's surrender, a much larger French force than Humbert's had sailed from Brest for Ireland. Commanded by General Jean Hardy, it involved some three thousand men placed in eight frigates and the *Hoche*, a 74-gun ship of the line. Theobald Wolfe Tone, a leading member of the United Irishmen, travelled on the *Hoche*. The squadron was intercepted by a larger British fleet under Sir John Borlase Warren on 12 October off the north coast of Ireland and, with the exception of two frigates, was captured without loss. Wolfe Tone, along with 2,500 French soldiers and those serving in the French squadron, was taken prisoner.

There was a much darker side to the civility shown to the French prisoners. The Irish who had supported the rising were hunted down and many were killed. Several Irishmen had travelled with Humbert from France, including Mathew Tone, a brother of Theobald Wolfe Tone. The details of the trial and death of Wolfe Tone by his own hand are well known.[25] Less noted are the circumstances surrounding the capture and trial of his brother Mathew. Like Wolfe Tone, Mathew was tried by court martial and Denis Pack was involved in the process. In Mathew's case the court martial was held in Dublin on 21, 24 and 26 September 1798. The President of the court was Colonel Hugh Maginnis. Alongside him sat Lords Gosford and Enniskillen, Colonel Jones, Lieutenant Colonel Peter James Daly, Major John Armstrong and Denis Pack. Like Pack, Armstrong was an officer in the 5th dragoon guards.[26] Lieutenant Colonel Daly and Major Armstrong appear to have participated in the trials of both Tone brothers.

During the trial, a witness deposed that Mathew had been at Castlebar and at the scene of another small action at Collooney, County Sligo. He had then been encountered by a yeomanry cavalry officer, Thomas Armstrong, after the Battle of Ballinamuck. Mathew had been disguised in peasant's clothing but admitted he was an officer in the French service who had thrown away his clothing and sword. He argued that when he had first gone to France he had been imprisoned as a spy and further he had never been a United Irishman. He pleaded that he had been an unwilling participant in the invasion, but was bound as a French officer to follow orders. At the time of his capture he claimed he had formed the intention of giving himself up to a magistrate, and that he had readily disclosed his identity and role to Armstrong. Mathew's pleading was to no avail. He was convicted and executed at Arbour Hill on 29 September 1798.[27]

Denis Pack's promotion to major involved a transfer to the 4th (Royal Irish) dragoons. The regiment had been active throughout the Irish rebellion, fighting at Naas, Prosperous, Tuberneering and Vinegar Hill.[28] In 1799 it was posted to Northampton, to where Pack now also progressed. The 4th (Royal Irish) dragoons were designated to form part of a new Anglo-Russian force intended to 'liberate' Holland in late 1799. While that expedition did result in the capture of a substantial part of the Dutch fleet, the withdrawal of the allies from Den Helder in the face of adversity meant Pack's new regiment was not required to serve there. In early 1800 it was reassigned to Scotland, but Pack's career took another turn when he was promoted lieutenant colonel of the 71st regiment.[29] This involved a return to Ireland, where he took up duties at Arbour Hill (Palatine Square) barracks on 24 April 1801. Through use of the purchase system, he had risen since the time of his re-enlistment from lieutenant to lieutenant colonel in under six years.[30] Prior to 1800 Pack had served in three cavalry regiments. Henceforth he was to serve with the infantry. No evidence for the reasons behind this change of direction has been found. Were there better prospects of serving in a challenging theatre in the infantry? Was it a question of finance, given that the commission of a lieutenant colonelcy in the infantry cost about 70 per cent of that payable for the equivalent rank in the dragoon guards and about 65 per cent of the price in the Life Guards?[31] Pack was twenty-six years old in April 1801. Remarkable as this rise may seem, his progress was not unusual. The young Arthur Wellesley had advanced from ensign to lieutenant colonel in a similar fashion, being appointed lieutenant colonel at the age of twenty-four.

Denis Pack's involvement with the 71st regiment has meant that information which might otherwise have remained hidden is available to those interested in his career. The 71st regiment is most unusual in that there are at least six extant contemporaneous accounts covering the regiment's participation in major events in the Napoleonic wars. Where they overlap their stories are mostly, but not always, consistent. Whether diaries, correspondence or chronologies, these narratives refer to Pack on many occasions, sometimes with reference to the same event, but on other occasions a unique citation. Even more unusually, four of these accounts were by men from the ranks, one from an officer who had risen from the ranks, with one series of letters written by a young soldier who served under Pack as an ensign, but who continued to make reference to him when Pack was serving outside the regiment.[32]

From 1801 to 1805 Pack was based in Ireland with the 71st regiment. The regiment had been posted to Ireland in 1800 on returning from India to Scotland in a depleted condition. In Ireland it was brought up to strength by the transfer of 600 men from Scotch fencibles then serving in Ireland.[33] The regiment moved from Dublin to Arklow in the spring of 1802 and from there to Loughrea in County Galway in 1803. Then, in May 1804, it was removed to Rathkeale, County Limerick. The regimental records reveal a substantial number of men with distinctly Irish names joining the regiment in the early 1800s, undoubtedly recruited to what was ostensibly a highland regiment while it was on garrison duty in Ireland.[34] The regiment was not about to lose its Scottish character, however, for in October 1804 a second battalion was raised, based in Dumbarton. Its commander was Lieutenant Colonel Lord George Thomas Beresford, son of the 1st Marquis of Waterford and half-brother to William Carr Beresford, then commander of the 88th regiment.[35] Pack was to get to know the Beresford family intimately in the years ahead.

Chapter 2

The Cape Colony and the Rio de la Plata, 1806–07[1]

The British government, led by William Pitt, determined in 1805 to attempt to retake the Cape Colony from the Batavian Republic, effectively a client state of Napoleon's France. Great Britain had previously overrun the colony in 1795 but had returned it to the Dutch, under the Treaty of Amiens, in 1803. Its importance at that time was that it straddled the sea route to India, where Great Britain was in the process of consolidating and extending its power, the possessions there governed by the East India Company providing extensive and profitable commercial support for British interests.

To accomplish the capture of the Cape Colony the government outfitted a force of six thousand men, in two brigades, under the command of Sir David Baird. The first brigade, consisting of the 24th, 38th and 83rd regiments, was commanded by Brigadier General William Carr Beresford. The second brigade (the Highland brigade), consisting of the 71st, 72nd and 93rd regiments, was led by Brigadier General Ronald Craufurd Ferguson.[2] Lieutenant Colonel Denis Pack was in charge of the 71st regiment. Though their families clearly knew each other, it is not known whether Pack and Beresford were acquainted prior to this expedition. By the end of their voyage to the southern hemisphere they had shared some very testing experiences and become firm friends.

The expeditionary force was to be transported in a fleet under the command of Sir Home Popham. In the summer of 1805 the fleet was collected in the substantial natural harbour of Cobh (the port of Cork) in southwest Ireland. Pack and the 71st regiment assembled there and while waiting to sail Pack, now aged thirty-one, was painted in miniature by Frederick Buck.[3]

The fleet sailed from Cork on 31 August 1805 and, having made port first in Madeira and then Sao Salvador in Brazil to take on supplies, following two transatlantic voyages Popham's fleet sighted Table Bay on 4 January 1806. Heavy surf prevented a landing by Beresford's brigade at

Leopard's Bay (now Melkbosstrand) the next day. While Beresford was sent north with the 38th regiment and some cavalry to land further up the coast, the main force was successfully disembarked without serious opposition at Leopard's Bay on 6 January.

The small army marched towards Capetown and on 8 January Baird defeated the Dutch at Blauuwberg, with the capitulation of the colony following a week later. The contest at Blauuwberg was decided by a charge of the Highland brigade during which the 71st captured two guns. Pack withdrew the claim of the 71st to the value of these guns on the basis it should be shared by the entire Highland brigade, a move which was much appreciated by its commander, Brigadier Ferguson.[4] Pack was apparently unfortunate enough to be wounded but it cannot have been serious for he remained with his regiment. The author of an article written on Denis Pack in the first half of the twentieth century, who was familiar with the family and had access to papers which it has proved impossible to locate when writing the current biography, quotes Denis on the battle and his wound: ''twas but a miserable affair, not worthy the name of a battle, so I thought nought of my graze on the buttocks and stayed in command'.[5]

Following the surrender of Capetown, the 71st regiment was quartered at Wynberg, which Pack found dull although he was in good health. The rumour was that the 71st was to be sent to India, which, although Pack felt was a 'dreadful distance', was preferable to remaining in situ.[6] But he never did travel to India, for a decision by Sir David Baird and Sir Home Popham was to take Pack and the 71st regiment to South America and the Rio de la Plata, under the command of William Carr Beresford.

In Capetown the British had learnt of the stunning victory by Nelson over the combined French and Spanish fleets at Trafalgar the previous October. While French squadrons and privateers continued to prove dangerous until the end of the war in 1814, this defeat confirmed British naval superiority in such a way as to remove any threat not only of invasion of the British Isles but to the Royal Navy's freedom of movement.

For a number of years Sir Home Popham had been a strong advocate of British intervention in South America.[7] He was a friend of William Pitt and had other supporters in the government. The loss of continental trading opportunities made it important to open up fresh markets and Popham had a following amongst the mercantile sector. Now, however, he was about to engage in an entirely unauthorized operation, notwithstanding Britain had been at war with Spain since 1804. Sources in Capetown informed Popham that a large quantity of silver was being transported from the mines in what is today Bolivia to Buenos Aires for onward

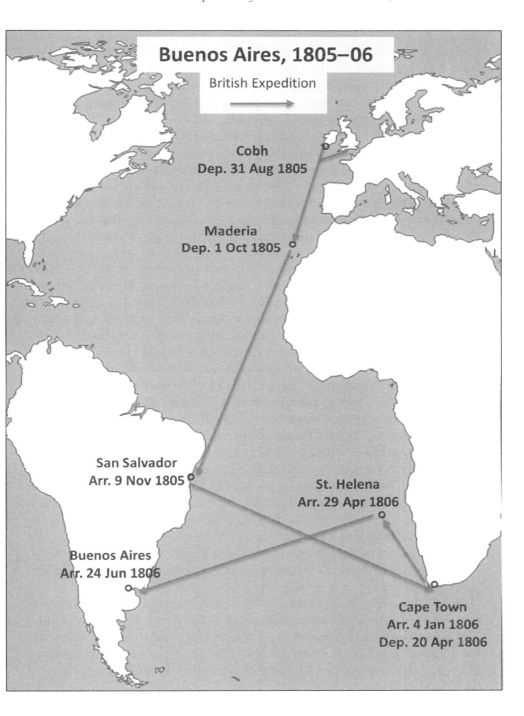

Buenos Aires, 1805–06

British Expedition

Cobh
Dep. 31 Aug 1805

Maderia
Dep. 1 Oct 1805

San Salvador
Arr. 9 Nov 1805

St. Helena
Arr. 29 Apr 1806

Buenos Aires
Arr. 24 Jun 1806

Cape Town
Arr. 4 Jan 1806
Dep. 20 Apr 1806

shipping to Spain. The information given to Popham also indicated that Buenos Aires had poor defences. There was no time to seek instructions from London. Popham persuaded Sir David Baird to authorize a small expedition which, while cloaked with respectability in the shape of advancing Britain's interests in South America, undoubtedly had the seizure of silver as an important objective. Baird authorized Popham to take part of his fleet and the 71st regiment, together with a picket of the 20th dragoons, on this undertaking. The first battalion of the 71st regiment amounted to 864 men. Overall command of this modest armed force was entrusted to William Carr Beresford. On the way to South America Popham called into St Helena, where he managed to convince the governor to supply him with some 250 additional troops, including artillerymen, giving Beresford an overall force, including marines, of some 1,400 men.

The expedition left Capetown on 20 April 1806, arriving in the estuary of the Rio de la Plata in early June. Beresford wanted to attack Montevideo first. As the strongest location on the coast, his logic was that it should be attacked while the British had the benefit of surprise. Further, Beresford felt it was a far better defensive position than Buenos Aires should the British need to hold such a position in due course. Popham argued in favour of an initial attack on Buenos Aires on the basis of its lack of defensive capability, the alleged existence of large supplies of food and undoubtedly the desire to capture the silver convoy. Pack and most of the senior officers supported Popham, though Pack was later to admit that, had he realized then the difficulties in navigating the river up to Buenos Aires, he would have voted with Beresford.[8]

In 1806 Buenos Aires was already a large city with a population estimated at forty to fifty thousand inhabitants. The fort contained thirty-five 24 pounder guns and other ordnance. It was, however, short of regular troops and, when told of the British landing, the Viceroy, Rafael de Sobremonte, abandoned the city, proceeding inland with 600 troops and valuables, including the silver recently arrived from the mines of Potosi. In his place he left Hilarion de la Quintana to organize the defence of the city as best he could.[9]

On 25 June Beresford, using small vessels because large ships could not safely approach the coast, disembarked his forces at Quilmes, some 12 kilometres from Buenos Aires.[10] In all, including marines from the fleet, he had approximately 1,450 men. The next day, while advancing on the city, they encountered a Spanish force estimated at between two and four thousand strong, including cavalry.[11] Keeping the St Helena infantry and the marines as a small reserve, Beresford sent Pack forward with the 71st regiment. The pipes were playing and a short sharp engagement resulted in the Spanish, having abandoned their guns, retreating behind the river Riachuelo, burning the bridge over the river as they departed.[12] On 27 June, having cleared the opposing bank with artillery fire, the British crossed over on rafts and later in the day the city surrendered, so that Pack was able to remark: 'The Viceroy fled, and we entered the town, and dined in his palace the same evening.'[13] Beresford's force had suffered one fatality and twelve wounded in the capture of Buenos Aires.

Initially the British received a warm welcome and it became clear that many locals disliked their own government. In accordance with his orders, Beresford proclaimed George III and assumed the position of lieutenant governor, as directed by Baird. Beresford allowed the garrison to surrender with the honours of war. He moved to protect private property and religious freedom and established a liberal commercial regime. All of these brought initial popularity. While he secured the Bolivian silver through a daring raid on Lujan, to which it had been taken prior to the British capture of Buenos Aires, he restored valuables seized with the silver to their owners in the city.[14] He was, however, acutely aware that his hold on the city was tenuous and he immediately wrote to both Baird in Capetown and the government in London seeking reinforcements. In doing so he praised the performance of the 71st regiment. It did not take the locals long to realize just how few troops Beresford had, a force that was reduced further when Popham recalled the marines to serve on board the fleet. Soon it became clear that the residents of Buenos Aires (*Portenos*) were not keen to exchange one colonial power for another, particularly one which had so little firepower that it was far from being able to guarantee their own independence from Spain.

Pack was made commandant of the garrison, and Beresford showed him his own orders which provided for Pack to assume command with the rank of brigadier general should anything happen to Beresford. It did not take long for unrest to develop, with attempts to blow up the barracks, the breaking of parole by Spanish officers, and attempts by the occupied to encourage desertion by, in particular, Catholic troops in the 71st regiment and the St Helena regiment. At the same time local armed forces were being assembled under Juan Martin de Pueyrredon on the right bank of the Rio de la Plata, and Santiago de Liniers on the left bank of the river. The threat was such that on 31 July Beresford dispatched Pack with five hundred men from the 71st regiment, fifty of the St Helena regiment and six pieces of artillery to tackle Pueyrredon's force. At the battle of Perdriel he scattered his opponents, but a lack of cavalry prevented a follow-up.

Worse was to come. Popham had naval patrols out in the Rio de la Plata to prevent de Liniers and his troops crossing over from the left bank. However, under cover of a storm on the night of 4/5 August, a force of over two thousand eluded these patrols and crossed over. With the addition of further local forces, de Liniers advanced on Buenos Aires, cutting it off from supplies. After a two-day running battle, during which Pack was injured, Beresford surrendered on 12 August, in order to avoid further bloodshed.[15] The surrender document provided for the repatriation of the British forces by way of Popham's fleet, but de Liniers was not able to uphold this agreement in the face of local political hostility and the soldiers were made prisoner. The municipal authority of Buenos Aires and subsequently the returned Viceroy of the Rio de la Plata, in the face of vociferous protests by both Beresford and Popham at the non-fulfilment of the terms of capitulation, argued both that Beresford had surrendered at discretion and that de Liniers had no authority to agree the terms.

Officers were offered parole, which they accepted after an initial refusal. They were able to maintain later that they were entitled to break that parole due to the circumstances in which the local government had broken the terms of surrender.[16] Parole was a courtesy not extended to other ranks and their treatment was mixed. They were sent to various jails. Some were abused and indeed Pack and William Gavin had to run the gauntlet of a hostile mob before being rescued by a 'worthy Spanish gentleman'.[17] There were also considerable acts of kindness shown to individuals, particularly by the Bethlehemite Brothers (Hermanos de Belén) who treated the injured.[18] Beresford, Pack and Beresford's aide de camp Robert Arbuthnot were offered accommodation by the city treasurer, the wealthy Don Felix de Casamayor. Nevertheless Pack, like Beresford and the other officers, felt not only aggrieved but humiliated. Pack, writing distraughtly to the colonel of the 71st regiment, Lieutenant General John Cradock, stated 'Much dependence could not be placed on Mr Liniers; instead of marching out with the honours of war, we literally marched to prison, and gave up our arms in a most ignominious manner.' He went on, however, to confirm that while their baggage had been plundered, many individuals had acted with kindness and generosity.[19]

Reinforcements, requested by Beresford from the Cape, arrived in the estuary at the end of September and joined Popham, who was still off Montevideo with his small fleet. This development seems, not unsurprisingly, to have hardened attitudes in Buenos Aires. The senior British

Rio de la Plata
1806–07

Catamarca

Colonia del
Sacramento

Montevideo

Arrecifes

Luján

Buenos Aires

Maldonado

400 km

200 mi

officers, including Beresford and Pack, were rounded up and sent on 10 October to Lujan, some 80 kilometres inland from Buenos Aires.[20] There they were lodged in the cabildo, the very location from which the British had seized the consignment of silver two months earlier. Other officers were sent to various estancias, all well inland from Buenos Aires. The troops for their part were moved to a number of different towns. The purpose was to prevent any rescue attempt.

Initially, the British officers quartered in Lujan were still at liberty on parole. They rode out, fished and played cricket and for a while were allowed to engage in correspondence. Their mail may have been carried by de Liniers' military secretary Captain Saturnino Rodriguez Pena, who attended on Beresford from time to time. In doing so he brought money from Buenos Aires for the officers, together with other supplies.[21] Pena also became the conduit between those in Buenos Aires who felt the British might have a role to play in the advancement of the objectives of some who were looking to loosen the bonds with Spain.

This relatively relaxed life was thoroughly disrupted by an assault in mid-January 1807 on two British officers, one of whom was Denis Pack. In the previous weeks a private in the 71st regiment had been assassinated, news of which had obviously reached Lujan. Now, however, Captain James Ogilvie of the Royal Artillery was shot while out riding with Pack, and then Pack, while trying to help him, was lassoed and brought to the ground.[22] Fortunately for Pack, two villagers then appeared and their assailant left the scene on horseback. Poor Ogilvie, however, soon expired from his wound, even though attended by Mr Evans, the assistant surgeon of the regiment. Ogilvie was buried beside the church in Lujan, with General Beresford reading the service.[23] Beresford protested these two outrages to de Liniers, who in his response referred to them as atrocious acts. He assured Beresford he had ordered a strong detachment of troops to pursue the assassins.[24]

While the British prisoners were being placed in the interior, Popham was seeking to make use of the reinforcements received from the Cape Colony. He attempted unsuccessfully to capture Montevideo in October and subsequently seized the town of Maldonado, which for a time became the British base. Further substantial reinforcements under General Sir Samuel Auchmuty arrived from England in early January 1807, having been dispatched before the news had been received there of Beresford's surrender. With this enlarged force Auchmuty captured Montevideo on 3 February. The reaction of the authorities in Buenos Aires was to order the seizure of Beresford's papers and the removal of him and other officers to Catamarca, over 1,000 kilometres from Buenos Aires. The decision to move the officers must have spurred Captain Pena and his colleagues to action. In possession of a free pass from de Liniers, he and Manuel Padilla, a politician who had collaborated with Beresford following the British occupation of Buenos Aires before changing sides, arrived at Lujan on 16 February. There they found that Beresford, Pack and the other officers in Lujan had left under escort that very day for Catamarca. Pena and his colleague pursued and caught up with the escort party near the estancia of the Bethlehemite Brothers at Arrecifes, 100 kilometres northwest of Lujan. Pena claimed he had orders to bring Beresford to Buenos Aires, but Beresford refused to leave without Pack. Pena and Padilla took both officers back to Buenos Aires, where they were hidden for a number of days before being smuggled from the city to a small boat, which took them out into the estuary. They transferred from the small vessel to HMS *Charwell*, which carried them to Montevideo.[25]

A court of inquiry held in Montevideo found that neither Beresford nor Pack had broken their parole in making their escape. As Pack put it in his submission, Beresford had told de Liniers and others that while they had given their parole, the British officers were not bound by that parole because of the violation of the surrender terms by the Spanish authorities.[26] As previously indicated, those authorities maintained that far from capitulating on terms, Beresford had surrendered at discretion.[27] Auchmuty requested Beresford to assume command of the force which was being prepared to attempt the fresh conquest of Buenos Aires, but Beresford demurred on the grounds that he wished to return to England to apprise the government of the situation in the Rio de la Plata. Auchmuty understood Beresford wished to advise the government of the existence of a group of people interested in securing independence from Spain, but Beresford also felt that the circumstances of his surrender meant he doubted he could assume the command.[28] Beresford in fact went further, writing to the mayor of Buenos Aires indicating that he would take no further part in the campaign, but would strive to do what he considered would make the inhabitants of Buenos Aires prosperous and happy.[29]

Pack was now free to serve again with the army. Auchmuty gave him command of a force comprising six companies of the 40th foot, four companies of light infantry, three companies of the 95th regiment (Rifles) and a squadron of the 9th dragoons with orders to attempt the capture of Colonia del Sacramento, a small town on the left bank of the estuary of the Rio de la Plata, almost opposite Buenos Aires. This was intended to guard Auchmuty's flank in case of any Spanish counterattack. Pack had no difficulty securing his objective, but in late April 1807 a Spanish offensive occurred. On the 22nd of the month Colonel Elio with 1,500 troops recently arrived from Spain attacked Colonia del Sacramento, spurred on no doubt by the promise of a reward for the capture of Pack, who the authorities in Buenos Aires claimed had broken his parole by escaping with Beresford.[30] This assault was thrown back by the garrison with minor British losses. Three weeks later Lieutenant General Sir John Whitelocke and further troops arrived in Montevideo from England, and Whitelocke, by virtue of his seniority, assumed overall command of the British army that eventually numbered in excess of nine thousand. He sent the balance of the 40th regiment to bolster Pack's force.[31] Pack then took the offensive and on 7 June with just over a thousand men attacked Colonel Elio's camp at San Pedro, about 18 kilometres from Colonia del Sacramento. The Spanish were not taken unawares but nevertheless a force of some two thousand was scattered, with over a hundred prisoners, six cannon and a standard being seized.[32] Pack lost only two men killed. In the defence of Colonia de Sacramento and in the battle at San Pedro Pack had demonstrated his abilities, showing initiative in command of a small force requiring rapid deployment. A slight historical curiosity occurred in relation to this achievement, in that Whitelocke issued a commendation and approbation of Lieutenant Colonel Pack and the forces under his command as part of his General Orders on 10 June, but those General Orders were not published in the *Gazette* in Great Britain at the time. This was because the dispatch was only received back in London after news of the disastrous outcome of the 1807 Rio de la Plata expedition had reached the capital. In 1809, following application by Pack for its inclusion in the history of events, Castlereagh authorized the making public of the account of the action.[33]

Whitelocke's primary objective was the recovery of Buenos Aires. Leaving only a garrison of 1,500 men in Montevideo, and having collected Pack and his men from Colonia de Sacramento, Whitelocke's forces crossed the estuary without opposition on 28 June.[34] They landed further east than Beresford and Pack had done a year earlier, near Ensenada de Barragan, so that the troops could be disembarked from the men of war and larger transports.[35] Additionally, Quilmes, where Beresford had landed, was now protected by a battery of guns. The march to Buenos Aires was an extended one. From Ensenada the force advanced in three columns, reaching Quilmes on 1 July; having crossed the river Riachuelo, they entered the suburbs of Buenos Aires on 3 July. The route from

Quilmes to the city was a familiar one for Pack and the light troops now under his immediate command.

Whitelocke decided to attack the city from the west using thirteen columns of troops. These columns had designated objectives but ultimately it was intended they would converge on the fort in the Plaza Mayor. In attacking the city Pack's troops formed the left wing of the central column (the Light Brigade), which was under the command of Brigadier General Robert Craufurd, who had arrived with further reinforcements in early June.[36] The right wing of the central column was led in person by Craufurd.

Pack's column of about six hundred men (a mixture of the 36th, 40th and 47th, the light company of the 71st with some riflemen of the 95th regiment) moved towards the river on Calle Santo Domingo. Their objective was the San Francisco church. Like others advancing in parallel columns, they were at first allowed to pass by those defenders hidden in

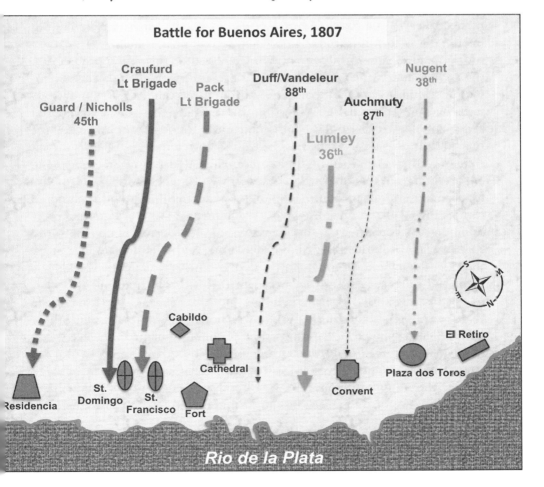

Battle for Buenos Aires, 1807

the adjoining buildings. Then fire erupted on both sides and from the roofs, causing devastation among the closely packed troops. Huge casualties were suffered also by those advancing towards the centre and the Plaza Mayor on the avenues and streets either side of Pack. On Calle Merced and Calle Santa Lucia the 88th regiment under Lieutenant Colonel Alexander Duff and Major Richard Vandeleur lost large numbers of men, not just to musketry but to burning oil, stones and other projectiles hurled from the roofs of buildings.[37] When they came within cannon range the tightly packed columns were decimated by grapeshot. Subsequently, they did manage to get into the buildings from which fire had been directed on the British columns. Having done so, they responded without mercy, bayoneting all those they could find. Pack, meanwhile, having advanced far towards the river, determined to turn left off Santo Domingo towards the Plaza Mayor. Unfortunately for him and his men, part of the order telling each column not to deviate from their line of advance had been omitted in the copying to both him and Craufurd. He turned towards the Plaza Mayor but as they reached San Ignacio church his force was torn to shreds by cannon placed in barricades and assaulted on both sides, preventing any attempt to advance towards the objective, the Franciscan church.[38] Pack and his second in command, Lieutenant Colonel Henry Cadogan, could only order a retreat.[39] Cadogan and his men became trapped in a house and, facing destruction, surrendered about midday. Pack and his remaining men found Craufurd, who had reached the Rio de la Plata via Calle Rosario relatively unscathed. Pack suggested they join with the forces designated to capture the Residencia, but Craufurd felt this smacked of defeatism and as a result they determined to take the church of Santo Domingo. This was duly done with some further losses. Based on subsequent developments, Craufurd confirmed at Whitelocke's court martial that he regretted the decision not to go to the Residencia, but in the absence of orders to do so he felt he should not go there.[40] Meanwhile, although the 87th and 88th regiments on Pack's left flank had both suffered severe losses in their efforts to advance, British troops had succeeded elsewhere, taking the Residencia, El Retiro and the Plaza de Toros (bull ring), during which large numbers of defenders were killed, wounded or captured. The problem remained, however, that there was no overall command in the city, with both Whitelocke and his second in command, Leveson Gower, based at Corrales, a small village outside the urban area some two to three hours' marching distance from the Plaza Mayor. The various attacking columns ground to a halt, positioned themselves in houses, lost men and were surrounded by the revitalized defenders with cannon. One group after another had to surrender. The submission of Cadogan's depleted force was followed by the capitulation of the remnants of Vandeleur's and Duff's columns of the 88th regiment. The British had failed in their central push to the Plaza Mayor. By mid-afternoon Craufurd determined that the Santo Domingo church was no longer tenable. He had lost a hundred men in defence of the convent, in addition to his earlier losses, and following consultation with Pack and other field officers Craufurd determined he had no option but to surrender and his force was then taken prisoner.[41]

The prisoners were searched and articles of Spanish origin taken from them but they were allowed to keep their own possessions. There were moments of acute danger for the men of the light company of Pack's 71st, such as when a gold crucifix from the convent was discovered to be missing. The prisoners were told they would be shot unless the crucifix was produced. As muskets were levelled at the prisoners the cross was found on the ground where they stood, although no culprit was identified, and the troops were imprisoned.[42]

Those of Pack's men who had made it to the convent with him, which Craufurd indicated was about seventy men, were amongst those who surrendered at the church of Santo Domingo. Given Pack's evidence that, having traversed the city, he had reached the Rio de la Plata with about six hundred rank and file, half of whom had been ticked off to go with Cadogan, it is clear that those who remained with Pack had suffered very heavily. Likewise, Cadogan himself stated that although he had perhaps two hundred and fifty men when he arrived at the Jesuit College, he only had about 140 men when he holed up in a house about 140 yards from the College. Further, when Cadogan sent ten men and an officer to try to communicate with Craufurd, all ten men were killed, only the officer escaping. When Cadogan surrendered only forty of his men were able to march out of the house they had occupied.[43]

Notwithstanding these setbacks, the British had enjoyed some success during the day. Two other columns had made good progress, occupying both the Plaza de Toros and the Residencia. Buenos Aires was still in play for both commanders, but both were likewise on risk. On the following morning, 6 July, de Liniers delivered proposed terms to Whitelocke. These called for a complete withdrawal of British forces from the Rio de la Plata, together with a full exchange of prisoners, including those held since Beresford's surrender in August 1806. Whitelocke was disposed to accept the terms, a proposal that was viewed with disquiet by some of his subordinates. The British force's occupation of the strategic points already mentioned, combined with the fact that Whitelocke still had an unused reserve under Colonel Thomas Mahon, led Lieutenant Colonel Richard Bourke, Whitelocke's Quartermaster-General, and others to urge Whitelocke not to make a hasty decision. He was prevailed on to propose a twenty-four hour ceasefire to recover wounded and dead. While the artillery was prepared for a heavy bombardment of the city centre, both Gower and Auchmuty, two of Whitelocke's most senior officers, felt the destruction of the city would be difficult, would incur further injuries and might not achieve any long-term objectives. The ceasefire did not bring immediate relief to Denis Pack. In the battle he had been wounded twice, but only slightly. He had, however, become an object of particular hatred to the locals. The animosity of the Portenos towards him had its origins in the previous year's campaign and a perception that he had broken his parole. When taken prisoner on this second occasion he had been brought to de Liniers' headquarters in the fort. A mob broke into the fort with a view to killing Pack, and he was only saved by priests and de Liniers protecting him. With de Liniers' assistance, Pack was disguised as a Spaniard and made his way back to the British lines, with the help of de Liniers' Quartermaster General, César Balbiani.[44]

On 6 July the correspondence exchanged between Whitelocke and de Liniers led to an armistice and ultimately a convention by which Whitelocke undertook to remove all British forces from the Rio de la Plata. In this decision he was supported by his two most senior army officers, Generals Gower and Auchmuty. He then sought the support of Rear Admiral Murray, who, having consulted with his own second in command, who advised him he could not second-guess Whitelocke, agreed to sign the terms. Following the signing of the convention, prisoners were exchanged and the evacuation of British forces began on 9 July. For his actions at Buenos Aires Whitelocke was court-martialled and cashiered. Why did Whitelocke, who still had between five and six thousand men, including his unused reserve under Colonel Thomas Mahon, agree to these terms?

Whitelocke's court martial was held at the Royal Hospital, Chelsea. Lieutenant General Sir William Medows presided and amongst the nineteen generals sitting on the court were Sir David Dundas and Sir John Moore. It ran with various adjournments from 28 January to 15 March 1808. The report of the proceedings, including the documents produced at the hearing, was printed in two volumes and runs to 830 pages.[45] In summary Whitelocke was charged on four counts:

1. The failure to organize properly the march from Ensenada to Buenos Aires, and incompetence in the way he approached the reduction of Buenos Aires which effectively prevented an amicable resolution of the conflict;
2. Failing to make the best military dispositions to ensure success and ordering an attack with unloaded muskets;
3. Failing to maintain contact with and support his troops during the attack; and
4. Unnecessary capitulation when possessing strong points on the flanks of the town, the arsenal, communication open to the fleet and an effective force of about five thousand men; and surrendering Montevideo without cause.[46]

In his defence Whitelocke maintained that de Liniers had intimated that the lives of both those who had surrendered on the previous day, and the prisoners from the 71st regiment were in danger if the British persisted in their attack, and this factor, combined with a view that it would be extremely difficult to hold the country in the face of almost universal hostility if his attack proved successful, led him to forgo the advantages achieved to date. He maintained he had lost 2,500 men in the attack. This figure contrasted with that supplied in his initial report on the battle, which referred to a total of 1,198 killed, wounded or missing.[47] He maintained that the enemy defences could not be destroyed by using cannon on the flanks, as too many houses were interposed between their respective positions. He would have had to attack again using similar tactics to those employed initially, and the likely losses would have made it difficult to hold Buenos Aires even if he succeeded in capturing the city. Having considered these factors, he determined that he could either retreat and re-embark, which would undoubtedly attract losses, or he could negotiate a treaty.

Many senior officers gave evidence against Whitelocke, but amongst the most damning was that of Craufurd, who felt his commander should be shot. He maintained that had Whitelocke supported his column, he would not have had to surrender. Further, had Whitelocke erected and used cannon in the captured Plaza de Toros and combined this with a naval bombardment, the town could not have held out.[48] Auchmuty felt that abandoning Colonia had been a mistake, though Whitelocke had done so to give himself a larger force with which to attack Buenos Aires. In fact, Auchmuty had advised the British government even before Whitelocke's arrival in South America that, based on Beresford's advice, Auchmuty did not think he had sufficient troops to reduce Buenos Aires, and if he was to attack that city he would have to leave Montevideo with too few men to defend it. He felt he needed fifteen thousand men to take and hold Buenos Aires.[49]

Pack's evidence, though nuanced perhaps because he was a relatively junior officer, was also critical of Whitelocke. Called on the twenty-third day of the court martial, he testified that Whitelocke had spoken to him twice before the attack on Buenos Aires.[50] On the first occasion he had asked to see the proposals for the advance, but Whitelocke's attention was then drawn to something else and the conversation was broken off. He and more senior officers doubted the prudence of Whitelocke dividing his forces and attacking in columns through the streets of the city. This plan seems to have been devised by Gower. Pack's second conversation with Whitelocke came when he was included in the meeting on the morning of 4 July to finalize plans for the attack on the city. Craufurd made it clear this was because of Pack's knowledge of Buenos Aires, as well as the weather they were likely to meet as they sought to advance.[51] It was of course winter in the southern hemisphere. Pack supported Auchmuty's proposal to postpone the attack from midday on 4 July to just before daylight on 5 July, not only because of its complexity and the need for all the commanders to understand it, but because this might assist a surprise attack which would not be possible in daylight. Pack testified he had spoken to Craufurd of his unease at a daytime attack, because of his concern about the inevitable loss of lives.[52] However, he appears to have felt he could not express his unease at the totality of the plan owing to his own lack of seniority.[53] Asked at the court martial to explain his concerns and his reasons for not raising them, he stated that he felt the army lacked sufficient artillery, scaling ladders, petards and implements for forcing doors. When cross-examined as to why he had not said anything to this effect, Pack said he believed Auchmuty had full knowledge of these requirements because he and General Beresford had discussed the project with Auchmuty when together for three weeks following their escape to Montevideo.[54] Pack also maintained that had Whitelocke utilized his reserve, the catastrophe of a surrender would have been avoided.

Whitelocke's defence, part of which alleged that Craufurd, Pack and Cadogan had taken the wrong direction on reaching the Rio de la Plata, was unsuccessful. There was horror that the attack on Buenos Aires had caused the loss of nearly one third of the British army in South America, with 2,824 men either killed, wounded or missing. The fact that his conduct might have saved the lives of several thousand prisoners helped him not at all. Of the four charges he faced, he was found guilty on all bar the second part of the second charge, namely ordering an attack with unloaded muskets. Whitelocke was cashiered and declared totally unfit and unworthy to serve His Majesty in any military capacity whatever, while his second in command, Leveson Gower, who many thought also culpable, never obtained another command.

The members of the 71st regiment imprisoned for a year in a variety of locations were released. They had endured mixed treatment during their captivity: considerable kindness in some instances but cruelty and severe hardship in others, and sometimes both kindness and cruelty. One of the best accounts from those serving in the ranks of the 71st is that of Balfour Kermack, who, after being roughly treated in Buenos Aires, endured a twenty-eight day march to San Juan at the foot of the Andes, during which his clothing and shoes disintegrated. He was then 'adopted' by the Bertaren family with whom he resided, while resisting their attempt to convert him to Catholicism. Finally, news of the convention allowing the repatriation of the regiment arrived.[55] Kermack and his fellow soldiers marched back to Buenos Aires and those who wished to do so were shipped home via Montevideo.[56] They arrived back at Cork on 27 December 1807 without uniforms or arms.[57] In the spring of 1808 they were re-equipped and presented with new colours and by the summer of 1808 were serving under Sir Arthur Wellesley in Portugal. However, 147 of these men with Irish names chose to stay in South America. While it would not be safe to assume that all those with Irish names came in fact from Ireland, it is clear that nearly one fifth (147 out of 844) of the 71st regiment on the 1806 expedition chose to remain in South America. Of the Irish, it is likely they were Catholics recruited in Ireland while the 71st was based there.[58] In choosing to remain they forfeited the prize money due to them in respect of prizes taken before surrender.[59] The 71st regiment left its mark in Rio de la Plata in other ways as well. The regimental bandsmen played daily in the Paseo de la Alameda in Buenos Aires during Beresford's occupation of the city, and later, when imprisoned, are credited with teaching a number of instruments to aspiring musicians.[60] These bandsmen achieved a popularity not accorded to their colleagues, which is reflected in the words of Mariquita Sanchez de Thomson y Mendeville, a young lady who witnessed from the balcony of her home the entry to the city of the 71st regiment on 27 June 1806:

> The regiment 71 playing their music entered the square commanded by Colonel Pack. They were most cute troops, a poetic uniform, shoes with bright red laces. Part of their legs are bared, a small skirt, a third of their cap was embellished with black feathers and a tartan lace as a hatband, a Scottish shawl like a band over a short bright red jacket.[61]

The regimental band itself, including twenty trumpeters, six pipers and a drum major, must have presented an impressive sight.

Pack had returned to England in November 1807. Neither he, nor the officers and men of the 71st regiment, forgot the great kindness shown to him and his men by the Bethlehemite Brothers (dedicated to the care of the sick), who looked after the injured and kept them safe at a time when not all others were well disposed to the British forces.[62] In 1809 the regiment gave two clocks to the Brothers: one a grandfather clock, which stands today in the church of San Pedro Telmo, the other an over-mantel clock about 15 inches high, which was later lodged in the Natural History Museum in Buenos Aires. The grandfather clock is late eighteenth-century Chippendale style, bearing inscriptions of gratitude on both the front and side of its long case.[63] On the over-mantel clock was inscribed 'Fugit irrevocabile tempus, Beneficiae haud fugit memoria' ('Time flees irrevocably, the benefits received will never be forgotten').

Pack for his part went even further in corresponding with Don Luis José Chorroarin, the Superior of the Convent of Santo Domingo. It will be recalled this was the same convent stormed by Craufurd and Pack and the scene of their surrender, leaving so many wounded to be attended to. Clearly the good works undertaken by Don Luis were much appreciated, for Pack sent him an English china coffee service in 1809.[64]

Chapter 3

The Portuguese and Spanish campaigns, 1808–09

Napoleon's pursuit of French hegemony in Europe was repeatedly frustrated by British intervention, through alliances bolstered by financial subsidies, and the activities of the Royal Navy. Prior to the campaigns in the Iberian Peninsula starting in 1808, the British army had not enjoyed any significant success in these wars on the European continent.[1] Its navy had, however, not only protected British maritime trade, but even before Trafalgar (1805) had prevented any substantial French intervention in the British Isles. Napoleon determined to strangle British trade by preventing commerce between the British Isles and the European continent, a move which would restrict Great Britain from subsidizing other European nations in their attempt to resist French domination. In 1807 there remained on the western periphery of Europe two outposts of resistance to Napoleon's continental blockade of Great Britain: Denmark and Portugal. Both maintained significant navies, coveted by Napoleon, who was attempting to rebuild his own navy following the battle of Trafalgar. The British removed the threat in northern Europe through the capture of the Danish fleet following the bombardment of Copenhagen in the summer of 1807. Napoleon then turned his attention to Portugal.

Portugal had been the object of French attention since it had supported Spain in the conflict with France in the Roussillon campaign of 1793–95. Spain had made a separate peace with France, leaving Portugal isolated. Napoleon had formed the view as early as 1800 that French control of Portugal would be 'the greatest damage we could inflict upon English commerce'.[2] He incited Spain to invade her neighbour in 1801, when Portugal failed to comply with Napoleon's demand that it abandon its long-standing alliance with England. This short war resulted in Portugal having to give up territory east of the Guadiana river to Spain and the payment of a financial penalty to France of 20 million francs. That, however, was not enough for Napoleon, who then pressurized Portugal to leave the British alliance. To further his aims, between 1802 and 1805 he sent in turn two very tough ambassadors to Portugal, the Generals Jean Lannes and Jean-Andoche Junot, neither of whom fitted the classical model for a diplomat. Desperately, Dom João, acting as regent for his incapacitated mother Queen Maria, sought to preserve Portuguese neutrality. By 1807 there was no further room for manoeuvre, and Dom João was forced to make a choice: surrender to Napoleon's demands or a French invasion.

A French force under General Junot overran Portugal in November 1807, though the royal family and the administration escaped to Brazil with British assistance. A month later the British government, with Portuguese cognizance, took over the island of Madeira, an important supply point on the way to the Cape Colony, India and South America. The island was controlled by Britain until the end of the war.[3] In early 1808 France sought to establish its authority in Spain, where Napoleon replaced the Bourbon monarchy with his brother Joseph Bonaparte. Following riots in Madrid on 2 May 1808 that were suppressed with severity, widespread resistance to French rule broke out in Spain. Soon Portugal followed suit, with Junot confined to holding Lisbon and other strong places, while sending out punitive expeditions in an attempt to quell the unrest.

Great Britain's desire for new commercial markets, combined with the fact that it remained at war with Spain at the beginning of 1808, meant that, notwithstanding recent experience on the Rio de la Plata, South America still appeared an attractive proposition for intervention. Not only had the cabinet determined to support anti-Spanish risings there, but it was already becoming concerned about potential French interference and influence in the Spanish colonies.

Francisco de Miranda, a Venezuelan soldier and politician, had long sought to obtain British assistance in his objective of liberating the Spanish colonies in South America. Having served in the Spanish royalist and French revolutionary armies, Miranda escaped to England in 1798. Finding British support at first lukewarm, Miranda went to the United States of America and organized two unsuccessful invasions of Venezuela in 1806. Returning to England, he found much greater enthusiasm to support a rising in Venezuela, and in the early summer of 1808 a force of ten thousand under Sir Arthur Wellesley was assembled at Cork in Ireland, from where it was planned to cross the Atlantic. The opportunity offered by resistance to French rule in Spain and Portugal led, however, to the decision to support these two countries in their battle with Napoleonic France. This strategic choice meant that while Britain sought greater trading freedom in South America, its priority was not to weaken the Spanish hold on its colonies at this stage. The force earmarked for

Venezuela was now redirected to assist Spain and Portugal. Denis Pack and the 71st regiment were part of Wellesley's army.

The 71st had moved back to recently built barracks in Cork from Middleton in early 1808. Pack joined the regiment there from London, having ensured clothing was sent on to the men. New regimental colours, to replace those lost in Buenos Aires, were presented to the regiment on 26 April by Lieutenant General John Floyd.[4] In a stirring address Floyd commended their fighting abilities, recognizing that the 71st had been loath to surrender at Buenos Aires:

> It is well known that you defended your conquest with the utmost courage, good conduct, and discipline, to the last extremity. When diminished to a handful, hopeless of succor [*sic*], and destitute of provisions, you were overwhelmed by multitudes, and reduced by the fortune of war to lose your liberty and your well defended colours, but not your honour. Your honour seventy-first regiment remains unsullied. Your last act in the field covered you in glory. Your generous despair, calling upon your General to suffer you to die with arms in your hands, proceeded from the genuine spirit of British soldiers. Your behavior [*sic*] in prosperity, your sufferings in captivity and your faithful discharge of your duty to your King and country are appreciated by all.[5]

Within a couple of months of receiving their new colours the 71st and Pack were joining the fleet at Cobh (the deep water harbour of Cork) to be transported to Portugal as part of Wellesley's army.[6] Wellesley originally intended the 71st to be brigaded with the 40th and 91st.[7] Wellesley's own force was to be joined by others under Major General Brent Spencer, as well as brigades under Brigadier Generals Acland and Anstruther.[8]

The 71st was embarked on transports off Cobh on 5 June, and remained there for some five weeks while the convoy was assembled. Close quarters on one of the transport vessels does not seem to have caused the author of *Vicissitudes in the Life of a Scottish Soldier* any difficulty. In fact this soldier in the 71st rather enjoyed that time.[9] The fleet departed on 12 July but, between waiting for others and the wind, did not reach the Portuguese coast until the end of the month, after a fourteen-day voyage.[10] On sailing from Ireland, as well as the two field officers, Pack and Major Henry Cadogan, the regiment had 8 captains, 23 subalterns, 5 staff, 50 sergeants, 21 drummers and 875 rank and file.[11]

On 3 August, along with other troops, the 71st disembarked on the coast of Portugal just north of the estuary of the river Mondego.[12] The landing there in the Atlantic surf was difficult and there were a number of fatalities. One of the earliest of the 71st ashore was William Gavin, sent by Pack to try to purchase mules. After a 'complete ducking and a terrible fright', he made it to land, only to find all the horses and mules had been procured by the French.[13] There was a march variously put at 7 to 12 miles through deep sand. The heat was such that a number of men died of thirst, even though the soldiers were welcomed by crowds of Portuguese with fruits.[14] When they reached their camp in a wooded area, there was plenty of water and no shortage of provisions.

Pack and the 71st were not involved in the occupation of Obidos on 15 August. Further, the 71st was only peripherally involved in the Battle of Roliça on 17 August, where it was brigaded under Major General Sir Ronald Craufurd Ferguson on the Anglo-Portuguese left.[15] The brunt of the fighting at Roliça took place in the centre and on the right of the allied line and, although Roliça is one of its battle honours, the 71st was not one of the regiments mentioned by Wellesley in his victorious post-battle dispatch.

Wellesley received welcome reinforcements with the landing of Anstruther's brigade at Maceira on 19 August and that of Acland a day later. He now had a British force of sixteen thousand men at his disposal, together with some 1,500 Portuguese under Colonel Nicholas Trant. A further force under Sir John Moore was expected shortly. While he was to be superseded imminently as commander of the army, successively by generals Harry Burrard and Hew Dalrymple, Wellesley now held a numerical advantage over Junot. The latter, however, had marched from Lisbon and, commanding a force of some fourteen thousand, attacked Wellesley's position at Vimeiro on Sunday, 21 August. The battle of Vimeiro was to prove a very hot engagement for Pack and the 71st regiment. The French attacked both the centre and the left wing of Wellesley's force. Ferguson's brigade (the 36th, 40th and 71st) was again positioned on the left, in the first line, when the French under General Junot launched their attack. The men of the 71st were instructed to prime their arms and lie down to avoid the French artillery. When the enemy infantry approached, the regiments of the brigade charged and broke the advance. As the French were forced to retreat, six of their cannon were captured. These were defended, notwithstanding a French counterattack when the 71st and 82nd regiments obliged the French to retire again. The 71st lost 119 killed or wounded in this combat. The battle was a signal defeat for the French, ultimately resulting in their evacuation of Portugal under the terms of the controversial Convention of Cintra.[16] In his dispatch

Wellesley singled out a number of regiments and officers for special mention, including the 71st and Pack.[17] Indeed at the end of the battle he rode up to the regiment and, speaking with Pack, praised it.[18] Subsequently the regiment was granted the battle honour of Vimiera [*sic*]. There were stories of individual bravery at Vimeiro in the regiment, but one event which was remembered long afterwards involved a number of men going to look for water.[19] They discovered the wounded General Brenier, whose horse had been shot from under him, with his aide de camp and an orderly trying unsuccessfully to extricate him.[20] All three were taken prisoner, along with the aide de camp's beautiful Arabian horse. The man who caught the horse wished to claim it as a prize but allegedly was deprived by Colonel Pack of his entitlement 'on account of his well-known intemperate habits'.[21] Further controversy, however, surrounded the manner of General Antoine François Brenier's capture and his subsequent treatment.

Corporal Mackay obtained the credit for capturing General Brenier, but there was disagreement at the time as a number of accounts had an Irish soldier, Private Gavin (Gaven in some accounts) capturing the general but Mackay taking the credit.[22] At some stage the French general offered either Gavin or Mackay his watch and purse for saving him, but the offer was refused or else Mackay prevented Gavin accepting the money. While Brenier was being secured, the orderly who had been trying to help him sprang onto his own horse and made good his escape. Mackay then took Brenier to his commanding officer, Pack, who, on being told of the generous conduct of the corporal, is said to have remarked that British soldiers fought for honour and not for money.[23] The net result was that Mackay received a commission as an ensign in the 8th West India regiment and later a gold medal from the Highland Society.

There ensued a degree of respite for Pack and the 71st. After Vimeiro the regiment marched to Torres Vedras and from there via Mafra to Lisbon, where the men camped at the Queen's Park, 'a large green in the vicinity of Lisbon'.[24] Immense crowds turned up and Colonel Pack ordered the regimental band to play for them.[25] On the next day the men received an issue of new tartan trousers, having worn their predecessors day and night for weeks on end. In Lisbon their duties included the protection of French troops awaiting repatriation to France under the terms of the Convention of Cintra from the vengeance of the Portuguese.[26] They were not entirely successful for a number of sick Frenchmen were killed, and reportedly the protection offered by the British made it unsafe in turn for British soldiers to go out in groups of two or three.[27] During that time a number of deserters from the French army enlisted in the 71st. These were not native French but Swiss, Germans and Italians.[28]

In the autumn, with Generals Dalrymple, Burrard and Wellesley facing investigation back in London as part of the Inquiry into the Convention of Cintra, Sir John Moore was appointed to command the British army in Portugal. Instructed to help the Spanish, if possible, he determined to take twenty thousand men into Spain, leaving some ten thousand to defend Portugal. Moore divided his army into four columns, which, it was arranged, were to meet at Salamanca in Spain. Pack and the 71st were part of the force of some six thousand men under Lieutenant General Sir John Hope, which, with all the cavalry and most of the artillery, took a circuitous route through Abrantes, Badajoz, Almaraz and Escorial before reaching Salamanca. Logistics demanded Moore follow the risk of dividing his force and the quality of the roads led to the cavalry and most of the artillery being sent with Hope. On 27 October Moore left Lisbon, the same day as the 71st set out under Hope.[29] Initially Moore had hoped to link up with the Spanish forces operating out of Madrid, but this objective was destroyed by Napoleon's explosive campaign resulting in the fall of Madrid on 4 December and the ensuing British retreat to La Coruna in late December and early January. Even while marching to join Moore at Salamanca, the 71st and other regiments were harried by the French. Their travails were only beginning for the 71st suffered with the rest of the army retreating in snow and icy rain in a 'march of death' through the mountains of Galicia.[30] Joseph Sinclair of that regiment described the suffering graphically:

> There was nothing to sustain our famished bodies, or shelter them from the rain or snow. We were either drenched with rain or crackling with ice. Fuel we could find none. The sick and wounded that we had been still enabled to drag with us in the wagons, were now left to perish in the snow. The road was one line of bloody footmarks, from the sore feet of the men; and, on its sides, lay the dead and the dying. Human nature could do no more.[31]

In these atrocious conditions Denis Pack's servant Mrs Cahill gave birth to a 'fine boy' in the snow.[32] She was luckier than another new mother who died on the descent from Monte del Castro. Sinclair again provides the commentary:

> In the centre lay a woman, young and lovely, though cold in death, and a child, apparently about six or seven months old, attempting to

draw support from the breast of its dead mother. Tears filled every eye, but no one had the power to aid … At length one of General Moore's staff officers came up, and desired the infant to be given to him. He rolled it in his cloak, amidst the blessings of every spectator. Never shall I efface the benevolence of his look from my heart, when he said 'Unfortunate infant, you will be my future care.'[33]

Pack's regiment lost men not just to the elements but also in crossing the river Esla at Benevente on 28 December, and in the fighting at Lugo on 5 and 6 January 1809 when the French caught up with them.[34] It was so cold at Lugo that the men were forced to stay ready all night on 5 January, alternately standing on the lee side of each other, like penguins sheltering from the wind. Events on this march indicate that although Denis Pack had a reputation for irritability, he was also the type of officer who looked after his men, and they in turn cared for him. On the retreat to La Coruna, when fording a river, a fellow officer ordered one of his men to carry him across. Spotting this, Pack told the officer to get down and ford the river himself. Bivouacking outside Lugo with rain coming down in torrents, one soldier reported: 'I threw myself down in the mud, on the lee side of a stone dyke, as the best shelter I could find. Certainly there was no respect of persons here: the elements are remarkably impartial in such cases as these; and on looking round the field I saw Colonel Pack squatting close by my side.'[35] Sometime later, when the men struggled into Betanzos, Pack was leaning out of the window of a house looking for stragglers from the 71st regiment and he allocated them houses depending on which company they belonged to.[36] When one of the regiment captured and killed a bullock, there does not seem to have been any criticism from Pack, who asked for its heart and was given the kidneys as well.[37] Officers as well as privates suffered desperately from lack of sustenance on occasion.[38]

The army arrived at La Coruna on 11 January 1809 to find no fleet of transports waiting to carry it back to England. Fortunately, Moore also found the governor and citizens of the town friendly and supportive, notwithstanding the fears they must have harboured of French retribution when the British departed. The fleet of naval and transport vessels dropped anchor in the bay on the afternoon of 14 January, whereupon the embarkation of the cavalry, heavy artillery and sick began immediately. Fighting with Soult's encircling French force took place on 15 January, and a full battle was fought on 16 January before the army was finally loaded onto the ships on the night of 17 January. The 71st had been involved in skirmishing prior to the arrival of the fleet but was posted on

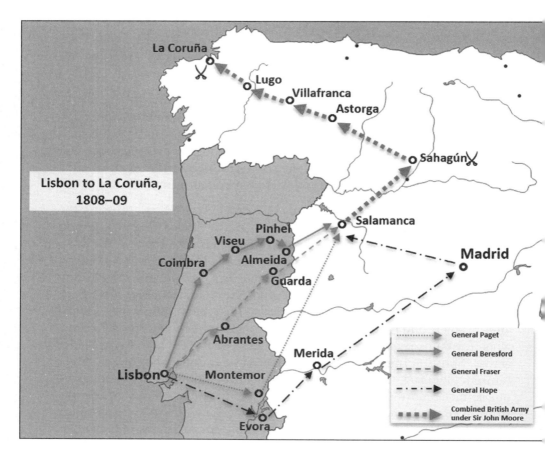

Lisbon to La Coruña,
1808–09

General Paget
General Beresford
General Fraser
General Hope
Combined British Army
under Sir John Moore

the extreme left of the British line on 16 January and saw little action.[39] Moore died in the battle on 16 January but his second in command, Lieutenant General Baird, who was also wounded, wrote to Pack from Portsmouth at the end of January conveying the thanks of the two Houses of Parliament to the army for its performance at La Coruna.[40] Pack and the regiment were entitled to the battle honour 'Corunna'.[41] Two weeks after the battle Pack and his regiment were back in England. On their return from La Coruna the regiment was sent to Ashford barracks in Kent to recover and to replace men lost in Portugal and Spain. One man of the 71st who did not make it back to England was Balfour Kermack, who had fought alongside Pack in southern Africa and the Rio de la Plata. He had become detached from his regiment, and with a small number of colleagues ultimately made it back to Portugal, where he continued to serve with the army in a battalion made up of stragglers.[42]

Light infantry, frequently used as a screening force, had been used by the Austrians, Prussians, French and British to a limited extent in the second half of the eighteenth century, but the British had seen how useful they were in the American War of Independence. More recently Sir John

Moore had admired their abilities in Corsica and Egypt, leading to the establishment of the light infantry division in which the 43rd and 52nd regiments were combined with the 95th. Schooled to a high degree, their training under Moore relied more upon mutual respect than the lash, their commander insisting that prevention of crime was superior to punishment of any misdemeanours. In 1809 the 71st was added to this elite group by being transformed into a light infantry regiment.[43]

Chapter 4

'Walcheren Fever', or the disintegration of a British army, 1809

English accounts of the French revolutionary and Napoleonic wars, perhaps understandably, tend to concentrate on naval success and the achievements leading to the liberation of the Iberian Peninsula. There were, however, repeated disasters involving British landings in the Low Countries, an area including Belgium and the Netherlands today. Denis Pack had taken part in the débâcle involving the Duke of York and the Earl of Moira in 1794–95, leading to the retreat to Bremen. France had established the Batavian Republic in 1795, effectively a client state. In 1799 an Anglo-Russian expedition to Den Helder had ended in retreat and evacuation, though it did manage to capture part of the Batavian fleet. In 1806 Napoleon had installed his brother Louis there as king but was surprised when Louis failed to turn out to be an obedient and manageable surrogate in the newly designated kingdom of Holland. Ultimately, this led to Louis's removal in 1810, but before then Great Britain had sought to advance its own position in that quarter once again.

In 1809 British eyes turned towards the Scheldt estuary, where part of the French navy was based, along with the remaining Dutch fleet. The menace of a second major French naval base, in addition to Brest, directly adjacent to England was a cause of serious concern in circumstances of a threatened invasion of the British Isles. Early in the year it became clear that a substantial number of vessels were being built and fitted out in both Antwerp and Flushing. The cabinet, at the urging of Castlereagh, then secretary of state for war and the colonies, determined on an expedition to attack and destroy both shipping and fortifications on the Scheldt. This campaign was the centrepiece of British strategy that summer, intended to assist Britain's allies, the Austrians, as well as destroy any maritime threat from the Scheldt.[1] A force of thirty-nine thousand under the Earl of Chatham (a larger force than that sent with Wellesley to Portugal in

April 1809) was prepared and conveyed to Walcheren island by a fleet of over two hundred vessels, including thirty-five ships of the line and twenty-three frigates. In itself the outfitting of two major foreign expeditions so soon after the return of a badly mauled army from La Coruna was no mean achievement. The British plan was to seize Flushing on the island of Walcheren, and to then proceed upriver to Antwerp to destroy the fleet and fortifications there. The first part of the plan was easily achieved, with Flushing captured by 15 August, but caution and lack of ambition seem to have afflicted the British commanders, in complete contrast to their French counterparts. Any opportunity to advance on Antwerp was lost as the expeditionary force succumbed in increasing numbers to 'Walcheren Fever'. Generally assumed to have been a combination of malaria and typhus, this proved not only debilitating but deadly. The notion of proceeding to Antwerp was abandoned by the end of August. Over 5,000 men had died and when the whole of the invasion force had been brought home later in the year only 4,500 men were still fit for duty. Denis Pack and the 71st formed part of Chatham's army.

In the period between his return home from La Coruna and the departure of the Walcheren expedition in July 1809 Pack appears to have been involved in a two-pronged scheme, designed to take him to the command of a cavalry regiment and to place his second in command, the Honourable Henry Cadogan, as lieutenant colonel of the 71st. Cadogan, who had acted as one of Wellington's aides de camp in the 1808 campaign, was well placed politically as the son of the 1st Earl Cadogan.[2] Further, two of Cadogan's sisters had married two of Wellington's brothers, Gerald and Henry.[3] Notwithstanding these connections, the representations made to Horse Guards failed to produce the desired results. The best Cadogan could secure was an offer of Pack's appointment as Quartermaster-General to the cavalry, a position involving a return to Portugal with Lieutenant General William Payne, on Wellington's staff at that time.[4] The alternative was an exchange into the cavalry, paying the difference. The trouble was that such an appointment might necessitate a period on half-pay or placement in a West India regiment. Clearly this type of arrangement did not suit Denis Pack. While he clearly hankered after a return to being a cavalry officer, he was keen to be involved in active service. He also stated he could not afford to pay the difference involved in an exchange.

The expedition to the Low Countries sailed from the Downs on 28 July. Forming part of a corps under Lieutenant General Sir Eyre Coote, the 71st regiment was heavily involved in the capture of various fortified places on Walcheren. It formed part of the Light Brigade, which landed first on 30 July to clear the way for the landing of the full army. They captured the battery of Den Haak, but then

> advanced too incautiously upon the town of Veer [*sic*], and had actually got close to the draw-bridge when the garrison sallied out upon the five companies he had with him, & in a few minutes opened so destructive a fire upon them from some field pieces, that 7 men were killed & 27 wounded, besides the Assistant Surgeon killed. They then made a hasty a retreat [*sic*] as possible but not without having a few prisoners taken by the enemy.[5]

On 1 August Pack and his regiment succeeded in taking Veer (Campveer), although not without further loss. The town surrendered following a particularly hard-fought encounter which left twenty-seven members of the regiment dead, and a further fifty-one regimental injured.[6]

On 14 August the outworks of the town of Flushing, which had been besieged, were carried by a party including companies of the 71st led by Pack.[7] The following day the town surrendered, although it took some days to implement the terms. Soon afterwards Pack was appointed commandant of the fort at Campveer. The 71st remained there until withdrawn on 22 December, following which the regiment once again returned to England. The campaign in the Scheldt estuary had proved to be an unmitigated disaster, from which Chatham's reputation never recovered. However, Pack and the 71st had proved their mettle once again. The *Historical Record* of the regiment shows a loss of just under one hundred officers and men on this expedition, much lower than some regiments.[8] It is not clear how many of these were lost to 'Walcheren fever', but a good number must have recovered for in early August there were reportedly 437 men in the regimental hospital. Those who did recover were to experience the ague later, presumably a reference to the recurring nature of malaria. While Pack himself had been ill with Walcheren fever and 'brought to death's door', he made a good recovery.[9]

Pack was clearly ambitious. Prior to going on the Walcheren expedition he had canvassed the position of aide de camp to George III. This largely honorary position had the advantage of promotion to colonel, and was duly achieved on 25 July 1810.[10] Earlier in the year Pack had already unsuccessfully sought a position with the British army in Portugal. When none was forthcoming, he had returned to Ireland to visit his family. He cannot have spent long there for he had been in contact with his friend Marshal William Carr Beresford, commander in chief of the Portuguese army, who was happy to appoint Pack a brigadier general in that service in

1810. He was given command of an independent Portuguese brigade made up of the 1st and 16th line regiments and the 4th caçadores serving alongside the Light Division under Brigadier General Robert Craufurd. The caçadores, like the 71st, were light infantry. In this capacity Pack was to serve with distinction for the next three years.

Pack's transfer to the Portuguese service marked the end of his direct involvement with the 71st regiment with which he had served on three continents over a ten-year period. Joining the 71st had been a successful career move. One of his last acts on behalf of that regiment was to resist its anglicization in terms of dress, when in April 1810 he secured permission for it to retain the traditional highland trousers and bonnet, along with the regimental pipers who themselves continued to wear the kilt.[11] This concession, and the retention of the designation 'Highland', was to prove a lasting achievement, ensuring the retention of the regiment's connection with Scotland.

The 71st regiment went on to play a prominent part in the war in the Iberian Peninsula. Brevet Lieutenant Colonel Nathaniel Peacocke succeeded Pack in command of the regiment but not for long.[12] He returned quickly to England in the autumn of 1810 to be replaced by Henry Cadogan as lieutenant colonel. Cadogan had previously commanded the second battalion of the regiment. Pack and Cadogan were to stay in touch until Cadogan's death at the Battle of Vitoria in 1813. Peacocke then returned as lieutenant colonel of the regiment only to be cashiered for cowardice at the battle of St Pierre in December 1813, where he was adjudged to have deserted the regiment.

Pack, notwithstanding his reportedly prickly nature, had been a popular commander and some at least hoped for his return to the 71st when it next served in Portugal. As late as 1811 John Vandeleur, an officer with the 71st, anticipated that Pack might replace Sir William Erskine as their brigade commander, stating 'it is the wish of the whole brigade, for Pack is a brave fellow'.[13] The appointment did not occur at that time for Pack was still with the Portuguese army. That there was even talk of it reflects the problem facing Wellington in the winter of 1810/11 when he was deprived of the support of a number of divisional, brigade and regimental commanders because they were on leave in Great Britain or Ireland, whether for recuperation from injuries or otherwise. Those absent included Rowland Hill, James Leith, Robert Craufurd and Stapleton Cotton. As these senior commanders returned to the Iberian Peninsula, Pack's lack of precedence meant the possibility of his appointment to command a brigade in the British army remained remote.

Chapter 5

Seguindo as ordens de Beresford*, 1810

Great Britain was faced with some difficult choices in early 1809. It had a tenuous hold on Portugal, now threatened with French invasion for a second time, on this occasion from the north by Marshal Soult. At the same time the French threatened England from the Low Countries, where logically Great Britain might best assist the other northern European powers in conflict with Napoleon. The British government determined on a two-pronged approach: the expedition designed to capture Antwerp, which ended in disaster, and the dispatch of further help to Portugal, intended not just to keep that country under British influence, but to give succour to Spain. Assistance to Portugal came in two forms. In January 1809 the government decided to respond positively to a request from the Portuguese Regency for a senior officer to rebuild and train the Portuguese army. In early February the government selected Major General William Carr Beresford to fill the position. It was not until late March that a decision was made to appoint Sir Arthur Wellesley to command a substantially reinforced British army in Portugal. As such he would command the combined Anglo-Portuguese forces. Arriving in Portugal in April, Wellesley succeeded in a campaign to clear Portugal of French forces in northern Portugal in May. In late July, with Spanish involvement, Wellesley was to win a tactical victory over the French at Talavera de la Reina, before being forced by superior numbers to retreat into Portugal. The winter of 1809/10 witnessed the commencement of the construction of the Lines of Torres Vedras, a defensive system designed to ensure the security of Lisbon, and in a doomsday scenario to enable the British army to evacuate the country.

William Carr Beresford, following his return to Great Britain from the Rio de la Plata, had led the occupation of Madeira in late 1807. He then joined the British forces in Portugal where he had undertaken a number

---

*Trans.: 'Following Beresford's orders'

of tasks in 1808. Subsequently, he commanded a brigade in Sir John Moore's army during the advance into Spain and the ensuing retreat to La Coruna.[1] Within two weeks of his return to England after the evacuation from La Coruna, he was informed that he had been chosen to command the Portuguese army. In March 1809, on arrival in Lisbon, Beresford was appointed Commander in Chief and Marshal of the Portuguese army. In that capacity he was to rebuild, reorganize and train a force of fifty-two thousand men which earned its laurels over the next five years, resulting in the recognition that its infantry was the equal of any other in Europe.[2] The task of rebuilding the Portuguese army and ensuring its ability to manoeuvre and fight was a considerable challenge. Many of the officers had left at or around the time of the first French invasion of Portugal under Junot in 1807. Some had gone to England, while others accompanied the royal family to Brazil. In early 1808 General Junot had dissolved the Portuguese army. At this time some of its best regiments entered the service of France, being posted to northern Europe, where as the *Legion Portugaise* they formed part of Napoleon's forces until 1814. Following the expulsion of the French from Portugal in the late summer of 1808, the Regency in Portugal had commenced the recall of the army, but, in recognition of the size of the task of rebuilding the army, requested the appointment of a British general, leading to Beresford's appointment. On arrival in Portugal Beresford commented:

> When I arrived here the army was in a terrible state ... One found it without discipline and without subordination. The soldiers were lacking in confidence in their officers who were negligent in their duties and had an attitude and behaviour which encouraged insubordination amongst the soldiers. There was completely lacking in the officers any strength or application of military laws, and the army I saw was an ungovernable machine.[3]

Beresford's approach to his task was to introduce English infantry and cavalry regulations to train the new forces and to combine training with strict discipline. The regulations were translated into Portuguese by one of his aides de camp, William Warre of the Anglo-Portuguese port family.[4] British officers and NCOs were seconded to the Portuguese army to carry out and oversee the regeneration of the army. To these were added a new wave of mostly young Portuguese officers. A number of the British officers who followed Beresford to Portugal in 1809 and 1810 had served previously with Beresford in the 88th regiment and/or in southern Africa and South America. The offer of a step up in rank, whereby for instance a lieutenant became a captain and a captain a major, was attractive to many young officers, but Beresford needed men with regimental command experience as well, and he must have been delighted with Pack's decision to join him.[5] Pack's commission as a brigadier general in the Portuguese service is dated 7 July 1810 and he was to serve in that capacity until July 1813.

Throughout the autumn and winter of 1809/10 Beresford oversaw the in-depth training of the Portuguese army by both British and Portuguese officers. Wherever possible he tried to ensure that if a British lieutenant colonel commanded a regiment, there would be a Portuguese major or vice versa. Drilled incessantly, the Portuguese regiments impressed Wellington when he and Beresford went on a tour of inspection over Christmas and New Year.[6] This inspection of the troops convinced Wellington that with a number of exceptions the Portuguese regiments could be brigaded with their British counterparts and in 1810 the 3rd, 4th and 5th divisions each incorporated a Portuguese brigade, while the Light Division contained two regiments of caçadores.[7] A Portuguese division was then created and put under the command of General John Hamilton on 5 March 1810. This division served on a regular basis with the 2nd division throughout the remainder of the war. Additionally, there were three Portuguese independent brigades fighting alongside the British army. Each of the independent brigades was made up of two line regiments and a regiment of caçadores.[8] Pack was appointed to command one of these independent brigades, the 1st Portuguese brigade, which, at the time of his arrival, was based close to the Portuguese frontier with Spain, where it acted in concert with the Light Division of the British army, then commanded by Robert Craufurd.[9]

Pack's return to Portugal coincided with the third and most intense French invasion of that country. Napoleon made it clear that the objective was to drive the British out of Portugal. To this end, a force of over sixty-five thousand men under Marshal Masséna was assembled in the environs of Salamanca in the early summer of 1810. In Spain there were additional French armies. Apart from the force centred on Madrid, responsible for the safety of King Joseph Bonaparte, the foremost amongst these forces were those led by Soult and Suchet, respectively engaged in the attempted conquest and pacification of Andalusia and Catalonia. In planning the attack on Portugal, Napoleon appears to have discounted the Portuguese army. His orders provided for Masséna to attack and destroy Wellington's army of twenty-five thousand. While they were as yet largely untried, the reconstituted Portuguese army in 1810 was able to contribute a further

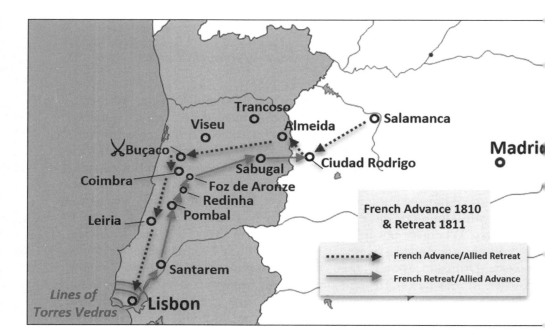

twenty-five thousand men to Wellington's force, while maintaining garrisons and small detachments elsewhere.[10] The French besieged and after a stout defence took the Spanish frontier fortress of Ciudad Rodrigo on 10 July. Masséna then moved forward to besiege Almeida, the Portuguese counterpart to Ciudad Rodrigo, sitting just inside Portugal. Confidently expected to hold out for three or four weeks, Almeida was virtually annihilated by a freak explosion in its own magazine on the first night of the siege proper, on 26 August. Its commander, Colonel William Cox, had no choice but to surrender the next day. The allies were fortunate in that Masséna, instead of moving forward into Portugal immediately, delayed his progress for several weeks. His advance then took him in a southwesterly direction until he came up against the Anglo-Portuguese army at Buçaco (Bussaco). The allied retreat involved laying waste to the territory being vacated, with fortifications, mills, bridges and other strategic sites being demolished and food destroyed.

Pack's appointment to the Portuguese army was important in that Beresford received many applications from more junior officers eager to seek advancement, but in Pack he obtained an experienced and trusted officer, who was also a personal friend. Pack was welcomed not just by Beresford. The Marshal's Quartermaster-General Benjamin D'Urban thought Pack 'a great acquisition, – an officer of tried service, sound judgement and proved intrepidity'.[11] Pack's new command consisted of the Portuguese 1st and 16th line regiments and the 4th caçadores (light infantry). In June the two line regiments of the brigade had been stationed at Trancoso, Beresford's then headquarters, north of but close to

Almeida.[12] D'Urban records that Pack had arrived at Trancoso by 2 July.[13] He would have been in time to witness the execution by firing squad of Bento José Garcia, one of the soldiers of the 1st regiment, who was convicted of killing one of his own comrades, the sentence being confirmed by Marshal Beresford on 4 July.[14] It would not be the last occasion on which the most severe of punishments was administered to soldiers from Pack's brigade, desertion proving particularly problematic in 1811, when it came to Wellington's attention.[15] Pack clearly spent some time at Trancoso for he was certainly there in August 1810 at the head of his brigade.[16] The 4th caçadores had only joined the brigade in July and it seems likely time was spent integrating all three regiments. Though operating in conjunction with the Light Division, his brigade was not part of Craufurd's desperate rearguard action on the Coa on 24 July. However, Wellington was sufficiently concerned about what had happened there to write to Beresford requesting he order Pack's brigade to be ready to march to Craufurd's assistance at a moment's notice.[17] In the event this did not prove necessary, though as a precautionary measure Wellington subsequently asked Beresford to move Pack's brigade into the pine woods in front of Celorico, unless Beresford was concerned such a move would leave Trancoso open. Celorico is some 20 kilometres south of Trancoso and it is unclear as to whether the brigade was in fact moved at that time, for on 2 September Pack, who was then based on the Rio Torto, a small tributary of the Douro north of Trancoso, was joined by Charles Synge as his aide de camp. Synge was then a captain in the 10th Hussars. He joined the Portuguese service, and his war notebook provides many insights into life with Denis Pack.[18] Even as Synge joined Pack, the allied army was retreating from the Portuguese frontier. In the retreat from Almeida, Pack's brigade was consistently involved in the depredation of the countryside with the objective of depriving the advancing French of material support. This was a process fraught with danger, for Pack's brigade was vastly outnumbered by the advancing French, whom Synge estimated at fifteen to twenty thousand. Pack's troops fought a minor engagement in Santa Comba Dao, at the junction of the rivers Criz and Dao southwest of Viseu, on 19 September, successfully destroying the bridges over both rivers having retired across them, and a few days later retreated further through Mortagua with the French close behind.[19] Here Pack's brigade joined the Light Division under Brigadier General Craufurd. The combined force reached the Serra do Buçaco on 25 September after several further days of resisting the probing of French cavalry. That day there were further clashes during which the 4th caçadores held their ground, with Wellington observing they 'showed that steadiness and gallantry which others of the Portuguese troops have since manifested'.[20]

Wellington chose to give battle at Buçaco. The Serra do Buçaco is a prominent ridge running north to south with its southern extremity anchored by the river Mondego. The Anglo-Portuguese army of some fifty thousand men faced a French army under Masséna of perhaps sixty-five thousand. The choice of a good defensive position compensated Wellington for the inferiority in numbers. There was some fighting on the evening of 26 September on the lower slopes of the mountain between the light infantry of the two armies, and Pack must have been concerned, for he referred to the French driving in 'our caçadore skirmishers like so many rabbits; would that I had the 71st to stiffen their backs'.[21] Early on 27 September the French launched their first major assault on the centre of the allied line, when Merle and Heudelet's divisions were hurled at Picton's 3rd division, which blocked the pass of Santo Antonio do Cantaro.[22] Along with the British 74th regiment, the Portuguese 21st threw back Heudelet's attack. Similarly, with the help of the 88th regiment, the 45th regiment with the 8th Portuguese performed heroically.[23] After protracted fighting, the French were thrown off this part of the ridge. Masséna's attention turned then to an attack on a more northerly part of the defensive line, near the convent de Santa Cruz do Buçaco. The divisions of Loison and Marchand were here launched against Craufurd's Light Division. Pack's brigade, on the right of the Light Division, became involved in some of the heaviest fighting, with the 1st and 16th line regiments as well as the 4th caçadores winning their spurs and the admiration of all. The French of Ney's 2nd division were pushed back by Craufurd's force, which included the 43rd and 52nd regiments.[24] The struggle and the bravery of troops on both sides was recorded by Charles Synge:

> Several other columns under Marshal Ney tried the same game on our immediate left – swarms of skirmishers clambered up the steep sides with desperate impetuosity regardless of a well-sustained fire of the Light Division and a Battalion of Caçadores of ours – as well as 8 or 10 guns some (ours) using only 'shrapnel' shells, which when they did burst on the calculated spot (which, however, was not invariably the case) caused immense loss – for some little time we thought the Light Division (every man of which we could see from our rock) overpowered – a small hamlet appeared to be disputed for some time and our Caçador Battalion on its right (but separate about a hundred yards) required some support which General Pack supplied from Sir

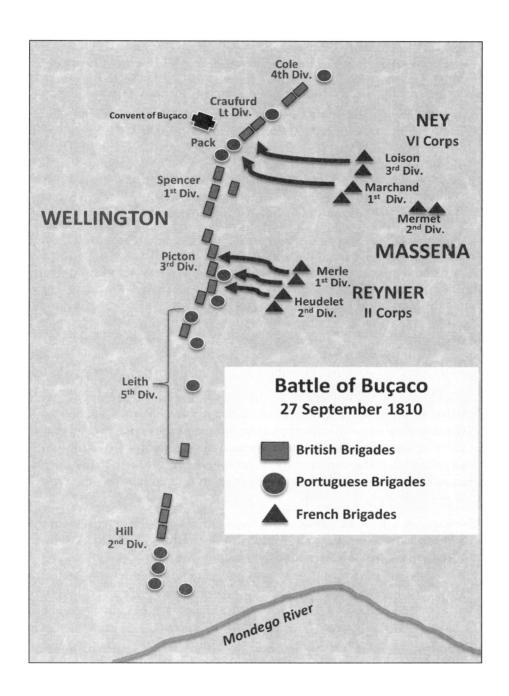

Battle of Buçaco

27 September 1810

British Brigades

Portuguese Brigades

French Brigades

Thomas Noel Hill's regiment. Indeed for a few minutes we doubted if the Light Division could maintain their ground – the struggle was desperate, the shouting, the roar of artillery, and the intense anxiety could never be imagined, still less described when suddenly the whole mass as if by some preconcerted signal dashed forward with a charge that nothing could withstand and such a cheer as broke out: the 1st Division in their rear ours from 'the rock' absolutely stopped my breath for an instant. The loss was considerable on our side but that of the enemy was immense – not more than half of general Pack's Brigade were engaged and that chiefly as light infantry – but we lost a good many amongst them a very fine young fellow a Captain of Grenadiers of Hill's regiment (Captain Mackintosh).[25]

Masséna, having suffered severe losses, withdrew. He then moved to out-flank Wellington by pursuing a route north through the mountains and then turning south to Coimbra, resulting in the allied withdrawal to the defensive Lines of Torres Vedras north of Lisbon. French losses at Buçaco were considerably greater than those suffered by the allies, but it is notice-able that allied losses of killed, wounded and missing were split evenly between the British and Portuguese forces, a reflection on both the make-up of Wellington's army and the intensity of the battle faced by the soldiers of both nations. Wellington praised both the Portuguese and Beresford at length, observing:

It has brought the Portuguese levies into action with the enemy for the first time in an advantageous situation; and they have proved that the trouble which has been taken with them has not been thrown away, and that they are worthy of contending in the same ranks with British troops in this interesting cause, which they afford the best hopes of saving.[26]

More specifically, Pack's brigade received praise from those serving on the ground in its vicinity. Captain Jonathan Leach of the 95th Rifles, part of the Light Division, observed in his memoirs:

General Pack's Portuguese brigade formed line and charged in a most regular and spirited manner under a cannonade of round-shot from the enemy's batteries. It shows what improvement they have made since British officers and good discipline have been introduced amongst them. I was quite hoarse with cheering and halloing. Whenever we saw the Portuguese about to charge, who were nearly a mile distant, we all set up a howl which undoubtedly spirited them on and they behaved uncommonly well, much better than the most sanguine could have expected.[27]

Pack must have been relieved, given the remarks he had expressed the previous evening when his caçadores were driven in 'like rabbits'. Further, Major Joaquim da Camara of the 16th regiment had abandoned the regiment before the battle, which must have unsettled Pack and drew down Beresford's ire, though he may have escaped with a peremptory, if embarrassing, public order to return to the regiment.[28] At Buçaco Pack's brigade was one of those singled out for praise, having 'showed great steadiness and gallantry'.[29] No one doubts the Portuguese fought well on the day, though Sergeant Anthony Hamilton suggested there may have been a degree of subterfuge involved with some British troops changing coats with the Portuguese in Pack's brigade.[30] Given that Pack's brigade was placed beside the Light Division, just on its right, it is possible this stratagem was used.[31] Hamilton served with the 43rd regiment, part of the Light Division, so would have been in the locality to witness events. The French suspected it. However, if this ploy was utilized, one would have expected to see more widespread reports on the topic, and Hamilton's uncorroborated report should be treated with caution. It is perhaps noteworthy that Charles Synge, who was serving with Pack at Buçaco, makes no mention of any such tactic in his notes on the battle.[32] British officers in the Portuguese army usually but not always wore Portuguese rather than British uniforms.

On the evening of 28 September Wellington's main force began the long retreat to the Lines of Torres Vedras via Fornos, Coimbra and Leiria.[33] The corps commanded by General Hill hitherto on the allied right proceeded through Tomar and Santarem to Alhandra. By 10 October the army had entered the Lines, a defensive cordon of two sets of fortifications, one behind the other, built to guard Lisbon and secure the Tagus estuary.[34] The allied army was not troubled much in that retreat by the French, although there was skirmishing and Pack had a horse shot from under him when the French drove the allies from Alenquer on 10 October.[35] Wellington's strategy involved the destruction of material that might be of use to the advancing French, with the local population retiring behind the Lines with whatever possessions they could bring with them. This migration was accomplished partially, so that substantial numbers reached the safety of the Lines, albeit with few possessions and in the knowledge that what had not been destroyed in advance of the arrival of Masséna's forces would thereafter be liable to be seized by the French soldiers. Those who chose to stay, or could not leave in time ahead of the French advance, suffered assault, injury and in some cases death. Wellington's strategy was more successful in some regions than in others. In Leiria, because of the reluctance of the Portuguese Regency to destroy that which could not be moved within the Lines, large stores of foodstuffs fell into the hands of the advancing French army.[36] On the other hand, General Koch reported that in the region of Mangualde (Beira), the fields had been set on fire and the villages were either deserted or destroyed.[37] Reportedly fourteen men and two women were killed by the French in Mangualde as they passed through the town. Other towns were not so fortunate. Redinha, with a population much smaller than that of Mangualde, suffered 341 deaths, of which 170 were women, during the French invasion.[38]

The two outer defensive lines protecting Lisbon stretched from the river Tagus to the sea. They presented a complex system of water defences, forts and redoubts, manned largely by Portuguese militia, enabling the army to encamp behind those forts with the prospect of being moved quickly to wherever there was a need. The whole was divided into six districts, with forces allocated to each district. Incredibly the French had no knowledge, or at the very least no detailed knowledge, of what they were facing until they were before the Lines. Part of Pack's brigade, the 4th caçadores, being light infantry, was ordered to occupy redoubts 11 (Moinho Céu), 12 (Passo) and 13 (Caneira) adjacent to Sobral de Monte Agraco and west of Arruda.[39] The remainder of his brigade occupied the great redoubt on Monte Agraco.[40] He was concerned they might be cut off from the rest of the army, but Wellington pointed out that he had had the redoubts stocked with provisions, including forage, to cover this eventuality. Unfortunately, these stores had been consumed by the first troops passing through the area on the retreat. Wellington assured Pack he had requested the Commissary-General to restock the redoubts with provisions and to make wood and forage available from Sobral. Perhaps more serious, given that the weather had turned very wet, was the lack of tents, which should have been supplied by the Portuguese government. In the circumstances Wellington agreed that temporarily piquets would guard the redoubts, with the remainder of the troops quartered in houses in nearby villages.[41]

The 71st regiment, having been restored following its losses in the Walcheren expedition of 1809, was sent to Portugal in the autumn of 1810. Six companies arrived in the Tagus on 25 September and disembarked at Lisbon the following day. They missed therefore the combat at Buçaco. Notwithstanding the achievements of his brigade at Buçaco, there was

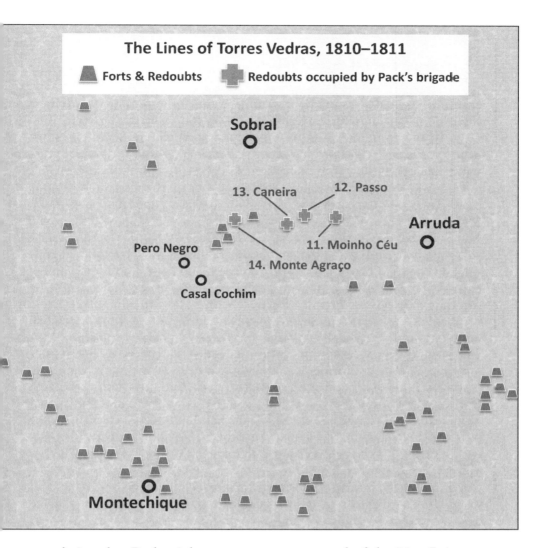

The Lines of Torres Vedras, 1810–1811

Forts & Redoubts   Redoubts occupied by Pack's brigade

Sobral

13. Caneira   12. Passo

Arruda

Pero Negro   11. Moinho Céu

14. Monte Agraço

Casal Cochim

Montechique

speculation that Pack might now resume command of the 71st. It is not apparent whether, or the degree to which, Pack was unhappy with his position in the Portuguese service at this time, but this is suggested in the *Memoir* authored by Pack's grandson. No contemporaneous correspondence between Pack and Beresford has been located, but their respective headquarters and those of Wellington were all within easy striking distance of each other, less than 10 kilometres apart. Further, while there does not appear to exist a definitive list of guests, it is highly likely Pack would have been invited to the dinner and ball which took place when Wellington knighted Beresford on behalf of George III at the palace of Mafra on 7 November. Pack was not only now a senior member of the army but a close friend of Beresford.[42] There was plenty of opportunity for Pack to have discussed his situation with Wellington and Beresford even if no request was made in writing in the autumn of 1810. There is evidence of an ongoing correspondence on the topic dating from June 1811. In any event Pack was prevailed upon by Wellington and Beresford to persevere with the Portuguese army at this stage and for several years thereafter, though he continued to seek a return to the British army.[43]

Pack was certainly in touch with members of the 71st at this time, however, as that regiment was part of a brigade stationed at Sobral under Major General Sir William Erskine when it joined the Lines.[44] There the 71st suffered two serious attacks on 12 and 14 October by Masséna's advance guard and, while the enemy was repulsed, the 71st suffered considerable losses. Quartermaster Sergeant William Gavin in his diary noted two events of interest in the story of Denis Pack. In the first of these he recounts how Major Thomas Reynell of the 71st foot fought in single combat with a French grenadier, overcame him, 'and laid him stretched on the ground'.[45] Reynell and Pack were to have a close association later. The second event recited by Gavin concerned a visit the quartermaster sergeant paid to his former commanding officer Denis Pack, whom he describes as his old friend and benefactor. Pack 'lived in a hut of sods with scarcely a bed of straw to rest on, but so devoted was he to his country that he appeared to be quite comfortable and cheerful; he received me with the warmest friendship'.[46] Pack may have been irritable on occasions but clearly he had a good relationship with many of his subordinates, whether officers, NCOs, or rank and file.

Masséna, having tested the Lines of Torres Vedras at Sobral, decided it would be too difficult to try to force them. On 15 November, having previously sent back his hospitals, supplies and heavy artillery, Masséna withdrew his army to the town and vicinity of Santarem, a distance of just under 60 kilometres. The Frenchman sent one of his most trusted generals, Maximilian Foy, back to France with a view to getting Napoleon either to send substantial reinforcements or to order his withdrawal from Portugal. In the event Napoleon sent additional troops, which reached Masséna in December, but these were too few to alter the situation materially.[47]

Wellington followed the French retreat to Santarem with caution. He was uncertain as to Masséna's designs. Was he headed back to Spain, preparing for the siege of Abrantes, a move into the Alentejo or the establishment of a new defensive position? Pack's brigade was one of those tasked with probing the French defences and trying to ascertain the Marshal's intentions. Ultimately the French dug in at Santarem.

Wellington initially thought of attacking Masséna. On the morning of 19 November Craufurd's Light Division was moving on the Rio Maior, while further inland and to the west of Santarem Pack's brigade was also converging on the Rio Maior, with Spencer and the 1st division in-between. The plan, which was predicated on the opposing force being Masséna's rearguard only, involved Pack and his force getting in behind the French right, while Craufurd and Spencer advanced across swampy ground in front of Santarem. Pack's brigade had marched from Almoster to Azambujeira, to a point on the heights above the bridge of Celeiro. There he was to be joined by a brigade of 9 pounders and a party of dragoons. A salvo from Pack's artillery was to be the signal for all three forces to advance. With difficulty, both Craufurd and Pack reached the Rio Maior but then ran into terrain that was so waterlogged as to render it impassable. It had been raining for days and as a result even the roads were waterlogged. Pack's guns became stuck in deep mud. Further, it appeared the French were in some force on the other side of the river. Charles Synge's papers reveal that Wellington, with Beresford and Spencer, came up to Pack's position and the commander-in-chief saw for himself the difficulties. Although the guns were then coming up, Wellington counter-manded his orders for the attack.[48] He was glad of his decision, later realizing that he did not have enough men to take on what transpired to be the main French force.[49] D'Urban, who was not afraid to criticize Wellington, condemned the operation and made it very clear that had it not been for the late arrival of Pack's guns, he thought the allies would have fallen into a trap

> which had been set for us and sacrificed the two attacking Divisions probably, certainly that of Pack, not only by determining to believe that a Rear Guard, which was in fact two corps d'Armée, and perhaps half of another, but by blindly making a straggling and unsupported attempt in defiance of local difficulties and with the Body of the Army at a distance. Good fortune has supplied what was deficient on the score of Prudence, and the late arrival of means for attack has averted the evils that would have followed.[50]

Spencer clearly also felt it was a wise decision to call off the attack and that the decision saved countless lives, if not the army, observing 'My dear Pack, as long as a man of this army lives, this day ought never to be forgotten to you.'[51]

With Masséna entrenched at Santarem, Wellington decided it was too dangerous for him to risk the allied forces in a pitched battle. He put the army in winter quarters, while using Pack's Portuguese brigade to monitor

French movements. Pack's brigade was withdrawn to Almoster, 10 kilometres west of Santarem, on 22 November.[52] Serious duties were relieved by frequent dinners, sometimes with overnight stays at other headquarters. Synge (whom it will be recalled was Pack's ADC) refers to evenings spent with Generals Spencer, Leith and Erskine, as well as Colonel Cadogan of the 71st and various more junior officers, including Major Thomas Reynell. Illness also took its toll. The most notable of those who had to return home that winter was Rowland Hill, but in general terms injury and illness often reduced the number of effectives in a regiment by 25 per cent or more. In late November Synge himself fell ill at Marmeleira and on 2 December was removed to Lisbon, where he was visited by his commanding officer. He returned to join Pack on 14 December but suffered a relapse on 23 December. Fortune then favoured him, for he was lodged in the home of the Countess of Rio Maior until the end of January, when he was able to rejoin the brigade.

Ultimately, it was the winter weather and starvation which enabled Wellington to force a French withdrawal without a pitched battle. Masséna's position in Santarem was made increasingly difficult by a partial encirclement by Portuguese forces which moved in behind his army. Thus, Buçaco itself was occupied by militia under General Manuel Pinto Bacelar, and Coimbra likewise by militia under Colonel Nicholas Trant, while the fortress of Almeida which the French had partially repaired was blockaded by forces under General Francisco da Silveira. In March 1811 the French retreated through the devastated Portuguese countryside, harried all the way by the army and the Portuguese militia, before reaching the relative safety of Ciudad Rodrigo and Salamanca. Pack's brigade was to the forefront of the pursuit led by the Light Division, engaging the enemy at Pombal (11 March), Redinha (12 March), Casal Novo (14 March) and Foz d'Aronce (15 March). At Foz d'Aronce Pack's brigade was detached to the left by Wellington, heading through the mountains to turn the French position. Virtually constant engagement with the enemy must have taken its toll, although Pack described to his friend James Butler not the numbers lost by either side, but the devastation wrecked on property and person by the French army on this retreat: 'The cruelties practised on the peasants by individuals were, I hope, till now unheard of almost – and as far as Murcella everything was systematically burned.'[53] He was not alone in describing the appalling actions perpetrated by the retreating army. Wellington referred to 'a barbarity seldom equalled' while Edward Costello, a sergeant in the 43rd regiment, gave vivid accounts from the various towns vacated by the French.[54] Costello was clearly horrified by the scenes he encountered:

> At night we encamped on the outskirts of a small village, the name I do not recollect, but the sights within it I can never forget. In searching for a small stream from which I might procure water, I fell upon a small fountain, close to which lay two or three murdered Portuguese; their brains and blood, which seemed freshly to have oozed from their mangled remains, had even streamed into the spring, and turned me away with disgust from the water ... As I however, approached into the plaza, the desolation thickened; all the havoc that can possibly be imagined in so small a compass lay before me – murdered and violated women – shrieking and dying children – and, indeed, all that had possessed life in the village, lay quivering in the last agony of slaughter and awful vengeance.
>
> These became every day scenes until we overtook the French rearguard at Pombal.[55]

Not surprisingly, the diaries and accounts of Costello and others carry gruesome accounts of retribution carried out by Portuguese on isolated, injured and straggling French soldiers.

The devastation caused by the retreating French exacerbated a problem faced by Pack's independent brigade, and probably increased his desire to rejoin the British army. The inefficiency, and indeed inability, of the Portuguese commissariat increased as the lines of supply became more extended. Soon Pack's brigade could not keep up with the Light Division for want of foodstuffs. Pack felt that if Beresford, rather than the Portuguese, was put in control of the British financial subsidy to Portugal then an army could be formed to put 'this country out of all danger'. However, the appalling state of the Portuguese commissariat combined with a bankrupt government meant no officer could serve with pleasure or advantage and Pack, writing to his old friend James Butler, indicated he had often wished himself out of the Portuguese service and intended to quit it as soon as he could do so.[56] Pack was not exaggerating. Even before Masséna began his retreat, while Pack's brigade was still in quarters, Wellington wrote to Charles Stuart, the British Minister in Lisbon, requesting him to bring to the Regency's attention the lack of bread for Pack's brigade. It had previously been agreed that the brigade should at all times have six days' supply of bread, but instead it did not even have one day's supply, and in every week it received none for two or three days. Quite apart from the fact the soldiers were malnourished, the problem was exacerbated because, as Wellington pointed out, Pack's brigade formed an advanced post and was therefore liable to have to act quickly in time of need.[57] The situation clearly did not improve once the army began to follow Masséna. On 16 March 1811 Wellington advised Lord Liverpool that notwithstanding repeatedly urging the Regency to take measures to supply the troops, it had failed to do so and 'it is literally true, that Gen. Pack's brigade, and Col. Ashworth's, had nothing to eat for 4 days, although constantly marching or engaged with the enemy'. Wellington advised he had been forced to get the British commissary to supply the troops, who would otherwise have perished. The knock-on effect was that he had been forced to halt the army for want of supplies.[58] Matters did not improve in the short term. On 25 March Wellington told Beresford that Pack's brigade could muster only 1,700 men against a nominal strength of 2,625. Two days later he complained again to Beresford that the Portuguese troops were falling off terribly, and there were 5,800 Portuguese infantry sick.[59] This meant he had lost a third of his Portuguese infantry, leaving him with only 11,586 effectives. On 30 March Wellington advised Charles Stuart that he had been obliged to leave Pack's brigade behind as 'he has had one day's rice, and one day's Indian corn or bread (mentioned in his last note, which I sent you), since I saw him, 12 days ago!! It is really a joke to talk of carrying on the war with these people.'[60] On 11 April Pack was still waiting for supplies at Mangualde, between Viseu and Celorico da Beira, whereas Wellington was up at Vila Formosa on the Portuguese-Spanish frontier.[61] There was simply little to be found locally to eat. Though his troops had demonstrated their ability to take on the enemy, Pack's disenchantment with the Portuguese service in 1811 is understandable. While seconded to the Portuguese army, Pack and his brigade were effectively under the immediate command of Wellington for the three years of his Portuguese service. At the same time, financial and administrative decisions regarding the regiments of the brigade continued to be dealt with by Beresford. This included promotions, discipline, pay, allocation of recruits and sick leave. The duality of this command structure does not appear to have given rise to issues between the three Irishmen, whose correspondence with one another was always cordial.

The French had been driven out of Portugal by early April 1811, save that they continued to occupy the fortress of Almeida, the subject of elementary repairs following its internal ruin the previous August. Pack's Portuguese brigade was one of those selected by Wellington to blockade that town, which Masséna sought to relieve in early May.

Chapter 6

Fuentes de Oñoro and the escape of the Almeida garrison, 1811

'Has the character of a more than ordinarily zealous and alert officer'[1]

Within four weeks of leaving Portugal, Masséna advanced again from Ciudad Rodrigo with the intention of relieving the blockaded fortress of Almeida. That he was able to do so was in part due to reinforcements received from Marshal Bessières's *Armée du Nord*, which now gave Masséna a numerical advantage over Wellington, who had detached the 2nd, 4th, and Portuguese divisions under Beresford to attempt the recovery of Badajoz. Wellington took up a defensive position in and around Fuentes de Oñoro on the frontier of Portugal and Spain. There the battle of the same name was fought over three days from 3 to 5 May 1811. Only on 8 May did Masséna finally withdraw back towards Ciudad Rodrigo. Wellington had sustained major losses, and it is noticeable that there was no vote of thanks by parliament on this occasion. He knew he was lucky to have emerged victorious. Fuentes de Oñoro was an allied victory in that the French failed to relieve Almeida.[2] One of Wellington's most difficult battles was to be followed by 'the most disgraceful military event that has yet occurred to us'.[3]

Pack's Portuguese brigade had not participated in the battle. On retiring from Portugal, Masséna had left a strong garrison in the fortress of Almeida, which the French had repaired and refurbished militarily following its partial destruction and capture the previous August. The garrison of Almeida, some 1,400 strong, was commanded by General Antoine Brenier.[4] The general had been a British prisoner, following his capture at the Battle of Vimeiro, until exchanged in 1809. Following the defeat of Reynier's 2nd corps at the Battle of Sabugal on 3 April, Almeida had been blockaded by Wellington. He appointed Major General Alexander Campbell, the commander of the 6th division, to take charge of the blockade.

In addition to his own troops, Campbell was allocated Pack's Portuguese brigade which had now made its way to Cinco Villas, about 6.5 kilometres northwest of Almeida. Pack reports having reached Cinco Villas on 10 April, at a time when Wellington had indicated he was still stranded through lack of provisions at Mangualde, about 100 kilometres to the west. Either this is a transcription error or Pack came up ahead of his brigade, for that only appears to have reached Cinco Villas on about 14 April.[5] Irrespective of the conflict in dates, it is clear Pack and his brigade were based at Cinco Villas until 1 May, when the brigade moved to Malpartida to take over the base of operations previously occupied by Campbell. Wellington required Campbell's 6th division for what was to prove to be the battle of Fuentes de Oñoro. Pack was given the assistance of a battalion of the 2nd regiment and a number of guns to assist him.

Pack and his colleagues were perfectly aware that Brenier and his garrison might try to break out of Almeida, and sought to guard against such an eventuality. His Brigade Orders of 17 April reflect with considerable accuracy both the likely conduct of and the number of French troops in Almeida:

> The Garrison of Almeida is supposed to consist of 1400 men, and the probability is that, after destroying the place, they will make an attempt to escape, which ought to be guarded against by every possible means, and must be frustrated by the attention, zeal, and care of the field officers that may be on duty with the picquets, which may be certain of the assistance of the Brigade and other troops that are kept in readiness to support them.[6]

The heavy responsibility placed on Pack caused him to write in a contemporaneous note: 'A more distressingly anxious command I never had.'[7] No sooner had Campbell's division moved off to support Wellington, and the Battle of Fuentes de Oñoro had begun some 8 kilometres away, than the garrison at Almeida began to send out picquets stronger than usual and frequent skirmishes ensued.[8] Pack sent out search parties and they arrested a number of peasants acting suspiciously. Then they caught a French commissary riding a mule and leading a horse in the vicinity of the fortress.[9] The confusion was compounded by rockets, guns and lights from the fort, Ciudad Rodrigo and Masséna's army. Pack was clearly on high alert for an attempt to break out of Almeida. In the event no attempt was made to escape the beleaguered fortress prior to Masséna beginning his retreat from Fuentes de Oñoro on 8 May, but these few weeks must have been stressful, given the quoted comment by a man who had gone

through the hardships of the campaigns in South America, the retreat to
La Coruna, the battle of Buçaco and the horrors of the fevers suffered in
multiple expeditions to the Low Countries.

Before retiring, Masséna sent Brenier a coded order to attempt to break
out of Almeida and rejoin the main army via a bridge over the river
Agueda at Barba del Puerco. In doing so he was to destroy the fortifications and guns at Almeida. Three soldiers volunteered to take the message
to Brenier on being offered 6,000 francs in the event of success.[10] Two of
them, disguised as Spanish peasants, were caught and executed as spies.
The third, a resourceful soldier named André Tillet of the 6th Léger
regiment, who kept his uniform, managed to reach the castle on 7 May.
That night Brenier signalled to Masséna, by firing his guns in an agreed
sequence, that the message had been received and that the break-out
would be attempted. It may be that Masséna was waiting for this signal
before beginning his retreat, though it may have been simply a question of
sending off stores and artillery before he marched himself for Ciudad
Rodrigo on 8 May. He ordered General Reynier with his corps to San
Felices, on the eastern side of the bridge at Barba del Puerco, in anticipation of Brenier's decampment.

Brenier's troops spent the next couple of days mining the foundations of
the fort, destroying or making unserviceable the guns and ammunition,
and preparing for their escape. On the night of 10 May at about 10pm
they broke out through the north gate of Almeida in complete silence,
whispering the passwords 'Bonaparte et Bayard'.[11]

Once Masséna began his retreat, Wellington sent back Campbell and
the 6th division to relieve Pack's brigade and to resume command of
the blockade of Almeida. For this purpose, Campbell had three brigades
amounting to just under five thousand men. In addition, Pack's brigade
would remain close by. Campbell and his staff arrived back at Malpartida
on 10 May, and he placed his troops in a ring around but not close to
Almeida. Hearing that a large French force was near San Felices, Pack that
day rode to Barba del Puerco. He probably did not see any signs of activity
on the right-hand bank of the river opposite him, because he does not
comment on it in his Notes.[12] It was only on his return to Malpartida at
9pm that evening that he found out Campbell had resumed overall command, the 36th regiment had moved into Malpartida, and Campbell had
dispatched Pack's Portuguese brigade back to Cinco Villas. Some picquets
from the 4th caçadores of Pack's brigade were still in position north of
Almeida and next to them were picquets of the 2nd regiment. Campbell
had positioned his other brigades west and south of Almeida.[13] His largest

British brigade was that of Hulse, which for unexplained reasons he placed south of the fortress, a direction which any escape was unlikely to follow, for fear of running into the allied army still encamped in or near Fuentes de Oñoro.

Realizing that there were no troops stationed to guard the bridge at Barba del Puerco, Wellington, at about midday on 10 May, sent an order to Major General William Erskine to have a battalion moved there. Erskine, at that time in command of the 5th division, was a questionable choice to lead a division. His eyesight was very poor, he drank heavily, even by the standard of the day, and he had already made a number of decisions at Casal Nova and Sabugal which could have ended in disaster during Masséna's retreat. On at least one occasion Wellington opined Erskine was mad, but he had considerable influence at Horse Guards, for when Wellington remonstrated against his appointment to the army in Portugal the reply was 'no doubt he is sometimes a little mad but in his lucid intervals he is an uncommonly clever fellow; and I trust he will have no fit during the campaign, though he looked a little wild as he embarked'.[14] This exchange highlights one of Wellington's difficulties in that he could not determine whom to appoint to serve with the army in the Peninsula, and if they had influence at home, he was obliged to accept some appointments which he no doubt would not have made. As late as 1813 he observed 'I have nothing to do with the choice of the General officers sent out here, or with their numbers, or the army with which they are to serve; and when they do come, I must employ them as I am ordered.'[15] Nonetheless he must have felt Erskine had some good qualities, for notwithstanding his conduct during Masséna's retreat from Portugal, in late April 1811 Wellington had offered him to Beresford as the commander of his cavalry, stating that, even though Erskine was very blind, he was cautious and 'you will find him more intelligent and useful than anybody you have'.[16] Erskine's mental state subsequently led to his leaving the army and he died on 14 May 1813, having thrown himself from the window of a house in Lisbon.[17]

When he received Wellington's order (probably about 4pm) to move troops to the bridge at Barba del Puerco, Erskine was apparently at dinner. Only some hours later did he dispatch his own order to Lieutenant Colonel Charles Bevan, commanding the 4th regiment. At the time the 4th regiment was tasked with guarding the fords over the Dos Casas river, a tributary of the Agueda. Bevan did not receive the order until about midnight and ultimately it was early morning before the 4th regiment was put in motion towards the bridge at Barba del Puerco. From where the 4th regiment was stationed near Fort Concepcion to the bridge is about 12 kilometres as the crow flies.

Brenier's escape plan was well thought out. His force was formed into two columns. He refers to these as the left and right column and it seems that once formed they marched in tandem, with the left column providing direction. A third group made up of sappers was tasked with setting off the charges intended to demolish the castle of Almeida. Once this was accomplished, it hurried to attach itself to the second column. Brenier also had a baggage train, which he placed at the back of the column. A short march north broke through the Portuguese and British picquets before Brenier turned east in the direction of Villar de Ciervo, crossing the rivers Seco, Touroes and Dos Casas. Shortly before reaching Villar de Ciervo he turned north for Barba del Puerco.

Pack, who was staying at Campbell's headquarters at Malpartida for the night, became aware of the commotion as the French force swept aside the picquets, which somewhat confusingly he refers to as divisions. There were three of these piquets, each under the command of a field officer. Because Brenier had been firing the guns of Almeida on previous nights, it would appear these field officers thought nothing untoward was taking place. Pack seems to have been the first to react, arriving on the scene just as the enemy had broken through the allied line. His post-engagement report to Major General Campbell and notes that he sent home to James Butler in Ireland tell the story of the events on the night of 10/11 May 1811.[18] Initially Pack may only have had about ten men with him, but he added eighty from the reserve which lay behind the centre piquet, that of the 4th caçadores. As Pack explained later, he always kept a reserve of two hundred men behind the central division, in effect a rapid reaction force. He quickly set off in pursuit of the French, sending back a sergeant to get Major Dursbach to bring up the rest of the reserve, which was drawn from the 1st Portuguese regiment.[19] Pack's objective was to harry Brenier in such a way as to slow down the French and at the same time to show those gathering together the pursuit party where the French were. Pack thought briefly of himself going to rouse the 'Queen's' regiment (2nd foot), one of those responsible for trying to prevent Brenier's escape. However, he thought better of it as he was concerned he might lose his way and he could more effectively direct others to his position by continual sniping at the retreating French. At about the same time he sent a courier back to Campbell to tell him where he had gone. Throughout the rest of the night Pack's men tried to stay in touch with the French columns, an endeavour made difficult in the dark and because the French showed admirable

discipline and sang froid. When fired upon they did not fire back but merely pressed on towards their objective in close formation.[20] A few Frenchmen were killed or wounded by Portuguese fire. The wounded were taken prisoner but the need to guard them only served to reduce Pack's own numbers. Towards dawn, Brenier halted his men near the village of Villar de Ciervo, allowing Pack to catch up. Captain William Beresford, deputy assistant quartermaster general of the 6th division, who himself had joined Pack a little earlier, discovered there were some British dragoons in that village, and went and had them turned out to join the chase on the flank of the French column. Skirmishing, they did cause some delay to the French move forward. Ultimately, just as the 36th regiment under Campbell and the 4th regiment under Bevan arrived on the scene, Brenier's men reached the bridge at Barba del Puerco. The first column seems to have crossed largely unscathed, but the second column suffered a considerable number of injuries and deaths as the men threw themselves down the steep slopes carved by the Agueda river to escape their pursuers. In his memoirs Baron Marcelin de Marbot, who was a cavalry officer with Masséna's army at the time, referred to the dangerous and desperate retreat in unequivocal terms. Having acknowledged Pack's role, he described the approach by the French to the bridge:

> The last of our columns had to pass through a defile opening into a quarry among steep and pointed rocks. The enemy was pressing on from all sides, and several sections of our rear-guard was [*sic*] cut off by the English cavalry. Seeing this, the French soldiers climbed nimbly up the steep sides of the ravine, and escaped the English cavalry, only to fall into another danger. The Portuguese infantry pursued them on the heights, pouring a murderous fire into them. When at length our men, on the point of being succoured by Heudelet's division, thought that they were in sight of safety, the earth suddenly failed under their feet, engulfing part of them in a yawning chasm, at the foot of a huge rock. The head of the ensuing Portuguese column incurred the same fate, rolling pell-mell into the gulf with our own people . . . when the foot of the precipice was explored, a fearful sight appeared. Three hundred French and Portuguese soldiers lay there dead or horribly mutilated. Some sixty French and thirty Portuguese alone survived the terrible fall. Such was the last incident in the laborious and unlucky campaign of the French in Portugal. They never entered the country again.[21]

The French losses were not insignificant, but it could have been much worse. Pack summed it all up: 'ten minutes sooner would have placed him [Brenier] in safety; ten minutes later, and his destruction would have been inevitable'.[22] The crossing of the river Agueda by Brenier's men was assisted by covering fire from men of Heudelet's division, part of Reynier's corps, in position on the east side of the bridge. Showing considerable bravery, but disregarding his own safety and that of his men, a follow-up party of the 36th under Lieutenant Colonel Basil Cochrane crossed the bridge in vain pursuit, incurring heavy losses before having to turn back.

Pack claimed that taking into account those killed, wounded, drowned or taken prisoner, Brenier must have lost nearly half his men, but it looks as if this claim is overstated. Brenier put his loss at 360 men (about one quarter of his force), about 150 killed and about 200 made prisoner. Understandably, he praised the officers of the garrison for what was a considerable achievement in bringing out to safety a thousand men in darkness over inhospitable terrain, and he requested the legion d'honneur for those who had not already been awarded it for previous actions.[23] Brenier's own leadership was noteworthy, and he was rewarded by being made up to a general of division and a baron of the Empire.[24] Unsurprisingly he took the title Baron de Almeida. In fact, he had been extremely lucky, for earlier on the morning he crossed the bridge at Barba del Puerco the 8th Portuguese regiment had stopped there, having been called out by its commander on hearing the explosions at Almeida.[25] The Portuguese saw nothing of note for they were well ahead of Brenier's party, but the 8th regiment had marched from Junca to Barba del Puerco, a distance far greater than Bevan and the 4th regiment had to cover: clear evidence that had Bevan acted when he received the order, he would have reached the bridge long before Brenier and his men managed their great escape.

Wellington heard about Brenier's escape the next morning. His initial reaction was one of puzzlement. Writing to Beresford before any reports came in, Wellington commented: 'I cannot tell how this occurred; the troops which had been taken from the duty of the blockade were sent back to it yesterday afternoon, and in the whole were 4 times more numerous than the garrison. However, I suppose I shall hear from Gen. Campbell soon.'[26] When more fully briefed Wellington was livid and remained angry for several days. Reports were made by those in positions of command, including Erskine, Campbell, Pack, Bevan and Iremonger, the latter in command of the 2nd regiment whose picquets had been brushed aside. Erskine's culpability in delaying sending on the order to secure the bridge was overlooked, but in truth had Bevan acted at midnight, when he says he received the order, his battalion could have reached the bridge before Brenier. Pack highlighted one issue in particular: the failure of the field officers in command of the picquets to appreciate the situation and react when initial contact was made with the French. Even the explosions in the fortress do not seem to have sounded alarm bells, because there had been gunfire on previous evenings. Without overtly passing the buck, Erskine, Campbell, Bevan and Iremonger blamed others. Remarkably, while Wellington railed that the blockading force 'had about 13,000 men to watch 1,400' and that 'they were sleeping in their spurs, even; but the

French got off', he did not take Erskine to task for his delay nor did he query why Campbell placed such a loose cordon around Almeida as to enable the escape to take place.[27] Erskine referred to Bevan not having marched to Barba del Puerco on the *evening* of 10 May as ordered, as if there had been no delay on Erskine's own part, and then said the 4th regiment had lost its way, as if that was a reason for it not arriving until 6am.[28] Erskine was a major general with friends in high places and Campbell was a friend of Wellington's, which may account for the failure to inquire further. Campbell was never again given a position of responsibility by Wellington, but that may merely reflect his ongoing health problems, which caused him to return to Great Britain later that year.[29] Despite his personal views on Erskine's health, Wellington still retained confidence in him, it would seem, for he was appointed to the command of a cavalry division serving under Rowland Hill in the south. Bevan felt he was unfairly blamed and sought an inquiry, which Wellington refused. It seemed Wellington disbelieved Bevan's assertion that the dispatch from Erskine had not been received until about midnight. Distraught, poor Charles Bevan shot and killed himself on 8 July in Portalegre, where he was subsequently buried with full military honours. Had Bevan acted immediately on receiving his orders in the middle of the night, he could have reached the bridge before Brenier, but holding it with just four hundred men might have been problematic with Reynier's regiments attacking him from the right bank. In the army there was a lot of sympathy for Bevan. Iremonger, the commander of the 2nd regiment, took no action at all, even though he was aware of an incident involving the picquets, other than to send out patrols that eventually came back to report the evacuation of Almeida. Lieutenant Colonel Basil Cochrane, who had led the futile pursuit across the bridge, was rebuked by Wellington.[30] Later that year he had to face a court martial for writing offensive letters to Campbell and refusing to withdraw them. Found guilty he was reprimanded and returned to his regiment.[31] He left the Peninsula for reasons of health later that year.

Years later Wellington still seemed to hold Bevan accountable.[32] Is it possible, however, that at the time he determined to bring the matter to a close as quickly as possible and to that extent avoided further enquiry? Wellington himself was virtually fighting a war on two fronts, having to keep politicians at home on side while fighting the French. He knew he had been lucky to win the battle of Fuentes de Oñoro, remarking to his brother 'If Boney had been there, we should have been beaten.'[33] Indeed, did he attempt to direct attention away from the battle and take the sting out of the Almeida affair at the same time, when he suggested to Liverpool

'Possibly I have to reproach myself for not having been on the spot' – or was that just Wellington micro-managing? He did have a reputation for being not entirely confident in his subordinates. Only a few weeks before Fuentes de Oñoro he had remarked to Beresford following the confrontation at Sabugal: 'In short, these combinations for engagements do not answer, unless one is upon the spot to direct every trifling movement.'[34]

Brenier's escape from Almeida, while not of great strategic importance, was more than an irritant to Wellington for it formed part of a trio of events that could have led to adverse reaction at home.[35] Wellington had hurried south on 16 May with a view to meeting the French threat in that quarter. He arrived at Elvas on 19 May to the news that Beresford had secured a victory at Albuera over Marshal Soult, but at huge cost to the British regiments present. Combined with his own losses at Fuentes de Oñoro and the upset of the garrison escaping from Almeida, these were difficult times, and Wellington was no doubt concerned about British political and public sentiment.[36] To his credit Wellington never sought to use Beresford's losses at Albuera to deflect from his own situation, though Henry Cadogan, now commanding the 71st regiment, remarked to Pack: 'Albuera has knocked Fuentes de Onor [sic] out of all recollection, and I even think it will, if timeously announced in England obliterate the remembrance of Almeida.'[37]

In a postscript indicative that even the upset caused by Brenier's escape would not interfere with matters of honour, Wellington the next day sent to Masséna a French captain he had detained while under a flag of truce on 3 May, suspecting he was a spy, together with four French soldiers in exchange for four English soldiers which Brenier had returned to Wellington under parole.[38]

Pack was the only senior officer to emerge with any credit from Brenier's escape. His quick and aggressive pursuit with a small force was remarked on by Wellington.[39] Having set off to follow Brenier's force with ten men, he had called up eighty of his own reserve on realizing the seriousness of the situation. Immediately after ascertaining the size of the column, he then called for the rest of his reserve and sent an orderly to Campbell to let him know the direction being taken by the Frenchmen.[40]

Wellington had ridden over to Almeida after its abandonment by the French. He was pleasantly surprised to find that the damage caused by mining the fort was not so bad that it could not be repaired. All the outworks were undamaged. Excepting in front of the gate, the counterscarp was uninjured, as was the exterior revetment of the rampart. Even where there was damage, the foundations were in good shape. Further, he found the French had left a great deal of ordnance and shot: 'better carriages and I think more ordnance, than when we left it'.[41] He determined to make it secure against a coup de main, ascertain the cost of repairs and then see if the Portuguese government would fund the restoration of the fortress. The work would require workmen and money, and Wellington made it clear he would supply neither.[42] Wellington appointed Denis Pack to command Almeida and directed he should keep a regiment there with advance posts at Barba del Puerco.[43] Wellington had decided to go south with two divisions to assist Beresford, leaving General Sir Brent Spencer in charge of the army on the Agueda. He did not think the French would try a further attack, but left Spencer specific instructions for a retreat should that prove necessary. Those instructions included provision for the blowing-up of Almeida so as to make it unusable by the French.

In fact, both Wellington and Beresford now faced a problem which threatened the efficacy of the Portuguese army and correspondingly Wellington's ability to use it as part of the allied weaponry. Massive desertion took place during the advance from the Lines of Torres Vedras. When one hundred recruits were sent up from Lisbon to join the 1st regiment with Pack in April, only fifty had reached their destination.[44] Beresford was at a loss to understand the reasons but wanted the cause investigated, fearing that Spanish guerrillas were offering inducements to persuade Portuguese soldiers to join them. It is perhaps more likely that desertion was driven by lack of provisions and pay. It seemed that if Beresford was not in Lisbon to exhort the Regency, matters stagnated.[45]

Pack had obviously repeated at this time a desire to return to the British army. He wanted to do so, however, as the commander of a brigade, not just a regiment. Beresford indicated that while Pack was likely to be given a British brigadiership, this would take time. Perhaps as a result Pack then sought to be put in charge of the Brigade of Porto. In turn that request was turned down on the basis that the Porto brigade was permanently attached to a division, whereas Pack's current brigade was independent.[46]

If he was disappointed at having to remain with his independent brigade, Pack did not let it interfere with his duties. With his characteristic energy, he set about investigating the requirements to put Almeida back into a state where it could again be used. He had estimates prepared by Captain French and forwarded these to Beresford, along with letters dated 28, 29 and 30 May.[47] Beresford responded by informing Pack that no re-edification was intended and that Wellington merely intended to make it a post for militia with two regiments having been ordered for that purpose.[48] The Portuguese Regency indicated it ultimately intended to restore the fortress but this was a long-term aspiration.[49] On 7 June on Spencer's orders Pack withdrew from Almeida, having caused some further damage to the fort, because of a fear that the French were now advancing again. Wellington was not impressed, not least presumably because he had written twice to Spencer in late May telling him that the Portuguese government had determined to repair the fort, and that pending the arrival of militia, Pack's brigade should remain there unless definitively threatened by the French.[50] He castigated Spencer, for he felt no move should have been made to blow up the fortifications until and unless the French made a definitive move towards the town.[51] That advance did not materialize and in July Wellington told Lieutenant Colonel Richard Fletcher, then commanding the Royal Engineers with the army in the Peninsula, to send a British engineer to Almeida to report on the damage, this in addition to a Portuguese engineer.[52] At this stage debris was cleared away from the ditch surrounding the castle.

In the interim the 6th division and Pack's brigade had moved south, crossing the Tagus, until they reached Portalegre. This was part of a general move southwards to join Wellington, who was undertaking a second allied siege of Badajoz – a move which led Marmont, who had succeeded Masséna in command of *L'Armée de Portugal*, to move his forces south to combine with Soult. Their juncture led Wellington to lift the siege and retire behind the river Caya, a watercourse running from north to south and joining the Guadiana just below Badajoz. By August Wellington had abandoned the notion of operations south of the Tagus. Leaving Hill with some sixteen thousand men there to guard against any attempt by the 5th French corps to cause trouble, Wellington turned his attention towards a blockade and hopefully capture of Ciudad Rodrigo. To this end he brought his forces further north and began a loose blockade of Ciudad Rodrigo on 10 August, undertaken by the Light and 3rd divisions. Marmont reacted by assembling a force of over fifty-thousand, with a view to inserting a relief convoy into the city. Wellington found himself in a dangerous position, with an inferior-sized army, on paper about forty-six thousand strong, strung out over a wide area. He himself was based at Fuenteguinaldo with the 4th division and Pack's Portuguese brigade close by, although once again Wellington was concerned that the Portuguese Regency was failing to supply it and other Portuguese brigades properly. In this respect he requested Beresford, then back in Lisbon, to ensure that the government sent money to the commissaries of the brigades so that they could make purchases in Spain; he warned darkly that otherwise they would starve or Wellington would have to relinquish his plans to prevent Ciudad Rodrigo being resupplied.[53]

On 24 September Ciudad Rodrigo was relieved and replenished by the French. Marmont began to probe Wellington's placement of his forces with a view to ascertaining his intentions and if appropriate to take advantage of the situation. Marmont's actions resulted in two engagements at Espeja and El Bodon respectively on 25 September. In the latter action it was with difficulty that Wellington extracted the 3rd division and 21st Portuguese line regiment. He then had some fifteen thousand men at Fuenteguinaldo but by the evening of 25 September Marmont had twenty-thousand men across the Agueda. Wellington was in considerable danger. He recalled the Light Division to join him but Craufurd did not react with any sense of urgency and it was only the following day that he joined Wellington. While Wellington moved back into Portugal to a better defensive position, Marmont retired without further engagement on 26 September to Ciudad Rodrigo and then Salamanca. The allied army then went into quarters, with Pack's brigade placed in the vicinity of Almeida once again.

Ultimately, in October Wellington ordered the carrying-out of more substantial works at Almeida. An additional reason to properly secure the fort at this time would have been the decision to store siege equipment there brought up from Lisbon via Porto and Lamego, and intended for the planned siege of Ciudad Rodrigo. The rebuilding of Almeida enabled Wellington to mask the purpose for which his siege equipment was planned. Wellington ordered that 200 rank and file British and 200 rank and file Portuguese troops, together with NCOs and officers, be employed to carry out works to improve the defences of Almeida.[54] The work took a number of months and the workers were drawn from different divisions and brigades by rotation. The men chosen were preferably to be masons and the regiments on which they were drawn included Pack's brigade.[55]

Pack had further enhanced his reputation in 1811. This did not stop him reiterating his wish to return to the British service. Before that would happen, he would acquire additional laurels in Spain in 1812.

Chapter 7

Ciudad Rodrigo to Salamanca, 1812

By December 1811 Pack's brigade was in winter quarters. Wellington, however, had an ambitious plan to besiege and capture Ciudad Rodrigo before the French, also in winter cantonments, could bring up sufficient numbers to threaten the allied army. The British siege train was brought to Almeida as surreptitiously as possible, with word being spread that the equipment was for the fortification of Almeida. The fortress there was now reported by Wellington to be once again a place of security capable of resisting attack. Just before Christmas Pack's brigade, along with the soldiers of the 1st, 3rd, 4th and Light divisions, was ordered to make fascines, gabions and piquets, all required for siege purposes.[1] Fascines were tied-up bundles of wooden branches used for shoring up trenches and around guns. Gabions were open-ended barrel-like structures made of interwoven branches, usually with sharp stakes at one end so that they could be driven into the ground. These would be filled with dirt and stones and placed to protect trenches and walkways from enemy fire. Piquets were pointed stakes that would be used to protect outposts. They gave their name to small groups of soldiers placed to give early warning and guard larger groups.

Wellington was greatly encouraged by intelligence he was now receiving that Marmont was sending elite cavalry and infantry both to France, for Napoleon's projected attack on Russia, and to Spain's Mediterranean theatre to support the campaign there.[2] In early January 1812 Wellington moved up the 1st, 3rd, 4th and 5th divisions to join the Light Division, which was already enforcing a blockade of the city, and on 8 January commenced the siege which led to the storming of Ciudad Rodrigo on the night of 19 January. Pack's brigade was intimately involved in the siege, being paired with the Light Division on trench duty. The brigade was also involved in the assault, but might not have been in a position to play any part had it not been supplied with provisions at Wellington's behest on 3 January. On that day Pack had explained to Wellington that, unless

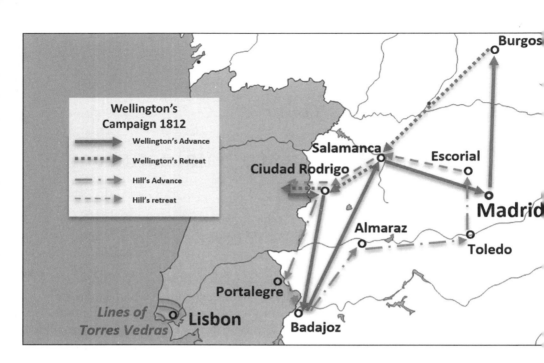

money or provisions were forthcoming immediately, he would have to move his brigade to the rear. Wellington issued a peremptory order to the British Commissary General to supply the brigade, and to seek reimbursement for the cost of doing so from the Portuguese government.[3] Pack must have felt thoroughly frustrated that, once again, his ability to participate was threatened by the failure of the Portuguese commissariat. The saving grace was his apparent ease of access to Wellington, who took immediate action to rectify a parlous situation. In December Wellington also gave Pack 200 dollars from the Portuguese Relief Fund for the inhabitants of Freixo to assist them in the shortfall they would now experience from the removal of troops in their area.[4]

By 19 January two breaches had been made in the walls of Ciudad Rodrigo. The 3rd division was designated to lead the assault of the main breach, while the Light Division was tasked with attacking the lesser breach. On this occasion Wellington ordered two false attacks to be undertaken by Portuguese troops. Pack's brigade, made up of the five battalions of the 1st and 16th line and the 4th caçadores, was sent to the Santiago gate on the southern side of the fortress. Lieutenant Colonel O'Toole headed a column of the 2nd caçadores with the light company of the 83rd sent to cause a diversion at the castle gate, a demanding task involving a crossing of the main bridge over the Agueda under the guns of the enemy.[5] While these two moves were intended as deflections to draw French troops away from the breaches, both forces were at liberty to develop their positions should the opportunity arise.[6]

Preparing and waiting for the attack to commence must have been stressful. Synge later described to his children the 'bivouac scene at General Pack's table and the promise that all survivors should meet at supper so very lightly given'.[7]

When the signal was made, Pack and his men quietly stole to their attack position. After a hasty consultation they determined to try to make their attack the real one. The fate of the city was determined by the success of the Light Division in storming the lesser breach. At about the same time the 3rd division broke through the main breach. Separately, however, both Pack's brigade and the force under O'Toole gained entrance to the city. Pack's troops seized the Santiago gate fortifications and held them against attempts to eject them. In his dispatch to Lord Liverpool the

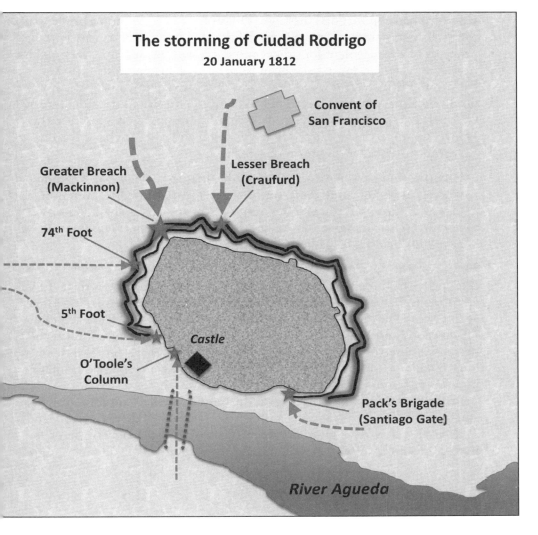

The storming of Ciudad Rodrigo
20 January 1812

Convent of San Francisco

Greater Breach (Mackinnon)

Lesser Breach (Craufurd)

74th Foot

5th Foot

O'Toole's Column

Castle

Pack's Brigade (Santiago Gate)

River Agueda

day after the capture of Ciudad Rodrigo, Wellington declared: 'All these attacks succeeded; and Brig. General Pack even surpassed my expectations, having converted his false attack into a real one: and his advance guard under the command of Major Lynch, having followed the enemy's troops from the advanced works into the fausse braie, where they made prisoners all opposed to them.'[8]

He went on to praise the 1st and 16th Portuguese regiments of Pack's brigade under Lieutenant Colonel Noel Hill and Colonel Neil Campbell respectively for their part in the storm.[9] When parliamentary thanks were voted to the conquerors of Ciudad Rodrigo on 10 February 1812, Pack was mentioned by name.[10]

Two senior officers, Major Generals Robert Craufurd and Henry Mackinnon died of injuries received at the storming of Ciudad Rodrigo. Craufurd had commanded the Light Division and Mackinnon a brigade of the 3rd division under Major General Thomas Picton. This opened up the prospect of advancement for others and Pack, with his star now very much in the ascendancy, must have been hopeful that his application to move back to the British army would result in the command of a brigade. It was not to be, however, for a week later Wellington was writing to Lieutenant Colonel Torrens at Horse Guards saying he proposed to appoint either Henry Clinton or Charles Alten to command the Light Division.[11] Referring to Pack, Wellington observed:

Pack has long wished to return to the British service but I doubt whether it would come to his turn to have a British brigade, even now that Craufurd and Mackinnon are gone. As soon as it shall come to his turn, I will remove him to the British service, and will apply to have him made a Brigadier General.[12]

Master of the two pivotal fortresses, Almeida and Ciudad Rodrigo, on the northern border of Portugal and Spain, Wellington now turned his attention to Badajoz, the Spanish citadel opposite Elvas in the south. Once again, he endeavoured to hide his intentions as well as possible, sending off divisions and brigades individually so as not to draw attention to his designs. Some of these, including Pack's brigade, were sent south in a huge circular arc through central Portugal, a move which may additionally have been designed to secure them supplies.

In Pack's case the brigade marched from Freixo via Coimbra, Pombal and Thomar to Villa Vicosa and Elvas. It reached Elvas on 20 and 21 March, a few days after the investment of Badajoz on 16 March by Beresford under Wellington's direction.[13] Beresford's aide de camp,

William Warre, suggested that Beresford took the leading role at this stage because Wellington was 'rather unwell'. Wellington himself did not elaborate in his own correspondence other than to say 'I have not been able to go out.'[14] Badajoz was captured by Wellington on 6 April after a ferocious onslaught. Pack's brigade formed part of Wellington's reserve at the siege of Badajoz, and was part of a covering force. As such, Pack did not receive the 'Badajoz' clasp to the Peninsular Gold Medal. Wellington was adamant that active participation in a battle or siege was required to merit the award of a medal or clasp. It was only years later, in 1847, when the issue of a Peninsular medal for all participants was being discussed, that Pack's aide de camp, Charles Synge, wrote to Wellington stating he was entitled to the medal for Badajoz and that he had been present with Pack.

Synge's claim was based on his, and Pack's, presence at the assault and capture of Badajoz in unusual circumstances. Relying on extracts from his own notes, which he copied to Wellington, Synge wrote to the duke on 8 June 1847 explaining that while part of the covering force at Badajoz, he and Pack had dined with the duke on the eve of the storming of the city. After dinner they had gone with him to witness the assault. With the attack under way, the continuous crashing of the guns led the duke to suggest someone had better go and see the nature of the obstruction which had occurred. Synge volunteered to go with Lieutenant Colonel Colin Campbell.[15] The two men went to the glacis, where Campbell's horse was shot from under him. Campbell sent Synge back to explain the 'confusion' to Wellington. The cause of this 'confusion' appeared to be that the Light Division had not been able to enter through the small breach, though the 4th division was thought to have crossed its breach, and was preparing to attempt to enter the town. Synge had difficulty finding his way back to Wellington through the numerous killed and wounded, and at one stage his horse fell into a quarry. Ultimately, he found the duke, who, on being told the situation, expressed some anxiety and now requested Pack to go down with Synge to appraise the situation. Not long afterwards Wellington himself came down. Finding so many general officers hors de combat, Wellington requested Pack to reform the divisions 'on their original alarm posts and remain there till daybreak'. Just then, however, a messenger arrived shouting for the duke. This was an officer sent by General Picton to say the latter was in possession of the castle and, if Wellington could send him another brigade, he would make a diversion in favour of the breaches. This meant Pack did not have to implement Wellington's order, and a short time thereafter Badajoz fell to the allies.

Wellington's response to Synge made no direct reference to the sequence of events he had set out. Somewhat obliquely, he mentioned that Pack must have received many medals, and went on to suggest that if Synge made application, setting out why he was entitled to receive a clasp for the siege, he was sure he would obtain it. Synge presumably made that application for he duly received a clasp for the siege of Badajoz. Pack's Peninsular Gold Cross and clasps never reflected that siege, however, for by 1848 he was dead, and presumably when clasps were issued for general officers he made no issue of the fact that he was not included.[16] Synge's account of the storming of Badajoz would seem to indicate that it was a near-run thing.

Once again, at Badajoz as at Ciudad Rodrigo, Wellington had moved too fast for the French to assemble a force of sufficient size to threaten him. Soult did march up from Andalusia, and Wellington prepared to give battle at Albuera before Soult withdrew. Marmont, with *l'armée de Portugal*, marched into Beira, sweeping aside the forces left there. Although he reached Castelo Branco and Guarda, he too withdrew to Spain when Wellington sent forces to face him on 11 April, a corps led by the Light and 3rd divisions, which included Pack's brigade, moving north via Portalegre as part of the advance guard.

Leaving Hill to contain Soult in the south of Spain, Wellington assembled a substantial army of nearly fifty-two thousand. Wellington now had double the number of cavalry regiments previously available to the allies; one of the disadvantages felt at both Fuentes de Oñoro and Albuera had been at least partly remedied by reinforcements from Great Britain. Events in 1812 were to strengthen his convictions that the cavalry could not be relied upon in a scrape, notwithstanding some impressive performances at Villagarcia and Salamanca by English and Portuguese cavalry. Following the fall of Badajoz the Anglo-Portuguese army under Wellington marched on Salamanca in three columns. Pack's brigade formed part of the left-hand column under Picton. Wellington crossed the river Agueda on 13 June and reached the outskirts of Salamanca on 19 June. Marmont had already vacated the city, save for a garrison of eight hundred dispersed in three fortified buildings. Marmont, by the time of the battle of Salamanca, had an army of perhaps 49,500, some two thousand less than Wellington.[17] The French general, however, had difficulty feeding his men, which prevented a close concentration of his force. The similarity in numbers gave neither side the confidence to risk a battle at this stage. For a whole month the two armies marched and countermarched, trying to outflank each other, the only noteworthy achievement of the allies being the subjugation and taking of the three fortified buildings in the city, giving them absolute control of Salamanca. Marmont retreated across the Douro (Duero) and between early and mid-July the two forces faced each other across this river. By 21 July Wellington was contemplating retiring to Ciudad Rodrigo, following days of parallel marching by the two armies in apparent deadlock. Then a Spanish battalion withdrew from the bridge at Alba de Tormes over the river Tormes, enabling Marmont to seize it and cross there and elsewhere. Wellington heard that Marmont expected further reinforcements within the week. He therefore determined that if he could not attack Marmont the following day, he would not wait for Marmont to gain an advantage in numbers but rather retreat to Ciudad Rodrigo. He ordered his baggage train to leave at dawn on 22 July.

The early part of the day witnessed sporadic fighting around the Santuario de Nuestra Senora de la Pena de Francia ('the chapel') on the heights near Calvarassa de Arriba, which the French had seized during the previous night. The allies held Calvarassa de Abajo and it was Pack's 4th caçadores that were sent to sustain the Brunswick Oels at the chapel, where Wellington stated they maintained their position throughout the day.[18] This is important in the light of Pack's involvement in the main battle later, as it has frequently been assumed he had his entire brigade with him on the afternoon of 22 July. There is a potential conflict of evidence here, for Pack in one of his reports on the battle seems to suggest that in the afternoon the caçadores of his brigade moved to the right and were involved in a sustained action for two hours, the result being that their ammunition was expended and they could not rejoin the brigade.[19] Synge for his part suggests that one hundred of the 4th caçadores took part in the attack Pack later mounted as part of the main battle. What seems to be clear is that whether the 4th caçadores, or part of them, were still at Calvarassa de Abajo, or had moved during the early afternoon to the right of Pack and had come under sustained fire there, the 4th caçadores as a unit were not with Pack's brigade that afternoon.

Further manoeuvring for position by the two sides during the morning saw the French division of Bonnet secure the Greater Arapile, while the allies seized the lesser Arapile. At this stage Wellington contemplated an assault on the Greater Arapile, but was apparently deterred from doing so by Beresford. This in itself was enough to cause comment: 'Marshal Beresford, no doubt, was the cause of the alteration from what he urged. Yet, at the same time, Lord W. is so little influenced, or, indeed, allows any person to say a word, that his attending to the marshal was considered singular.'[20] Beresford had spotted the *placement* of the French troops on and behind the Greater Arapile and convinced Wellington that the odds were not propitious. William Tomkinson, then a relatively junior cavalry officer, went so far as to suggest Wellington was a little nervous, perhaps because it was the first time he had commanded the attacking rather than defending army.[21] Pack in his battle report also refers to the morning attack being deferred but makes no reference to Beresford's role in that decision. Once again Wellington considered retiring to Ciudad Rodrigo. Then Marmont's manoeuvres gave him the opportunity he had waited for so patiently and the end result was the substantial destruction of Marmont's army, though not without several hard-fought and defeat-threatening incidents, in one of which Denis Pack was centrally involved.[22]

The engagement commenced with Pakenham and the 3rd Division, along with the Portuguese cavalry, attacking and substantially destroying the French left, which had become detached from the main army. Then Leith's 5th division, including Spry's Portuguese brigade, advanced on Maucune's division and, combined with Le Marchant's heavy cavalry, threw it into confusion with horrendous losses. Early in the battle Marmont and his second in command, General Bertrand Clausel, had both been injured. For some time the French effort lacked direction and it was only with the return of Clausel, commanding the French 2nd division, that French resistance for a period threatened the British positions. It was on the French right and allied left that Clausel and Bonnet threatened for a time to turn the tide of the battle.

The 4th division, commanded by Major General Lowry Cole, one of the heroes of Albuera, was to the left of Leith and the 5th division. Cole's division was thus facing the French right. To Cole's left and guarding his flank lay Pack's Portuguese brigade, composed of the 1st and 16th Portuguese line, but missing, as we have seen, at least part, if not all of the 4th caçadores. That brigade therefore had probably no more than two thousand men. While Cole was advancing on Clausel's division, Pack was ordered by Wellington to take the Greater Arapile occupied by Bonnet's fresh troops, well established on top of the hill, with the advantage for the French that to reach them the Portuguese had to climb a vertical lip variously described as between 3 and 4ft high. This required them to lay down their muskets while scrambling over the lip into a withering fire. The virtual parity of numbers between attackers and defenders was overturned by a strong defensive position, and the Portuguese disadvantage increased by the order given not to load and fire muskets but to use bayonets.

Why did Wellington engage in such a risky manoeuvre when he had huge unused reserves behind Cole and Pack in the shape of Clinton's 6th division, Anson's brigade and the 1st division a short distance further away? Pack's Portuguese brigade was the logical spearhead to attack the Greater Arapile but it needed support, which it did not receive until both the 4th division and Pack's brigade had been thrown back in confusion.

Possibly assisted by their cavalry, the French infantry threw back the 4th division in confusion. When Pack's Portuguese were driven off the Greater Arapile, the effect was to expose further Cole's left to Bonnet with devastating consequences. Cole's broken troops retreated in haste, losing cohesion and suffering accordingly. The day was saved by Wellington's decision to send the 6th division forward, and the remnant of the 4th passed back through it as it advanced. The success was contributed to by Beresford personally leading Brigadier General's Spry's 3rd Portuguese brigade across from the 5th division to attack the French on the left flank of Clausel's division in an effort to shore up Cole and the 4th division.[23] Initially giving Cole's 4th division a breathing space, ultimately Spry's Portuguese formed part of the British assault which took the heights and ensured a French retreat. Shortly before they gained the heights Beresford himself was wounded in the chest and spent many weeks recuperating in Salamanca and Lisbon.[24]

Given that the repulse of the 4th division and Pack's brigade might have affected the overall result of the battle, it is worth looking further at the circumstances under which he came to advance on the Grand Arapile and the difficulties he encountered. In doing so we are fortunate to have his own reports and the writings of his aide de camp, Captain Charles Synge.[25]

Pack had with him the 1st and 16th Portuguese regiments. These were two of the best regiments in the Portuguese army, having proved themselves on a number of occasions. They had participated in the battle of Buçaco, Masséna's retreat from Portugal and the capture of Ciudad Rodrigo. The fighting pedigree of the 16th regiment stretched back to Wellington's march on and capture of Porto in 1809.[26]

The broad sequence of the unfolding battle was that it commenced on the allies' right with the 3rd division. The 5th division and then the 4th division engaged the French centre. The 3rd division advanced at about 3.45pm but it was not until 5.45pm that Cole and the 4th division moved off against Clausel and part of Bonnet's division. The rest of Bonnet's division held the Greater Arapile and it was against this latter force that Pack moved. Cole's caçadores (7th) and British light infantry at first pushed back the French but ultimately, when under fire from the front and their left (the Greater Arapile), the 4th division broke and retreated.[27]

The circumstances and timing of Pack's attack on the Greater Arapile are unclear. Pack says he was ordered to attack the hill by Wellington, a statement that is supported by Wellington's post-battle dispatch to Lord Bathurst in which he states 'I ordered ... and Brig. General Pack should support the left of the 4th Division, by attacking that of the Dos Arapiles which the enemy held.'[28] Synge says the brigade was to give cover to Cole's 4th division and any further action was discretionary. Synge also says that Pack received a message from Cole seeking assistance, but that Pack realized it would take at least half an hour to get to Cole and to attempt to do so would expose his own left flank to Bonnet's troops on the Greater Arapile. On this basis Synge indicates Pack determined the better course was to attack the Greater Arapile in the hope this would take the pressure off Cole.[29]

The second aspect of confusion concerns the number and type of troops at Pack's disposal. Pack says that two companies from each regiment advanced in line with snipers in front under the command of Major Fearon, followed on the right-hand side by the fusiliers of the 1st regiment under Colonel Hill and on the left those of the 16th regiment under Lieutenant Colonel Vidigal, with the grenadiers of both regiments under Colonel Neil Campbell forming the reserve. Synge tells us that Pack prepared as if storming a fortress. One hundred men of the 4th caçadores under Major Peter Fearon made up the storming party with two companies (four hundred men) of grenadiers from each of the 1st and 16th regiments in support. These were commanded by Sir Neil Campbell. Behind the grenadiers in two columns came the 1st and 16th regiments under Sir Noel Hill and Colonel Pizarro respectively. The remainder of the caçadores were to make their way up the flanks of the hill. A slight change of plan then involved splitting Fearon's party into two, with Fearon commanding the left and Synge the right. One difficulty with this account relates to the 4th caçadores, who Wellington says were on the heights of Nuestra Senora de la Pena, and Pack says were off to the right with their ammunition expended. The explanation may be that one hundred of the caçadores had indeed returned to the brigade and were thus involved in the assault on the Greater Arapile. A second difficulty arises by virtue of Denis Pack's official reports (there were two) which imply that the grenadiers formed the reserve.[30] He also refers in this report to the advance being made by 1,700 men and two pieces of artillery.

That could be consistent with not having the caçadores present and with holding back his reserve of grenadiers.[31] A further small discrepancy in Pack's reports and those of Synge concerns the naming of the officer leading the 16th regiment. Pack tells us that it was Lieutenant Colonel Vidigal and not Pizarro.[32] Pack was correct.

The third issue concerns the wisdom of the deployed formation and the order providing for the arming of the troops. There is uncertainty as to the formation involved. Pack and Synge both agree in effect that the first line was a type of forlorn hope, as used for storming a fort. The formation of the troops behind this extended line is not agreed, but what is clear is that when they reached the brow of the hill were exposed to such a withering fire that they turned and could not be reformed. On the basis that the men were advancing uphill, and in the absence of knowledge regarding the mini cliff and lip at the top, Pack ordered that muskers not be loaded and that bayonets be used. The logic behind this decision was simply that if the troops stopped and fired, loaded and fired, there would be no prospect of a quick advance. There is no dispute that this was the order, and as such Pack's decision was not remarkable. The consequences, however, were terrible. When Synge and his advance party arrived at the 3 to 4ft cliff, the only way to get over it was for each man to lay his weapon on top of the lip and pull himself up. In doing so, he was rendered defenceless. Synge very sensibly says that he turned to Colonel Hill seeking that men from his column would come up and give covering fire, only to be told that they too had fixed bayonets and no load. The result was predictable.[33] Bonnet's men fired from 10 yards away on those trying to climb over the lip, then charged. The storming party fell back on those behind them and chaos ensued. The French jumped down on top of the confused men and the rout was complete. Bonnet's troops had the sense to follow only so far, before returning up the hill, having seized what valuables they could from the dead and wounded, including Synge, whose thigh was broken in a fall from his horse.[34] Synge was taken prisoner but left for dead, having been stripped of clothes and valuables. Fortunately for him, Synge was found as the allied army launched a fresh attack, with the introduction of the 6th division. Remarkably, he was discovered by Pack, who at first did not recognize him, before enquiring 'My dear Synge, is that you?', to which the latter responded 'Yes, General, here I am'. Pack then organized for the staff surgeon to come and attend to Synge.[35] The young Irishman's wounds were serious and his survival uncertain. He spent several months recuperating in Salamanca[36] before travelling back to Ireland. In 1813 he rejoined his regiment, and was present in the final battles of this war.[37]

Finally, the wisdom of sending this one brigade armed only with bayonets up the hill to meet massed French regiments, having had to escalade a small wall of 3 to 4ft high, which necessitated laying down one's weapon, is suspect, if either Wellington or Pack was aware of the number and disposition of the French troops awaiting the brigade. Pack referred to hidden French reserves emerging on the brigade's front and flanks when they were within thirty paces of the top, but could Wellington or his staff see the existence, if not the extent, of those reserves from their vantage point on the Lesser Arapile? It will be remembered that Beresford had observed the *placement* of French troops on and behind the Greater Arapile that morning. Pack's depleted brigade met the 120th line while climbing over the lip at the summit of the hill, but Bonnet had 4,600 men in nine battalions immediately available, with further troops a short distance away. Bonnet's three battalions of the 120th regiment were able to pay the Portuguese back in similar fashion for the treatment the French had received on reaching the crest at Buçaco. At Salamanca, however, unlike Buçaco, the defence crumbled elsewhere and the attackers proved to be the victors. Later, Pack in his journal suggested Wellington expected too much of his 'Hidalgos' and indicated he had some apprehension about his orders, but these comments could also reflect a desire to deflect criticism of the way in which Pack organized the attack on the hill:

> My caçadores stood well at Busaco [*sic*] and Ciudad Rodrigo, much to my wonderment, but my mind misgave me somewhat when I received the order to attack the hill at Hermanito, the strongest part of the enemy's position; it is the duty of a soldier to obey and not to question, hence we advanced up the hill and were within thirty paces of the top when the hidden French reserves leaped on us from the rocks on our front and flank. I did what in me lay, but the Lisbon volunteers disappeared sooner than smoke ... No one admires Lord Wellington more than myself, but I fear he expected overmuch from my Hidalgos, whose courage is of a vastly changeable nature.[38]

This is a mild enough criticism of Wellington, but an expression of an extraordinary lack of confidence in his Portuguese troops who had proved themselves many times and were to do so again. It is also a comment totally at odds with the contents of his official reports on the battle in which he praises the conduct of the troops as a whole, while singling out Synge, who was severely injured, for particular praise.[39] William Grattan of the 88th regiment was very dismissive of the performance of Pack's Portuguese brigade, but Grattan failed to realise the nature and extent of the force Pack's Portuguese faced at Salamanca, insisting that it was 'a few hundred Frenchmen'.[40] Indeed, four Portuguese brigades – Pack's, Spry's (5th division), Stubbs' (4th division) and Resende (6th division) – suffered 451 dead out of a total Portuguese killed of 506 men, and 956 injured out of a total Portuguese injured of 1,035. These regiments were in the thick of the fighting.[41] Of these, Pack's regiments lost 102 killed and 257 injured on the day. Pack's own courage was not in doubt. Synge makes it clear that Pack was in the thick of the action, and when Pack found Synge he was attempting to lead a second attack on the Greater Arapile. In Wellington's post-engagement dispatch to Lord Bathurst, Pack is one of those mentioned favourably.[42] William Tomkinson, then a young cavalry officer in the 16th light dragoons, observed that although Pack was repulsed, his brigade drew the fire from both the 4th and 6th divisions.[43] Likewise John Aitchison, then an ensign in the 3rd Guards, but later to become a full general, observed that while Pack's attack failed, it diverted the attention of the enemy from the 6th division, which would otherwise have been taken in the flank during its own advance.[44] Later Pack was to receive the thanks of both houses of parliament for his part in the battle of Salamanca.[45]

Synge's account was written up years later from notes made contemporaneously. There are apparent errors of recollection, such as the name of the colonel leading the 16th regiment and perhaps the suggestion that Major Fearon led one hundred of the 4th caçadores at the head of the attack, given that Fearon was attached not to the 4th caçadores but to the 1st regiment.[46] Do these contradictions affect Synge's credibility in such a manner that one should treat with caution his remark that Wellington's orders to Pack gave the latter discretion? On occasions Wellington did give senior officers such as Beresford and Hill discretion, but his inclination was more to seek to micro-manage. It is not inconceivable that while Pack's primary instruction was to guard the left flank of the 4th division, he was told that if the opportunity presented itself to capture the hill he should take it. Seeing Cole was in trouble and the difficulty and danger of trying to reach him, Pack then decided on the assault. The trouble with this thesis is that neither Pack nor Wellington mentions the alleged discretionary nature of the order. Of course, given the failure of the attack on the Greater Arapile, Pack may not have been inclined to highlight his role in the decision-making. The *Memoir* of Pack's life prepared by his grandson throws no light on the conduct of the battle other than to rely on the history of the contest as recounted by William Napier. Nevertheless, we have Pack's own contemporaneous and later assertions that he received an order 'to attack the hill at Hermanito' without any elaboration about discretion.[47] Synge certainly bore no malice towards Pack, in fact he was most supportive of him. He admired his senior officer, so any inconsistencies are likely to have arisen through the lapse of time rather than any other cause.

Wellington's victory was complete and exceptionally well managed. General Maximilien Foy, who probably had more experience than any other French general of Portugal and Spain, wrote of the battle:

> The battle of Salamanca is the most masterly in its management, the most considerable in the number of troops engaged, and the most important in results, of all the victories the English have gained in these latter days. It raises Lord Wellington almost to the level of Marlborough. Hitherto we had been aware of his prudence, his eye for choosing a position, and his skill in utilizing it. At Salamanca he has shown himself a great and able master of manoeuvres. He kept his dispositions concealed for almost the whole day: he waited till we were committed to our movement before he developed his own: he fought in the oblique order – it was a battle in the style of Frederick the Great.[48]

The battle is remembered for the great successes of Pakenham's 3rd division and Le Marchant's heavy cavalry, but half the allied losses took place on the left wing of Wellington's army, an indication of the fierceness of the fighting there. Only exhaustion prevented a more aggressive follow-up. The French forces under Clausel retired northwards, and Wellington determined to make Madrid – and Joseph Bonaparte – his next target.

Chapter 8

The siege of Burgos and the retreat to Ciudad Rodrigo, 1812

'The worst scrape I ever was in'[1]

The battle of Salamanca was followed by the allied march on Madrid. Before turning south, Wellington pursued Clausel and the remnants of the French army northwards for some days to Valladolid. Aware of both King Joseph and Soult at his back with their respective armies, and concerned about lengthening communication lines, Wellington determined to capture Madrid if possible. Leaving some forces at Valladolid, and the 6th division at Cuellar, Wellington marched on Madrid via Segovia with the rest of his forces. These included the two independent Portuguese brigades, those of Pack and Bradford, the 1st and 10th Portuguese brigades respectively. On Wellington's approach to Madrid, Joseph left precipitately for Valencia, accompanied by most of his military force and the Afrancesados. Wellington entered Madrid virtually unopposed on 12 August. A force of 1,700 men had been left in the Retiro, to the east of the city. The fortifications there included a star fort, but the defences were not strong and, following an initial attack on the evening of 13 August, the defenders surrendered the next day. The attack was made by men of the 3rd and 7th divisions, so Pack's brigade was presumably not used, and he leaves us no record of any personal involvement in the confrontation there.

The allied army was welcomed by the liberated population of Madrid.[2] While three weeks of festivities took place, Wellington was acutely aware that the French were likely to attempt its recapture, and that his own position would be threatened if Clausel, Joseph and Soult could coordinate their forces. Hill, for the time being, remained in the south with twenty-one thousand men monitoring Soult. With Joseph in Valencia, Wellington determined to march north and confront Clausel, if possible before there could be any junction of French forces. He then hoped to return to defend Madrid. He left the 3rd, 4th and Light divisions together with Spanish forces to cover Madrid on the basis that Hill would move east towards Madrid if Soult abandoned Andalusia and the siege of Cadiz. Wellington took north the 1st, 6th and 7th divisions. On hearing that the French were approaching Valladolid, he had earlier sent on to Arevalo the 5th division, and Ponsonby's heavy cavalry, together with Pack and Bradford's Portuguese brigades.

Leaving Madrid on 1 September, Wellington was again in Valladolid on 7 September. By the latter date he knew that Soult had raised the siege of Cadiz, abandoned Andalusia, and was marching east to join with Marshal Suchet, then headquartered at Valencia. He was deeply conscious of Soult moving up from the south, and Hill having an inadequate force to meet the French with confidence. Accordingly, Hill was directed towards Madrid. On 8 September Wellington gave Hill instructions to move north of the Tagus so that Hill would be in close communication with both Wellington and the force in Madrid.[3] Meanwhile Wellington proceeded north to Burgos with considerable optimism, stating to his brother Henry that 'unless some accident happens, they [the French] will not be long on this side of the Ebro'.[4] Likewise Wellington wrote to Stapleton Cotton 'Matters are going on famously.'[5] These comments, while ultimately proving overly confident, were understandable in the context. The French under Clausel had approached Valladolid in Wellington's absence but declined a confrontation, retreating all the while before the allies until taking up a position north of Burgos, leaving a strong garrison in the castle there. On 16 September Wellington was joined by the army of Galicia, twelve thousand men under José Maria Santocildes. On 18 September the allies reached Burgos. Wellington determined to besiege the castle, not wishing to leave it in his rear. Pack was to play an important part in the events of the next two months, though the outcome was not one for which he would have wished.

The castle of Burgos was set on top of a steep hill dominating the town, and was surrounded by two, and in places three, sets of walls, the whole protected by an unfinished hornwork on the neighbouring hill of San Miguel.[6] Wellington had just three 18-pounders and five howitzers – wholly inadequate artillery for the siege of a fortress held by an enterprising and determined commander with perhaps thirty guns.[7] Wellington was completely outgunned.[8] In order to give himself a gun platform from which to attack the castle, the allied commander determined on his arrival to capture the hornwork. Crossing the river Arlanzon on 19 September,

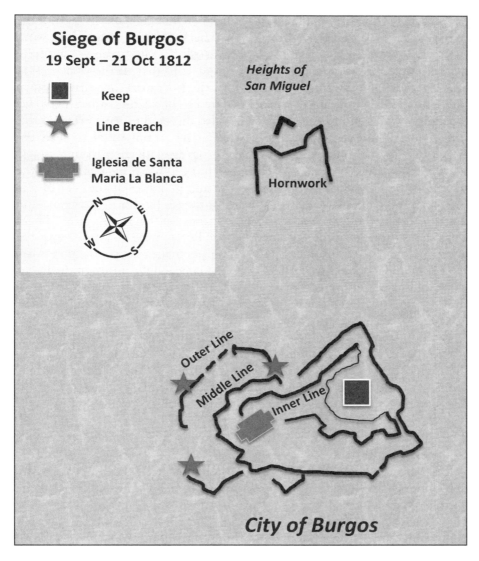

Pack's brigade was used to force the French to abandon their outposts on San Miguel.[9] The siege was then commenced by the 1st division and Pack's brigade, while the rest of the army formed a covering force to prevent any attempt by the French to intervene. On the first night of the siege the allies attacked the hornwork. The assault was undertaken by a party of three hundred men of the Black Watch (42nd regiment) and troops from Pack's brigade with orders to attack the front of the hornwork, with a party made up of further Black Watch and men from the 24th and 79th regiments led by Major Charles Cocks assigned to work their way round to the rear of the hornwork. Cocks's troops may have been intended as a feint, but were certainly told that, if the opportunity arose, they should attempt to break into the hornwork by cutting down the palisades. To this end they were ordered to be accompanied by twelve carpenters with felling-axes. They were also directed to stop French reinforcements being sent from the castle.[10] Pack volunteered to lead the attack.[11] The Portuguese failed to make progress with their frontal attack, but Cocks converted his approach into a full assault. This resulted in the taking of the hornwork via a small gorge and palisades at the rear of this fortification. Very severe losses were suffered by both attackers and defenders, but the prize was the platform desired by Wellington. There were suggestions in some quarters that the Portuguese had not shown the necessary degree of resolve, but Wellington makes no such suggestion. He commended Cocks in particular for the successful capture of the hornwork, but also mentioned favourably Denis Pack and the two colonels of the 1st and 16th Portuguese regiments, as well as the commander of the 4th caçadores serving with Pack, for their part in a 'very gallant affair'.[12]

Wellington was now able to erect his gun platform, with the additional advantage of having a number of French guns seized in the hornwork. On the night of 22 September an unsuccessful attempt was made to escalade the outer wall of the castle by volunteers from the 1st division. On this occasion the 9th caçadores from Brigadier General the Conde de Rezende's brigade were ordered to mount a diversion on another part of the wall. This did not take place and the frontal attack was also mismanaged. Pack's troops were not involved.

Even before the failed attack on the outer wall Wellington wrote despondently to Beresford, recuperating from his wounds suffered at the battle of Salamanca: 'I hope that we may take this place; but I doubt it. I have neither officers nor good troops, the whole of which I have left behind me; and I can undertake nothing with hopes of success without great loss.' Later, in reports to England, Wellington was to blame the inexperience of his troops again. This condemnation of his soldiers was in stark contrast to his earlier praise of them when writing to Home Popham on 2 October.[13] While some of the blame may have been attributable to the actions of other individuals, the reality was that Wellington did not prepare for this siege. Even later, when attempting to shield the government from blame for the dismal end to the year, Wellington stuck to the line that his own fault had not been a lack of preparation, but that he had taken the wrong troops with him.[14] Wellington's failure to prepare for the siege is remarkable for someone who had earlier demonstrated that he had learnt the lessons of previous failures so well as to be able to reduce two huge fortresses in Ciudad Rodrigo and Badajoz, before the enemy had time to react.

Worse was to follow the failure of the initial attempt on the outer wall. Wellington's guns proved ineffective and two of the three 18-pounders he had brought with him were damaged by the defenders' accurate gunnery. Wellington ordered mining of the walls, and some limited success was achieved against the outer line of defences, which were assaulted on 4 October. On this occasion a lodgement was achieved in the outer wall, notwithstanding a counter-attack, but at substantial cost. Wellington now turned his attention to the penetration of the second line of defence. The early optimism he had shown was gone, however, with Wellington writing to Bathurst, Beresford and Hill expressing his doubts as to whether he could take the castle.[15] He repeatedly disparaged the troops he had brought with him, but was particularly negative about the Portuguese at this time, telling Beresford 'something or other has made a terrible alter-ation in the troops for the worse'. He put it down to a lack of pay, railed against the Portuguese Regency and particularly Dom Miguel Forjaz, secretary for war and foreign affairs, who claimed the men had money in their pockets. Wellington requested Beresford, who was back in Lisbon recuperating from wounds he had received at Salamanca, to look into the matter.[16]

On 8 October Pack's brigade suffered again when these troops formed the working party sapping forward. They were being guarded by soldiers of the King's German Legion when the French launched a sortie which not only destroyed the works being undertaken, but once again resulted in a serious loss of life to the allies. It was on this occasion that Major Cocks was killed while directing the legion. Wellington had been particularly fond of Cocks and regarded him highly. He, along with Pack and other senior officers, attended the funeral.

Wellington was now running short of ammunition, in spite of supplies received from the north coast of Spain. Morale was falling and despon-dency set in. A fifth attempt was made to capture the castle, again using a mine on the second ring wall, on 18 October. Like its predecessors, the attempt was unsuccessful, and incurred further substantial losses, resulting in Wellington deciding to abandon the siege. The possibility of being trapped between a rejuvenated *Armée de Portugal* now under General Souham, who had superseded Clausel, and the combined forces of Joseph and Soult was too dangerous. Each French army was estimated to contain over forty thousand men, outnumbering Wellington and Hill respectively. Wellington determined to abandon the siege, acknowledging 'the ability with which the Governor conducted the defence, and the gallantry with which it was executed by the garrison'.[17] He ordered Hill to withdraw from Madrid and join his own army on the long retreat to Ciudad Rodrigo, a city from which he had started so promisingly at the beginning of 1812.

Retreat is often a difficult manoeuvre. It is frequently commenced with an attempt to disguise the intention, particularly in order to get to safety heavy equipment, stores and the injured. Wellington was a master at obscuring his intentions. The method of doing so was to convert a siege into a blockade, while maintaining the fiction of the siege, for which the command was given to Denis Pack. In addition to his Portuguese brigade, Pack was given the 11th, 24th, 53rd, 58th and 61st British regiments, the 9th caçadores under Lieutenant Colonel George Brown, and the Spanish battalions of the Asturias and Guadalajara.[18] This was a substantial command, reflected in Wellington's memorandum to Pack of 20 October. Pack was left one of the captured French guns and a howitzer to keep up the pretence of a siege, but he was under orders to be prepared to march 'at a moment's notice', with the exception of five hundred men, to be English and Portuguese in due proportion, together with Brown's caçadores and the Spanish battalions. When Pack marched, Brown was to be left in command of this rearguard. The hornwork was to be mined and sprung on withdrawal.[19]

The allied retreat began on 21 October. It had clearly been conceived before Pack's appointment the previous day, though Wellington in a note to Pack on the afternoon of 21 October makes it sound as if the decision had just been made when he began the communication by writing,

> I am sorry to say that I am afraid I shall be obliged to give up our position here in consequence of the intelligence which I have received from General Hill of the movements of the enemy in the south; and unless I should receive a contradiction of the intelligence, I propose to march this night.[20]

While making his own preparations for a speedy departure, Wellington continued to micro-manage Pack's task, giving him specific instructions. He told Pack to send the baggage of his troops to Frandevinez, a small village about 10 kilometres west of Burgos on the Valladolid road. He was to leave with his force when the moon rose, with specific instructions as to which troops should leave first and those that should remain in the trenches until evacuation at five in the morning, when the mines in the hornwork should be blown by a mounted officer who should ride away. The strategy was to keep hidden from the French until the last possible moment the abandonment of the siege, and to gain as much time and space between the retreating army and the French pursuit. The strategy appears to have been largely successful. John Aitchison, serving with the 3rd Guards, one of the earlier regiments to pull out, observed: 'As soon as the sun set we began to move, and notwithstanding it was fine moonlight we passed under the guns of the castle within range of grapeshot without being discovered, and before daybreak on the 22nd the whole of our army was three leagues in rear of Burgos.'[21] Pack's force presumably kept the castle defenders engaged, for another commentator refers to hearing 'the thunders of the artillery of the castle vibrating in my ears' and 'the angry lightning from the cannon of the besieged castle' while hastily preparing his departure.[22]

On the morning of 22 October Souham discovered that Wellington had departed Burgos. He began a pursuit of the allies, harrying them continuously with his cavalry, which enjoyed numerical superiority. It is 330 kilometres from Burgos to Ciudad Rodrigo, and much of the journey was undertaken in appalling weather. Serious losses were sustained by the retreating army, but the infantry at this stage kept its shape and the King's German Legion in particular stopped the French vanguard on a number of occasions. The weather, however, had already begun to take a toll on men, animals and equipment. Rain and knee-deep mud hampered movement. Guns were abandoned having been spiked, and animals were shot.[23] Rearguard actions were fought in or near Torquemada, Palencia and Villamuriel. Food was in short supply, but the demon drink reared its head as the grapes had been harvested and pressed. In villages as they passed the soldiers broached casks, with men and some officers availing themselves, often indiscriminately, of their contents. Lieutenant Colonel Alexander Dickson, then in command of the Portuguese artillery, described the situation in Torquemada 'where such a scene of drunkenness occurred as would have disgraced even a Billingsgate rabble. The wine vaults were broken open by the troops & hardly 500 men in all the troops in my brigade, the 1st and 6th Divisions, were effective.'[24]

The scenes described by survivors were reminiscent of the retreat four years earlier from Salamanca to La Coruna, and Pack experienced the hardships of both journeys. William Grattan of the Connaught Rangers (the 88th), one of Pack's fellow countrymen, published his memoirs in 1847, thirty-five years after the events he described. His account of the retreat from Salamanca to Ciudad Rodrigo even at that remove leaves no room for doubt as to the difficulties faced:

> The rain fell in torrents, almost without any intermission; the roads could no longer be so called, they were perfect quagmires; the small streams became rivers, and the rivers were scarcely fordable at any point. In some instances the soldiers were obliged to carry their ammunition boxes strapped on their shoulders to preserve them, while passing a ford which on our advance was barely ankle deep. The baggage and camp kettles had left us; the former we never saw until we reached Rodrigo, and the latter rarely reached us until two o'clock in the morning, when the men, from fatigue, could make but little use of them. The wretched cattle had to be slaughtered, as our rations seldom arrived at their destination before the camp kettles, and when both arrived, there was not one fire in our bivouac sufficient to boil a mess. Officers as well as soldiers had no covering except the canopy of heaven; we had not one tent, and the army never slept in a village. We thus lay in the open country; our clothes saturated with rain, half the men and officers without shoes, nothing to eat, or at all events, no means of cooking it . . .
>
> What I have related took place on the 16th. The following days matters became worse, the rain continued to come down in torrents, and in the passage of one river, out of ten that we forded, a woman and three children were lost, as likewise some baggage mules, which the women of the army, in defiance of the order against it, still con-trived to smuggle into the line of retreat. The rations arrived alive (I mean the meat), as usual after midnight, but no kettles reached us for an hour after the poor famished brutes had been knocked on the head. Each man obtained his portion of the quivering flesh, but before any fires could be re-lighted, the order for march arrived, and the men received their meat dripping with water, but little, if anything, warmer than when it was delivered over to them by the butcher. The soldiers drenched with wet, greatly fatigued, nearly naked, and more than half asleep, were obliged either to throw away the meat, or put it with their biscuit into their haversacks, which from constant use, without any means of cleaning them, more resembled a beggarman's wallet than any part of the appointments of a soldier. In a short time the wet meat completely destroyed the bread, which became perfect paste,

and the blood which oozed from the undressed beef, little better than carrion, gave so bad a taste to the bread that many could not eat it. Those who did were in general attacked with violent pains in their bowels, and the want of salt brought on dysentery.[25]

The allied troops were no doubt fortunate that there was enough wine left for the French to discover during their pursuit. Fortune also favoured them in another way, in that after recapturing Valladolid Souham's pursuit was cautious and slow moving. Wellington, who was now marching to join up with Hill, was in no doubt that he had had a lucky escape, writing to Beresford on 31 October: 'You will see what a scrape we have been in, and how well we have got out of it. I say we have got out of it, because the enemy show no inclination to force the passage of the Duero.'[26]

It was not long, however, before the French did force the crossing of the Duero at Tordesillas and Toro and the retreat continued. By 7 November Wellington was at Pitiegua, 25 kilometres from Salamanca, with Hill in close contact. The following day he was at Salamanca and Hill crossed the Tormes at Alba, less than 20 kilometres away.[27] It was outside Salamanca that the allied and French armies squared up to each other on now familiar countryside. On this occasion Pack's brigade was part of the second line. The combined French armies now under the command of Soult made no move to attack. Instead they secured the continued withdrawal of the allies by threatening Wellington's communications with Ciudad Rodrigo. Concerned that he might be cut off from that fortress, Wellington withdrew on 15 November, making his way to Ciudad Rodrigo, all the time harassed by enemy cavalry. The elements remained daunting, though rain was for a time replaced with freezing but dry weather. Ultimately the army reached Portugal, where it was put in cantonments for the winter. Wellington had successfully extracted the army from a difficult situation, but at a very substantial cost. In addition to the two thousand casualties suffered at the siege of Burgos, somewhere between two thousand five hundred and five thousand men had been lost on the retreat.[28] The vast majority of the losses at the siege were sustained by the 1st division and Pack's Portuguese brigade, the part of the army directly engaged in those operations.[29] Losses in battle on the retreat were estimated by D'Urban to be less than eight hundred and fifty men, but large numbers had been lost to sickness or capture by the French. Wellington raged at the cause he perceived for the losses incurred in the retreat from Burgos – a lack of commitment and discipline by British and Portuguese officers – but it is difficult to argue that the siege of Burgos itself had been properly planned and thought out.

The French had ended a most difficult year by driving the main allied army out of Spain and back into Portugal. However, in spite of a disappointing end to the campaign, in eleven months the allies had recovered Ciudad Rodrigo and Badajoz and won a crushing victory over the French at Salamanca. They had successfully required the French to raise the siege of Cadiz, captured (and in many cases destroyed) over three thousand guns, and ensured that twenty thousand French prisoners had been sent to England during that period.[30] Wellington, having intercepted correspondence from Soult to Joseph Bonaparte advocating that Portugal be made the seat of war, felt able to observe that while the campaign had not turned out as well as he had at one stage expected, it had still so favourable a result as to render Soult's suggestion out of the question.[31]

In 1812 Pack and his brigade had participated in all the major actions bar Badajoz, where his brigade was part of a screening force. At the storming of Badajoz he had been personally present. At Ciudad Rodrigo his unit had successfully gained entrance to the fortress in the final assault. When the French escaped from Almeida, Pack was one of the few officers to emerge with his credibility intact for leading the pursuit with a handful of men, while at the same time organizing the chase. At Salamanca he had taken his brigade to attack a difficult position held by a superior force of French veterans. There may be some doubt as to whether Wellington gave Pack a direct order to attack the Greater Arapile or left it to Pack's discretion, but though the Portuguese were thrown back in disarray, there is no sign that Wellington ever blamed Pack for this setback. Indeed, he was mentioned in the post-battle dispatch. Finally, at the unsuccessful siege of Burgos, Wellington used Pack and his brigade to establish the siege, to assault the hornwork and to cover the retreat. These events clearly demonstrate the faith Wellington now had in Denis Pack, a faith which was to be justified in the years to come.

Chapter 9

Spain and the Pyrénées – an ambition realized, 1813

'The battle thunders, and the hills reply;
The smoke in wreathing columns seeks the sky;
Dark Maya startles at the central roar,
And Roncevalles' echoes wake once more.'[1]

Wellington and Beresford were among the few field officers who did not return home between 1809 and 1814. Both men had an aversion to officers going home unnecessarily. There was no issue if an officer was seriously ill or needed time to recuperate from dangerous wounds, in which case a request for leave would be granted. One reason given for requests to go home was pressing business: a suggested reason which found no favour with either Wellington or Beresford. Stemming the flow in the months where there was likely to be no campaigning was not easy, particularly with officers who possessed friends in high places. Some wanted to see spouses or other lady friends; others sought to use political influence to gain promotion. Wellington told Beresford in October 1809 that the solution he had adopted with regard to officers in the British army going home was to oblige them to declare the nature of their business and fix the date of their return, and if they did not return by that date he would court-martial them for being absent without leave.[2] When Brigadier General Craufurd sought permission to go on leave in December 1810, Wellington put real pressure on him not to go, warning Craufurd he might lose command of the Light Division: 'Adverting to the number of General Officers senior to you in the army, it has not been an easy task to keep you in your command; and if you should go, I fear that I should not be able to appoint you to it again, or to one that would be so agreeable to you, or in which you could be so useful.'[3]

Craufurd persisted in his request. Wellington did not change his views. At the end of January 1811 he wrote to Craufurd stating that while he

could not refuse leave of absence to those who said their personal atten-
dance at home was required, he would not give his approval:

> I see no reason why I should depart from the rule which I have laid
> down for myself in these cases. Officers (general Officers in partic-
> ular) are the best judges of their own private concerns; and although
> my opinion is that there is no private concern that cannot be settled
> by instruction and power of attorney ... I cannot refuse leave of
> absence to those who come to say that their business is of a nature
> that requires their personal superintendence. But entertaining these
> opinions, it is rather too much that I should not only give leave of
> absence, but approve of the absence of any, particularly a General
> Officer, from the army.

Wellington went on to emphasize the inconvenience to the service of
absentees and the difficulty in finding proper substitutes, and then concluded: 'I may be obliged to consent to the absence of an officer, but I
cannot approve of it. I repeat that you know the situation of affairs as well
as I do, and you have my leave to go to England if you think proper.'[4]
Craufurd went to England in February 1811, returning at the end of April.
Notwithstanding this absence, he was welcomed back by Wellington.[5]

Beresford was equally difficult on the subject of leave involving absence
from the Peninsula. When one of his fellow countrymen, Brigadier
General Charles Miller, sought to return to Ireland two weeks after being
appointed Governor of Minho in northern Portugal in mid-November
1809, Beresford responded that public service demanded sacrifice, stating
that had Miller made the application prior to his appointment it might
have been possible but that the Portuguese government needed the British
officers. Beresford concluded: 'I don't doubt that you will cheerfully
occupy your post until a more favourable occasion.' All this in spite of the
fact that Miller had said he understood that if he went, he could not expect
to retain the position of Governor of Minho, and furthermore his assertion that if he was not in Ireland to sign some deeds for the sale of a
property by 1 January he feared foreclosure on a mortgage.[6] Miller chose
to stay in Portugal, rendering valuable service, before losing his life later
in the war.

In December 1812 Denis Pack applied for leave to go home. The
reasons he gave have not been ascertained, but it is possible that he was
frustrated at his inability to obtain the command of a brigade in the British
army despite Wellington's assurances that, subject to seniority, as soon as
one became available Pack could transfer back from the Portuguese army.

While Pack was reportedly severely wounded nine times during his career, there is no evidence he was wounded at Salamanca or Burgos.[7] However, William Gavin, an officer in the 71st, visited Pack in Bury Street, London in March 1813, recording that Pack was confined to his room as he was recovering from a wound received in Portugal, so perhaps an old wound was giving him trouble.[8]

Wellington continued to deplore 'the inconvenience felt by the constant change of the officers employed in every branch of the service in this country' and he diagnosed a primary cause of officers' requests to go home:

> One of the principal causes of these changes is the practice of going to England to apply for promotion which ought to be acquired by service here; and I acknowledge that I do not see the utility of my forwarding the recommendations of the heads of departments of those officers whom they deem deserving of promotion, if to these recommendations are to be preferred the claims and applications of those who quit the service here, to go home to make them.[9]

This letter was written in December 1812 so it seems Wellington had become no more relaxed about leave of absence by virtue of his improved military position vis à vis the French. Nevertheless, Pack's request does not seem to have irritated either Wellington or Beresford, or indeed caused them any qualms. Pack seems to have applied to Wellington for permission and the commander-in-chief mentioned in a letter to Beresford of 29 December that he rather thought 'I referred Pack to you for leave, letting him go if you should have no objection.'[10] Permission was given and Pack spent several months away from Portugal once the troops had been placed in winter quarters. We know he stayed in London for some time but there is no suggestion in the correspondence found to date that he went home to Ireland; indeed, his reference to his aide de camp Charles Synge going to Ireland is suggestive of Pack not having been there.[11]

Pack clearly used his time in London to cultivate contacts at Horse Guards for, while he was there, Lord Bathurst, then secretary of state for war and the colonies, offered him the command of a small expedition to act in conjunction with the navy on the coast of North America with, he understood, the local rank of major general. The United States of America had declared war against Great Britain on 18 June 1812, an event which resulted in further demands of a financial, military and naval nature on a country already involved in a life or death struggle with Napoleon. This meant that prior to the defeat of Napoleon in 1814 Britain resorted to a primarily defensive war in North America. However, troops were furnished to assist with the defence of Canada, and British squadrons caused considerable interference off the east coast of the United States. Pack declined the offer of this command, clearly preferring to wait for his chance with Wellington. Arriving back in Lisbon in late April 1813, he wrote to Wellington saying that although he had been flattered by the offer, he had felt he could not accept without Wellington's approval, and in any event he would have regretted parting 'from a Commander-in-Chief to whom I had been so long and sincerely attached'.[12] In response Wellington stated: 'Colonel Bunbury and I are highly flattered by the preference of the service in this country to that which has been proposed to you by the Secretary of State. I think you are right, but at all events I am very sensible of the kindness of your motives in refusing to accept the offer.'[13] Wellington was clearly receptive to Pack making his point again about his wish to command a brigade in the British army in the Peninsula, for within days Wellington was writing again to Pack to tell him he had not forgotten his wishes. Although there were two brigades currently vacant, the one in the 2nd division would have to go to Major General Oswald if Sir John Leith did not return, and the second in the 7th division would have to be given to Thomas Fermor as he was senior to Pack. However, Wellington went on to add that if no general officer was sent out from Britain, Pack would 'be removed to the British army, as you desire'.[14]

Recently honoured with the award of the Portuguese Order of the Tower and Sword (Torre e Espada), Pack proceeded to resume his command of his brigade then at Penafiel, where it had overwintered, recuperating and making good the losses incurred in the siege of Burgos and the harrowing retreat to Portugal.[15] He was just in time, for within weeks Wellington was to take the offensive against the French armies in Spain once again. The 1st Portuguese brigade would be deeply involved in the campaign leading to the Pyrénées and beyond. For Pack the year 1813 must have been fulfilling, notwithstanding the constant dangers.

Wellington did not begin to move the allied armies into Spain until mid-May. His forces were well equipped and well fed, having benefited from a quiet winter while supplied with clothing and food. British control of the sea to bring goods into Lisbon and Porto greatly facilitated the resupply of the army. Thanks to the efforts of Beresford and Dom Miguel Forjaz, secretary for war and foreign affairs in the Lisbon-based Regency, the Portuguese army was also in good shape. Clothing and equipment had been replaced, and after some difficulties arrears of pay were reduced to

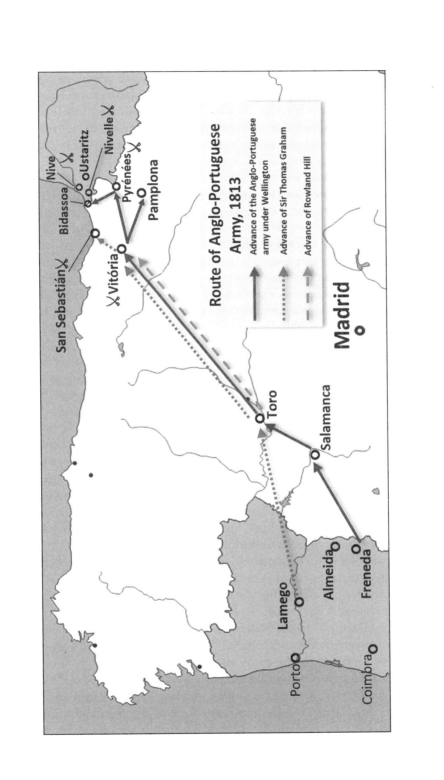

Route of Anglo-Portuguese Army, 1813

Advance of the Anglo-Portuguese army under Wellington

Advance of Sir Thomas Graham

Advance of Rowland Hill

San Sebastián

Bidassoa

Nive

Ustaritz

Nivelle

Pyrénées

Pamplona

Vitória

Toro

Salamanca

Madrid

Lamego

Almeida

Freneda

Porto

Coimbra

the level in the British army. In contrast, the French armies in Spain faced further reductions to replace troops lost by Napoleon in the Russian campaign of 1812. Virtual parity of numbers, and on occasion local superiority, gave Wellington the opportunity to move forward aggressively. In doing so, he deceived the French into thinking he was making a straightforward advance to Burgos via Salamanca.

Wellington himself did not leave Freneda until 22 May, but on 13 May he sent his main force forward under Sir Thomas Graham. Graham moved north across the Douro at Lamego and then through the Portuguese province of Tras os Montes, far to the west of any serious French force. From there he marched via Braganza, reaching Zamora in Spain on 1 June. When Wellington left Freneda he accompanied Hill with the 2nd and Portuguese divisions. He marched northeast via Salamanca, before joining up with Graham again at Toro on 2 June. Having outflanked the French once, he undertook the same move again, this time marching northeastward in four almost parallel columns, all passing west of Burgos. From east to west these columns were Hill's, Wellington's, Graham's and the army of Galicia under General Giron. Wellington marched via Amusco, Villadiego and Masa, learning on the way that the French had fired Burgos in an only partially successful attempt to destroy the fortifications. Joseph Bonaparte and Jourdan had contemplated trying to fight at or near Burgos but the French forces were still not collected together, and Joseph withdrew first to the Ebro, from where, finding he was again outflanked, he moved north to Vitoria.

On this long march from Portugal Pack and the 1st Portuguese brigade accompanied Graham's force, amounting to some twenty thousand men.[16] From Braganza to Zamora, via Miranda do Douro, and on to Sotresgudo which they reached on 10 June, the army faced tough marches over hilly country. On reaching Sotresgudo the allies needed to halt in order to allow provisions to be brought up. The scarcity of food was exacerbated in the Portuguese brigades due to inefficiencies of supply, a difficulty that seems to have only partly been made good by Wellington's direction on 5 June for Spanish or Portuguese troops serving with British corps to be supplied by the Commissary General of the British army, at the expense of their own governments, with bread, wine and forage corn received from villages through which the army passed.[17]

At the battle of Vitoria on 21 June the lead was taken by the allied right under Hill. The brunt of the fighting was borne by the 2nd and 3rd divisions, and this is reflected in the figures for the killed and wounded on the allied side.[18] Pack's brigade was part of Graham's vanguard, including the

1st and 5th divisions, charged with attempting to encircle the French right. The vanguard was more lightly engaged than the other allied columns, and losses were correspondingly few, but Graham was criticized in some quarters for not pushing forward with sufficient energy. Pack's brigade along with Colonel Longa's Spanish troops were with General Oswald in the fiercely contested taking of the têtes du pont at Gamarra and Abechuco.[19] The allies overwhelmed Joseph's army at Vitoria, resulting in the flight north to France of the soi disant king and his entourage. In the retreat of the French army Graham's forces, including Pack's brigade, crossed the Zadorra river from the north and pursued the corps of Reille and Lamartiniere through Arriaga and into the woods around Zurbano. The caçador battalions of both Pack's and Bradford's brigades there engaged the French but the pursuit was broken off and the French were able to retire in disarray but without further trouble. Graham reported that the Portuguese troops behaved admirably, mentioning in particular the 4th caçadores (part of Pack's brigade) and the 8th caçadores (part of Spry's brigade).[20] Beresford applauded the performance of a number of Portuguese brigades in the battle of Vitoria, including Pack's brigade.[21] Pack was well pleased with the performance of his Portuguese troops, though his language suggests he had remained somewhat apprehensive before the battle: 'Wonders will never cease; my 4th regiment of "caçadores" distinguished themselves by driving the enemy at the point of the bayonet from the heights. Sir Thomas Graham could scarcely believe his eyes.'[22] The 4th caçadores had performed with particular distinction, as Pack noticed in his post-battle report to Beresford's adjutant general: 'the conduct of the brigade under my command in the glorious day yesterday has my entire approval, particularly the 4th Caçadores battalion'. He also praised the performance of Lieutenant Colonel Edmund Williams, the commander of the 4th Caçadores.[23]

Wellington pursued the main body of the French army towards Pamplona. On reaching Salvatierra, he directed Graham to take part of his own corps, including Pack's brigade, north towards Villafranca with a view to intercepting any French attempting to use the Bayonne road to reach France.[24] Wellington had already sent two Spanish divisions directly north from Vitoria on the Bayonne road. They were not just chasing the French escaping from Vitoria, but were aware that also operating in the area was the division of Maximilien Foy. Unfortunately from the allied perspective, a failure to coordinate the advance of Graham's troops meant that by the time they reached and attacked Villafranca on 24 June, most of the French seeking to retire by that road were on the way to Tolosa. The

French fought repeated rearguard actions while waiting for reinforcements to come in to protect the remnants of the French convoy heading
for France. The most serious of these actions was at Tolosa on 25 June
where the Portuguese brigades were once again heavily involved. The
4th caçadores were at the heart of the action when capturing an important
hill with two companies of the grenadiers of the 1st regiment. Together
with their lieutenant colonel, Williams, they were once more praised by
Pack.[25] Pushing the French back across the frontier along the Bidassoa
river, Graham settled down to besiege St Sebastian. The Portuguese
brigades were part of the force at San Sebastian, but Denis Pack was on
the move.

On 3 June Wellington had been sent from London notification of the
brevet promotion to major general of a number of officers including Pack.
Horse Guards, aware that this would give Wellington more officers of this
rank than he required in the Peninsula, gave him some hints as to what he
might wish to do but left it to him to determine which officers to retain
and which to send back to England.[26] In July Wellington appointed
Pack to command the Highland brigade and his official association with
the Portuguese army came to an end.[27] What were the factors that led
Wellington to appoint Pack to the command of the Highland brigade?
Pack had no known associations of a direct kind with Scotland, but while
commanding the 71st regiment he had clearly developed a rapport with
the Scots officers and other ranks. The respect in which he was held by
those officers was manifested later when he was elected a member of the
Highland Society of London, an organization dedicated to the distribution of charity to Highlanders.[28] In this capacity it established in 1817 a
school for boys orphaned in the Napoleonic wars, a project likely to have
been close to Pack's heart, given the care with which he sought to look
after his men. It will be recalled that Pack had also fought for the retention
of highland dress for the 71st regiment when others were minded to
supersede it in 1810. The membership of the Highland Society of London
reflected primarily the great Scottish highland families, and only existing
members could propose new members.

In June 1813 the Highland brigade was composed of the 42nd, 79th and
91st regiments, together with one company of the 5/60th, and formed part
of the 6th division under Major General Sir Henry Clinton.[29] The key to
Pack's appointment to command the Highland brigade is clear from
a letter written by Wellington's adjutant general, Edward Pakenham,
to Pack on 6 July 1813. Prior to this appointment to command the Highland brigade, Pack had clearly indicated a preference to command light

infantry, a desire perhaps based on his experience with the 71st regiment. Though his wishes were not met in this respect, in that in June 1813 the Highland brigade was made up of regular line regiments, his new appointment was a singular recognition by Wellington of Pack's talents. In the letter of 6 July, Edward Pakenham noted that given the poor health of Henry Clinton, Pack might well find himself commanding a division. Pakenham's words proved correct only too quickly, for Clinton, who had been absent from the army through illness from January to June 1813, was again absent from late July until October of the same year.[30] Pack's appointment to command the Highland brigade demonstrated Wellington's micromanagement of a situation whereby, because of his confidence in the appointee, he was prepared to thrust a man who had hitherto not commanded a British brigade into a situation where he felt there was a strong likelihood that he would soon lead an allied division.

The Highland brigade had not been involved in the battle of Vitoria on 21 June, for it had been appointed to guard the stores and artillery which were unable to keep pace with the main part of Wellington's force. Following the battle, it was ordered up to assist in the blockade of Pamplona, one of the few remaining cities in northwest Spain still in French hands. In this situation Pack found himself, within days of being appointed to lead a British brigade, commanding the entire 6th division. Pack's force formed part of the outer ring of those blockading Pamplona once the Spanish army of Andalucia under Captain General Enrique José O'Donnell and Major General Carlos d'Espana had arrived and encircled the city. The headquarters of the 6th division was now in Lesaka, some 75 kilometres from Pamplona, while most of the 6th division was based in and around Santesteban, 25 kilometres nearer the encircled city.[31] Pack's new command was soon to face the first major counter-attack by the French under Marshal Soult, appointed on 1 July commander in chief of the French armies in southwest France and northern Spain ('*L'armée d'Espagne*'). Soult mounted a multi-pronged offensive through the passes and valleys of the western Pyrénées at the end of July. He wished to relieve Pamplona, and the allied army risked getting caught between Soult's forces and the garrison.

The main attacks were through the Maya pass, guarded by General Hill and the 2nd division, and that of Roncevalles, where General Cole was stationed with the 4th division. Initially the French met with considerable success, forcing the allies to abandon the passes at Maya and Roncevalles. In a further setback for Wellington, the force under General Graham was repulsed in his attempt to storm St Sebastian. Moving eastwards from

St Sebastian, Wellington assumed direct control of operations against Soult. Pack was directed to move two brigades of the 6th division to give support to Hill and to place the third brigade at St Estevan (Santesteban/ Doneztebe). On 27 July he was directed to hold Olague, 15 kilometres north of Pamplona, under all circumstances.[32] Wellington's instructions to Pack on the day are a good example of the manner in which the commander-in-chief micro-managed affairs. They dealt with the treatment of the reserve of small arms ammunition, communications with the commanders of other divisions, and even the taking of meals, as well as the need to hold Olague. Later on the same day Wellington directed the 6th division to make its way to Ollocarizqueta, a village about 10 kilometres north of Pamplona. Soult occupied Sorauren on 27 July and on the following day Wellington, having joined the army, recalled the 6th division from Ollocarizqueta and it

> had scarcely taken their position when they were attacked by a very large force of the enemy which had assembled in the village of Sorauren. Their front was, however, so well defended ... that the enemy were soon driven back with immense loss from a fire on their front, both flanks and rear.[33]

As the battle progressed, Pack led an unsuccessful attack on the village of Sorauren with light companies from the Highland brigade and others, including the Portuguese brigade in the division, commanded by Major General Sir George Madden.[34] Pack and the regimental major of the 91st, Donald McNeill, were severely injured in this attack on 28 July.[35] In Pack's case he was wounded in the head, one of the more serious wounds he received during his service. He was reportedly hit while standing beside one of the guns of the artillery brigade attached to the 6th division.[36] Pack's sense of humour was shown by his recounting that 'if the ball had struck any other but an Irish head, it would certainly have broken it'.[37] Pack was evacuated to Errenteria down near the coast, where he was still recovering when John Vandeleur visited the village in early September. Vandeleur may well have made the journey specifically to see his 'good friend Genl. Pack', as both officers hailed from Ireland and Vandeleur was then stationed quite near St Sebastian, itself only 11 kilometres from Errenteria.[38] Madden was also wounded, but was able to continue in his command. Wellington overcame Soult following a three-day battle. Madden's 7th Portuguese brigade was involved again on 30 July when Sorauren was taken from the French, and their retreat over the Pyrénées back to France commenced.[39] The Portuguese brigade of the 6th division suffered substantial losses in the three days but their performance was acknowledged by Beresford in an Order of the Day dated 11 August 1813:

> His Excellency Marshal Beresford saw with pleasure the good conduct displayed by the regiments under the orders of Marechal de Campo George Allen Madden at the memorable battles of the 28th and 30th of last month, near Pampluna; and assures the General, the officers and men, that their bravery met with his perfect approbation; particularly the conduct of the 9th regiment of caçadores, which constantly merits distinction.[40]

Yet this strong performance by Madden and the Portuguese brigade seemed to count for little, for in appointing Pack to command the 6th division in July Wellington had apparently breached the sacrosanct rule of promotion by virtue of seniority. Madden had been created a brigadier general in the Portuguese army prior to Pack's appointment to a similar position and, after Beresford and Major General Sir John Hamilton, Madden was the most senior British officer in the Portuguese forces.[41] His career, however, had been full of controversy, and whether as a cavalry officer now commanding infantry or for other reasons, Wellington certainly did not want him to command a division.[42]

The announcement of Madden's appointment as a major general (marechal de campo) in the Portuguese army appears to have been deliberately held back until a day after Pack's elevation was announced in the *London Gazette*, as part of the birthday honours promotions of June 1813. In that list Madden was made up to a full colonel in the British army. The British brigades in the 6th division were now commanded by major generals, and they did not wish to serve under Madden. Representations were apparently made to Wellington by Charles Colville, who, following the Battle of the Pyrénées, had replaced Sir Henry Clinton as commander of the 6th division.[43] The result was a decision announced by Wellington through the adjutant general's office on 14 August giving Pack precedence over Madden.[44] A furious Madden requested Wellington to reconsider his decision, pointing out he had been a brigadier general when Pack and others had only been lieutenant colonels.[45] Wellington realized he had done wrong but was still not prepared to have Madden command a division, writing to Beresford on 19 August:

> I enclose a letter which I have received from Major General Madden in regard to his rank. I was wrong in the decision which I had made, and I have altered it; but as it is quite impossible to leave the

6th Division liable to the chance of being commanded even for a day by General Madden, in which I believe you concur with me, I shall be obliged to you if you will remove him from it.[46]

Beresford then ordered Madden to relinquish the command of the 7th Portuguese brigade, because Madden's current rank was 'attended by great inconvenience to the general service'. He directed Madden to return to Lisbon, as he had no other command for him at this time.[47] Beresford did invite him to his own headquarters but this must have been out of compassion, for Madden was told that 'remonstrance would be hopeless'.[48] Thus the unfortunate Madden was deprived not only of his command of a division, but also of a brigade in the final eight months of the war. Pack in contrast was to enhance his reputation further.

The importance of the Battle of the Pyrénées, and its fierceness, is sometimes overlooked. Soult found the allies unprepared for his move back into Spain and, had his mission succeeded, he would not only have relieved the siege of Pamplona but might have been able to cause his adversaries serious difficulties. Wellington appreciated the situation, writing to Lord Liverpool: 'I never saw such fighting as on the 27th and 28th July, the anniversary of the Battle of Talavera, nor such determination as the troops showed.'[49] Having lost the battle, Soult retired over the Pyrénées into France, leaving Pamplona to its own devices. Wellington, for his part, began to prepare for an invasion of France. He did so with caution, concerned that the major powers other than Great Britain might enter into a peace settlement with Napoleon which would leave Wellington's army exposed to French military might. Indeed, at the outset of the 1813 campaign crossing the French border must have seemed a remote possibility, and to reach it in six weeks was a huge achievement. An indication that Wellington, whose modus operandi was to prepare to the utmost, was not initially thinking in the spring of 1813 in terms of an invasion of France that summer may be gleaned from the fact that in late August he was writing to Bathurst in England, asking the latter to help secure Cassini's map of France and his map of the Pyrénées, maps which he understood to be very scarce.[50] In late September, having received a map from London, he requested further maps of both the Pyrénées and the river Garonne, stating 'I wish I may not require them; but it is as well to have them at all events.'[51]

Following the Battle of the Pyrénées, the 6th division moved to join Picton in the neighbourhood of Roncevalles, guarding the Bastan valley and the Col de Maya on the border with France. Colville was delighted with his new command and observed that Pack was 'reckoned as an excellent officer, and whose wound being slight, though on the head, has returned to quarters'.[52] This remark is contradicted by evidence that Pack was hospitalized in early August following his head injury at Sorauren. In any event he was certainly back at the helm of the Highland brigade at the time of the crossing of the Bidassoa on 7 October. While the 6th division did an admirable job on that day of diverting Soult's attention by coming through the Maya pass, it was not involved in any sustained fighting as Wellington's main attack was at the estuary of the river, involving the allied left and French right. There the attack was led by the 1st and 5th divisions aided by Pack's former command, the 1st Portuguese brigade, now led by Brigadier General John Wilson.

Soult now fell back on his second line of defence, the river Nivelle, which empties into the Atlantic Ocean at St Jean de Luz. Moving inland, he had fortified various heights with redoubts and batteries, including La Petite Rhune, and the mountains behind Sare and Ainhoa all the way to St Jean Pied de Port. The fall of Pamplona was now felt to be imminent, although on 30 October Pack wrote to Sir James Willoughby Gordon, then quartermaster-general to the forces, stating he wished he could make his letter more acceptable by telling him Pamplona was in the allies' possession. He reported that the garrison had offered to surrender on 25 October, if allowed to march to France, but the terms had been rejected. Wellington proposed to move forward as soon as Pamplona had fallen.[53] In the event the allies did not have long to wait. The capitulation of Pamplona on 31 October left no French-held position of importance to Wellington's rear in northern Spain, and he determined to advance against Soult's fortified line on the Nivelle forthwith. Before this occurred, however, an event took place indicative of the recovered Pack's standing in Wellington's eyes. On 3 November Wellington held a dinner at headquarters to celebrate the fall of Pamplona, at which Denis Pack was the guest of honour. Pack reported on the evening as follows:

> Lord Wellington could not have chosen company I would sooner meet, Marshal Beresford, Sir Rowland Hill, Sir Henry Clinton and others. Lord Wellington was very polite and proposed my health after my recovery, which the rest were so civil as to acclaim. He then, as was his wont, said what was in his mind: 'Gentleman we have prospered, but we have now Soult, a man of mettle in front of us. I intend to prod that fat Marshal till he comes to my terms and I pray you help me to that end.'[54]

Wellington had intended to attack Soult's Nivelle line on 8 November, but owing to intense rainfall he postponed the move forward until 10 November. The main attack was launched at 6am against the French centre, under the command of Beresford with the 3rd, 4th, 7th and Light divisions, while Hill with the 2nd, 6th and Portuguese divisions with Spanish support targeted the French left. Traversing the pass of the Maya, the 2nd and 6th divisions did not have an easy time of it, notwithstanding their supporting role. Robert Blakeney, one of Pack's fellow countrymen and a lieutenant with the 28th regiment, who was himself injured in the battle, stated 'I saw one shell drop in the midst of a Portuguese regiment drawn up in our rear: it blew up twelve men, who became so scorched and blackened on their fall that they resembled a group of mutilated chimney sweeps.'[55] The pivotal position of La Petite Rhune, its associated redoubts and the bridge of Amotz were all secured, driving a wedge between the two halves of the French army, with Beresford's divisions capturing St Pée sur Nivelle. Soult was left with no alternative but to withdraw to his next line of defence, the river Nive, where his right rested on the strong fortress of Bayonne.[56] After the battle Wellington moved his headquarters to St Jean de Luz. Nivelle was an important allied victory, for it enabled Wellington to move his forces out of the Pyrénées, where the weather had already turned cold, with snowfalls that caused hardship to all involved.

Quartermaster General George Murray's comprehensive instructions for the attack on the Nivelle had been prepared and distributed even before the fall of Pamplona. The 6th division formed part of a corps under General Rowland Hill, along with the 2nd and Portuguese divisions and Pablo Morillo's Spanish division. The instructions for the 6th division, under the now returned General Henry Clinton, were to move from the valley of Maya in the night before the attack. On the morning in question the advance of the 6th division was led by James Douglas's (previously Madden's) 7th Portuguese brigade.[57] Pack's Highland brigade moved from Urdax, just inside Spain, down the right bank of the Nivelle, threatening Ainhoa and the French left. The 6th division, including the Highland brigade, suffered considerable losses, but Hill's force was able to join up with that of Beresford at St Pée sur Nivelle on the evening of 10 November after the battle. In his post-battle report to Rowland Hill, Clinton observed that during the advance Pack's brigade with the 8th Portuguese regiment formed his second line. In the attack on Ainhoa the Highland brigade under Pack supported the advance 'with the utmost steadiness, and proceeded to the top of the hill in as good order as if he had met with no other impediment than the steepness of the hill'.

(*Left*) Lieutenant Denis Pack, 14th Light Dragoons. (*Right*) Lieutenant Colonel Pack.
(*From* A Memoir of Major-General Sir Denis Pack)

Lieutenant Colonel Denis Pack miniature. (*Suzie Pack-Beresford*)

The sword of Lieutenant Colonel Denis Pack when commanding the 71st regiment. (*Spink & Son Lt*

Major General Sir Denis Pack's travelling basin. (*Christopher Clarke Antiques*)

ull-length portrait of Sir Denis Pack. (*Moya Maclean*)

British troops entering the citadel at Buenos Aires, 27 June 1806. (*Author's collection*)

Santo Domingo Convent, Buenos Aires. (*M.L. Maciel*)

Battle of Vimiera (sic),
Highland piper, by
B. Manskirch.
(*National Army Museum*)

Major General Sir Denis Pack,
by Ann Mee. (*Michael Ruderson*)

The Storming of Ciudad Rodrigo, 19 January 1812, by William Heath. (*Author's collection*)

The Battle of Salamanca, 22 July 1812, by John Augustus Atkinson. (*Author's collection*)

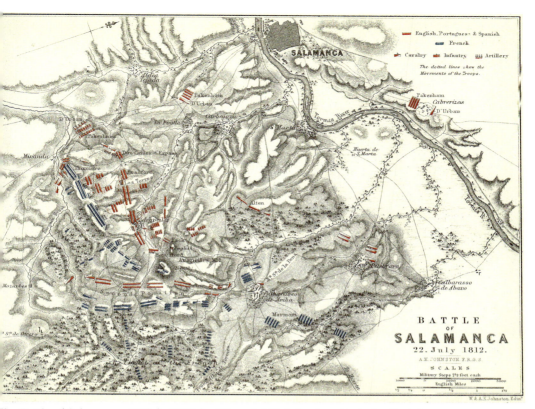

The Battle of Salamanca, 22 July 1812, by W. and A.K. Johnston. (*Author's collection*)

The Defence of Burgos, October 1812, by Francois Joseph Heim. (*Topfoto*)

The Battle of the Pyrénées, 28–30 July 1813, by William Heath. (*Author's collection*)

Plan of the Battle of Orthez, 27 February 1814, by Adolphe Thiers. (*Author's collection*)

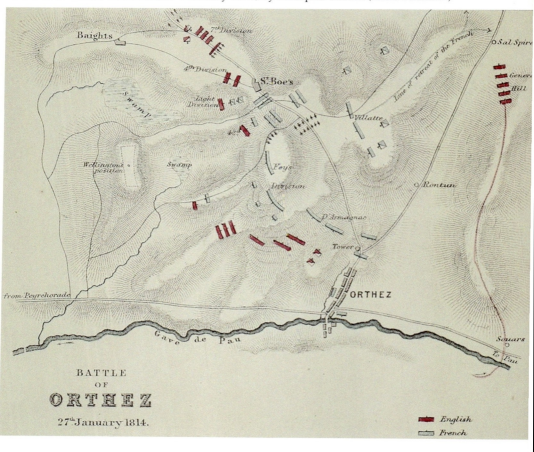

BATTLE
OF
ORTHEZ
27th January 1814.

English
French

'Field Marshal the Duke of Wellington giving orders to his Generals previous to a general action', by Thomas Heaphy, engraved by Anker Smith. Denis Pack is the fourth officer from the left at the back. (*Author's collection*)

Major General Sir Denis Pack, by Charles Turner, engraved by Joseph Saunders.
(*Suzie Pack-Beresford*)

Major General Sir Denis Pack's Peninsular War and Waterloo medals.
(*Spink & Son Ltd*)

Major General Sir Denis Pack's Portuguese
Peninsular War Medal. (*Spink & Son Ltd*)

Six light candelabrum by Paul Storr (London) 1817, bearing the Pack coat of arms and motto '*Fidus Confido*', presented to Major General Sir Denis Pack by the city of Kilkenny. (*Christies*)

The City of Waterford Freedom Box. (*San Antonio Museum of Art*)

The Duke of Wellington,
by Thomas Lawrence.
(*Heritage England*)

Plan of the battle of Quatre
Bras, 16 June 1815, by W. and
A.K. Johnston. (*Author's collection*)

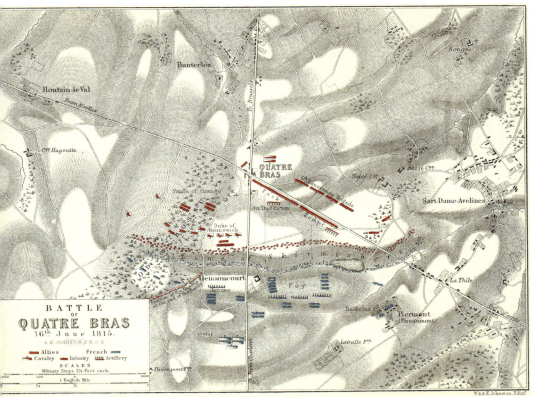

Marshal William Carr Beresford by William Beechey. (*National Portrait Gallery*)

Lady Elizabeth Louisa Pack *née* Beresford, artist unknown. (*Suzie Pack-Beresford*)

Denis Pack's octagonal pistol by Tathum & Egg, London; inscribed and with shoulder extension.
(*Olympia Auctions*)

Lieutenant Colonel Noel
Hill by George Dawe.
(*Cheffins, Cambridge*)

Monument to Denis Pack in St Canice's Cathedral, by Francis Chantrey. (*Author's collection*)

A redoubt on the same ridge that was attacked by one battalion of the Highland brigade and the 8th Portuguese was abandoned by the enemy. Pack was praised for his 'gallantry and judicious conduct'.[58] A week later Wellington told Clinton he was 'delighted with the attack of the 6th division' and that while he had not yet recommended any officers for promotion, he would 'not forget those of the 6th division'.[59] Writing home to Lord Bathurst with his report of the battle, Wellington praised the performance of the 6th division:

> I had the pleasure of seeing the 6th division under Lieut. General Sir H. Clinton, after having crossed the Nivelle, and having driven in the enemy's piquets on both banks, and having covered the passage of the Portuguese division under Lieut. General Sir John Hamilton on its right, make a most handsome attack upon the right of the enemy's position behind Ainhoué and on the right of the Nivelle, and carry all the intrenchments, and the redoubt on that flank.[60]

Later Wellington, when asked to describe his best battle, called the battle of Nivelle his 'best work'.[61]

It rained for five days following the battle, rendering the roads and other tracks a quagmire. Wellington determined to put the army into cantonments on 16 November, abandoning for the moment any further pursuit of Soult. The latter concentrated his now reduced forces behind the river Nive, with a strong position in Bayonne on his right. Pack and the 6th division were placed between Ustaritz and Arraunts. Beresford was now in command of the 4th and 6th divisions, so Pack would have been close to his old friend, whose headquarters were at Ustaritz. Wellington now moved his own headquarters to St Jean de Luz.[62]

The weather improved sufficiently for Wellington to make a further move forward in December. The final operations of the year involved the crossing of the Nive and the battle of St Pierre (outside Bayonne), a hard-fought encounter over four days from 9 to 13 December. On this occasion Hill's force bore the brunt of the fighting, with Beresford supporting him. In the first phase of the battle on 9 December the 6th division was part of Beresford's force which crossed the river Nive by pontoons at Ustaritz. Later that day Hill's and Beresford's forces linked up. Somewhat obliquely, Pack's obituary in *The Annual Biography and Obituary* tells us that while he commanded the Highland brigade at both the Nivelle and the Nive, 'though not actually engaged, he was present at the signal defeat of the enemy's desperate attack on Lieutenant General Sir Rowland Hill's corps, on the 13th December, 1813'.[63] What appears to have happened is that Wellington became aware that on the night of 12 December Soult 'passed a large force through Bayonne' in order to make a major attack on Rowland Hill's divisions the following day. Wellington then 'requested' Beresford to reinforce Hill with the 6th division and later the 4th division was also sent to assist Hill.[64] Although the 6th division crossed the Nive at daylight to join Hill, he did not really require these reinforcements to defeat Soult's latest initiative.[65] However, a substantial part of Pack's brigade was engaged.[66] Sergeant James Anton of the 42nd regiment (the Black Watch) had joined the regiment in the Peninsula in 1813. He described in his memoirs how the regiment supported the left of the 2nd division at St Pierre, recounting how their hapless colonel, Sir Robert Macara, led them into thick entangling undergrowth on the order to advance.[67] Having come to a standstill, they were withdrawn by General Pack, who sent them to attack by a different route. Anton suggested that the regiment lost a not inconsiderable number of killed and wounded in this fight.[68] Of Macara he observed that he was 'a brave man who feared no personal danger, but was not well acquainted with field manoeuvres or military tactics'.[69]

Anton's memoirs are informative on an aspect of these wars that is sometimes overlooked. Fraternization receives periodic reference, particularly when rival armies were bivouacked on opposing sides of rivers. However, there was another facet to the relationship with the enemy: helping your opponents wounded in battle. Many wounded were, of course, dispatched in the heat of the moment, but there are tales of assistance being rendered as well. Anton gives one such account at a time the armies were in the Pyrénées, reflecting 'the hand of kindness was equally extended towards the foe as to the friend' and 'in the morning, by order of Lord Wellington, the whole of the wounded of the enemy were carried into their own lines; and it certainly was gratifying to see those brave but disabled soldiers embracing those who had entertained them during the night, and kindly shaking the hand that perhaps inflicted the wound'.[70]

In the summer of 1813 the artist Thomas Heaphy had joined the allied army as it marched north from Vitoria. In the course of six months he was to paint many of the British officers, either singly or in groups. Judge Advocate General Francis Seymour Larpent referred to him as having made twenty-six portraits by October 1813. Perhaps one of these was the fine painting by Heaphy of Denis Pack against a background of mountains. Heaphy was at Bera in the Pyrénées in October when he was nearly captured, as a result of which he reportedly increased the price of portraits from 40 to 50 guineas.[71] Pack is also portrayed in Heaphy's masterpiece

'Field Marshal the Duke of Wellington KG giving orders to his Generals previous to a General Action'. In 1810 regulations had been introduced for the wearing of medals awarded to officers in the British army.[72] By notice dated 7 October 1813, the wearing of medals to commemorate battles was regularized. The regulation now introduced was designed to reduce the number of medals worn by introducing the cross when a recipient had received recognition for participation in four battles or sieges, with clasps for subsequent distinctions. Amongst those listed in the *London Gazette* of 7 October 1813 as entitled to wear a cross and one or more clasps was Major General Denis Pack.[73] For Pack 1813 had proved to be a momentous year. His Portuguese brigade had performed well at Vitoria, before he rejoined the British army shortly afterwards. Though seriously wounded at Sorauren, he returned to lead the Highland brigade with distinction at the battles of the Nivelle and the Nive.

Chapter 10

'Bonaparte's building must now fall and peace is at hand', 1814[1]

Though driven back on all fronts, Napoleon's armies continued to fight the allies through the spring of 1814. Following the disaster of Leipzig (16–19 October 1813) Napoleon was forced to defend northern France in the winter of 1813/14. He gained a number of minor victories in January and February, but the tide was running strongly against him and by early March the allies had advanced deep into France.[2] Even though Napoleon managed to gain the advantage over his opponents at Rheims on 17 March, it was but a temporary success. In southwest France, following the victories of the Nivelle and the Nive in late 1813, Wellington now blockaded Bayonne, and developed a strategy designed to stretch Soult's army by extending the front eastward. Soult moved his own headquarters to Peyrehorade on the river Adour in late December, leaving the heavily fortified city of Bayonne with a substantial garrison under General Thouvenot. Soult's strategy henceforth was to defend successive lines based on the large numbers of substantial rivers emanating from the Pyrénées. On the French side of the massif these run from south to north, before turning west and emptying into the Atlantic Ocean. In adopting this approach Soult did mount a number of small diversionary attacks early in the new year, but the French marshal's designs were rendered more difficult by the repeated demands from Napoleon to send regiments northwards to augment his own forces. Meanwhile, Wellington rested and strengthened his own army from late December until early February, a task greatly facilitated by the continuous arrival of supplies through the ports of northern Spain and St Jean de Luz. Wellington waited only for the weather to improve, and for a sufficient supply of money to pay the troops and debts, before seeking to advance again. When funds reached him in the second week in January, he waited only on the weather.

Only an entirely unanticipated development could now save Napoleon. Militarily his exhausted armies were outnumbered on all fronts. In desperation, he sent King Ferdinand of Spain back to that country, in the hope that Spain would then detach itself from the allies, but this move was unsuccessful. Nonetheless, Wellington remained wary that the northern powers might negotiate a separate peace with Napoleon, an event that would leave the British and their Iberian allies isolated.

Fine but cold weather arrived in southwest France on 10 February, and Wellington's advance began four days later. Pack's Highland brigade, which had been in cantonments in and around Villefranque following the battle of St Pierre, was part of a force under Beresford earmarked initially for the defence of the Nive (including the blockade of Bayonne) and the river Adour, thus freeing Hill to move eastward supported by Morillo's Spanish division.[3] Hill's force of some twenty-eight thousand men then proceeded to drive the French back over a series of not insubstantial rivers flowing north from the Pyrénées before they joined the Adour. In this manner the allies crossed the rivers Joyeuse, Bidouze, Saison and the Gave d'Oleron. With a view to forcing Soult's left flank and to give help to Hill's own extended forces, Wellington brought the Light and 6th divisions eastwards to join Hill.[4] By 24 February the 6th division was between Montfort and Laas on the Gave d'Oleron, and by 26 February Wellington's main army was substantially assembled on the left bank of the Gave de Pau opposite Orthez.[5]

In winter the Gave de Pau is deep and fast flowing on the south side of the town of Orthez, overlooked by a ridge of steep hills. The road crossed the Gave by way of a fortified bridge. While there existed fords both below and above the town, crossing these would have been difficult, if opposed. Soult, however, having partially blown the bridge, decided to defend the heights surrounding the town. Initially, Wellington was disposed to turn Soult's left flank by crossing the river above Orthez. On 24 February he ordered Beresford, who was downriver menacing the town of Peyrehorade, to distract the French by threatening their right wing. When the French retreated, blowing up the bridge at Peyrehorade behind them, Beresford crossed both the Gave d'Oleron and the Gave de Pau above where they join the Adour, on the night of 25/26 February. He then marched 20 kilometres upstream on the right of the Gave de Pau, and had linked up with some of Wellington's force by the evening of 26 February, a few kilometres outside Orthez. Wellington had managed to cross the Gave de Pau with the 3rd division, Somerset's cavalry and some artillery at Berenx (downstream from Orthez) earlier that afternoon.[6] While it was anticipated that Soult, who had failed to attack the allies while they were separated, would retire during the night, preparations were made to attack him if he was still in situ the next day. Wellington determined that the key

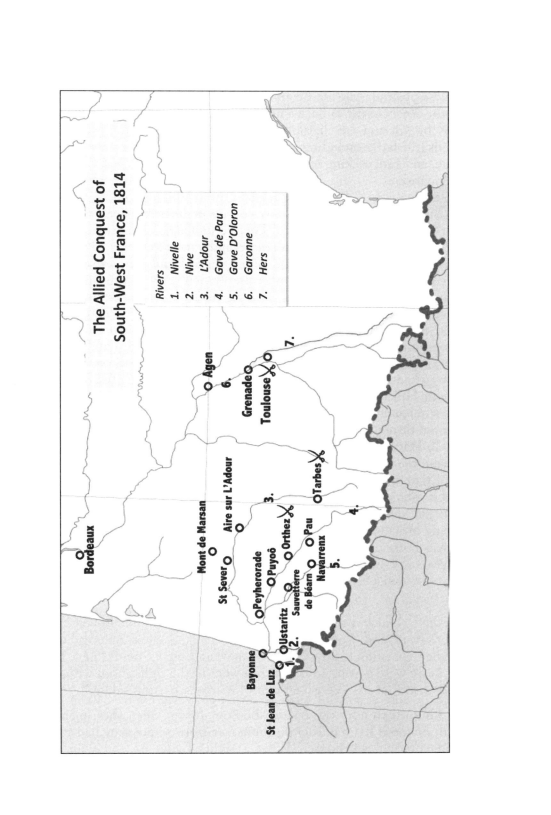

The Allied Conquest of
South-West France, 1814

Rivers

1. Nivelle
2. Nive
3. L'Adour
4. Gave de Pau
5. Gave D'Oloron
6. Garonne
7. Hers

to Soult's position was the heights on the French right, which was to be made the object of the initial assault. The attack was to be led on the allied left by the 4th and 7th divisions under Beresford, with the 3rd and 6th divisions (the latter including the Highland brigade) holding the centre of the line, and Hill seeking to cross above Orthez with the 2nd and Portuguese divisions.

At daybreak on 27 February Pack and the Highland brigade, as part of the 6th division, crossed the Gave de Pau at Berenx where a pontoon bridge had now been put in place. There it joined the 3rd division. While Beresford with the 4th and 7th divisions and Vivian's cavalry advanced on the heights and the village of St Boes, the 3rd and 6th divisions were engaged in holding the attention of the French centre. After initial success, and the capture of St Boes, Beresford's troops were denied further advance by Taupin's and Rouget's divisions. There the French artillery, heavier than that of the allies, managed to prevent allied progress. Wellington then ordered the immediate advance of the 3rd and 6th divisions to attack the French centre and the left of the heights on which the French right stood. The engagement became general along the whole line and, with Hill crossing the Gave above the town, Soult was threatened with encirclement and annihilation. He chose to retreat. Orderly at first, the retreat turned into a scramble in which the French were only saved by nightfall. Having crossed the Luy de Béarn at Sault de Navailles, Soult's now demoralized forces formed a further line of defence along the right bank of that river.

Orthez was no easy victory. In the absence of commentary from Pack, we have the views of Beresford, complemented by those of a soldier in the Highland brigade. Beresford paid tribute to the courage of the French on the day, observing 'I have not seen them fight so well for these two or three years.'[7] Private James Gunn of the 42nd regiment, the Black Watch (Am Freiceadan Dubh), recounted a charge of the Highland brigade at Orthez:

> I never saw such a sight before. Man and horse tumbled over each other, dead and wounded. We advanced and their infantry was getting in position to attack. But, from what cause we never knew, but just as we were getting into line they went to the right about without firing a shot at us. We gave them of course a parting salute.[8]

James Gunn then goes on to describe how, having been shot in the leg himself, he made his way back to the house from where they had started and on entering the house, 'What a sight! Lying on the floor were wounded men, and some in great pain. The most painful to hear was a stout Grenadier who lay beside me, shot through the belly, and crying out to the Doctor to put him out of pain. Next day, Frenchmen came with carts to bring us into hospital.'[9]

Allied losses in the action were 2,270. Wellington indicated that these were mostly sustained by members of the 3rd, 4th and 7th divisions.[10] In his extensive report on the battle to Lord Bathurst on 1 March, Wellington makes few references to the 6th division and none to the Highland brigade or Pack, but Pack was named in the vote of thanks of both houses of parliament on 24 March.[11] No account of the battle by Pack has been found to date.

Following the battle of Orthez, Wellington split his army, sending Beresford north with the 4th and 7th divisions, while he himself pursued Soult, who retired eastwards via Aire and Tarbes to Toulouse. Beresford's instructions were to secure Bordeaux if possible, Wellington having received news that there was a sizeable party there in favour of surrender. This proved to be the case. Having accepted the surrender on 12 March, Beresford hurried back to join Wellington with the 4th division, leaving the 7th division at Bordeaux and its environs. He rejoined Wellington on 26 March outside Toulouse, where he was to command the allied left wing, including the 6th division and the Highland brigade. For the allies, for the Highland brigade and for Pack, Toulouse was to prove a difficult and dangerous engagement, but first the 6th division was to face determined French resistance from Soult during his fighting withdrawal to La Ville Rose.

At Aire sur Adour the Highlanders drove the French from the town on 2 March. The allies had successfully crossed the river Adour the previous day. The rain was incessant and must have made life uncomfortable for officers and miserable for rank and file. That night and the next morning would witness two events that demonstrate both why Pack was a popular commander and his irascible nature. James Anton was Pack's orderly on the night of 1 March. Pack ordered a distribution of straw for the tents of the men setting up camp 'in a newly ploughed field, rendered a complete mire by the rain and hail which fell upon us with dreadful fury', so that they did not have to lie on wet ground. Pack himself was lodged in a nearby farmhouse, and Anton was lucky enough to have a good roof over his head as he slept in a cart shed. However, the next morning the guard was changed before the general's house without the required formalities being observed, and Pack, who had witnessed the whole proceedings from his window, ordered the confinement of the two men responsible, with

Anton himself being reprimanded for failing to prevent this irregularity. He was told to report the matter to Colonel Macara. When he did so, Macara seems to have felt Pack had overreacted, interrupting Anton's report with 'There is always something disagreeable occurring to the general's notice, very unpleasant indeed; but here he comes himself.' Whatever conversation took place between Pack and Macara, the men confined were released before nightfall.[12]

At Tarbes, where Soult had stopped to resupply his forces, the two armies clashed again on 20 March. Soult gave way but not before a stiff resistance in which the 6th division attempted unsuccessfully to turn the French right under Clausel.

Wellington abandoned an attempt to cross the river Garonne above Toulouse at the end of March owing to heavy flooding. Had he been able to make such a move, he could have encircled Soult's forces, preventing any further move eastwards and any attempt to join up with Marshal Suchet. Instead, on 4 April he put Beresford with the 3rd, 4th and 6th divisions, together with a cavalry detachment, across the river Garonne at Grenade, 30 kilometres northwest (downstream) of the city. A most dangerous situation then developed, for rising floodwaters caused the pontoon bridge to be taken up, thus dividing Wellington's army. Soult, however, failed to take advantage of the situation, and on 8 March a fresh pontoon bridge was laid nearer the city at the Château de Gagnac (Gagnac sur Garonne). Wellington then brought the remainder of the army across the river, with the exception of Hill's forces that were to be used to create a diversion in the southwestern suburb of St Cyprien and prevent any French attempt to break out southwards.

Leaving Picton with the 3rd division to demonstrate northwest of the city at the Jumeaux bridge, Wellington launched his main attack from the north. Beresford was sent with the 4th and 6th divisions, the latter including the Highland brigade, across the river Hers at Croix Daurade with a view to turning the enemy's position and capturing the heavy French entrenchments on Mont Rave, a hill that would effectively command Toulouse once captured. This involved a 3 kilometre trek over marshy land while exposed to French gunners on Mont Rave. At times Beresford's force was no more than 500 yards from the French guns and it suffered accordingly. The Highland brigade was fortunate at this point as it marched on the allied left and was the least exposed to French fire. However, the soft ground forced Beresford to abandon his own artillery. The attack was to be coordinated with one launched by a Spanish division under Freire. Unfortunately, contrary to instructions, Freire failed to wait

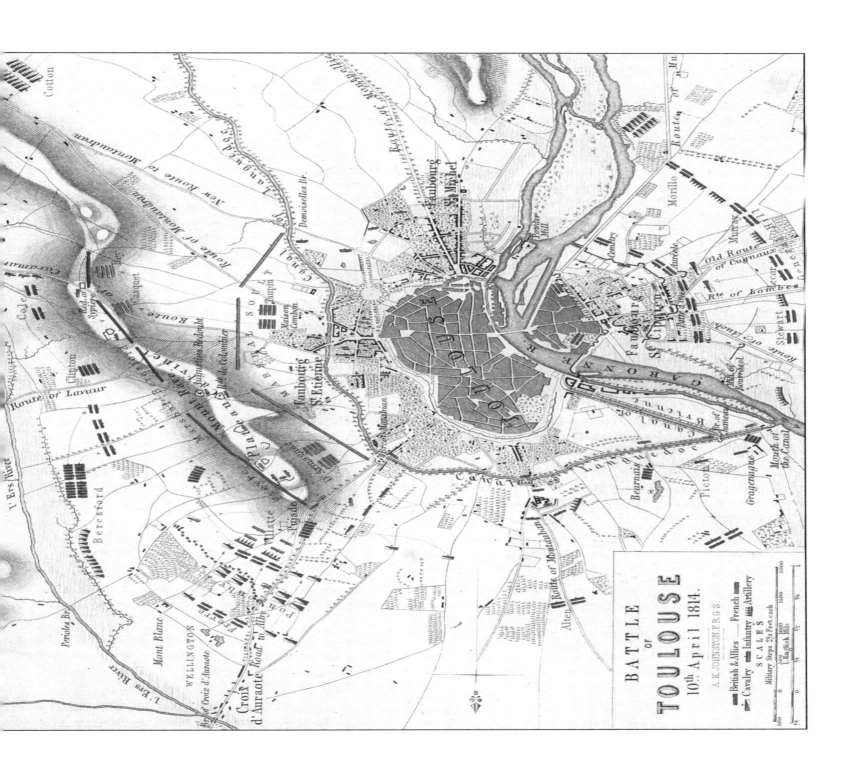

BATTLE
OF
TOULOUSE
10th April 1814.

A.K. JOHNSTON F.R.G.S

British &Allies ——— French ———
Cavalry —— Infantry —— Artillery
SCALES
Military Steps 2½ Feet each

for Beresford's advance and launched his own attack, which was repulsed with considerable loss. At this stage the French were streaming down the hill after the retreating Spaniards, and both the 4th and 6th divisions were faced about in line to receive them. The French were, however, recalled, enabling Beresford's force to continue its march.[13] Once they reached the southern end of Mont Rave, the 4th and 6th divisions attacked the French positions, which were made up of redoubts and earthworks. In an extremely hot engagement, lasting perhaps six hours, the tide of battle ebbed and flowed before the allies carried all the positions on the Heights of Calvinet and Mont Rave, with the remaining French forces retiring across the canal into the city. During this battle the brunt of the fighting was borne by the 6th division, with Pack and the Highland brigade to the fore, as is witnessed in many accounts.[14] Prior to the battle Pack reportedly addressed the brigade in the following manner:

> We are this day to attack the enemy; your business will be to take possession of these fortified heights which you see towards the front. I have only to warn you to be prepared to form close column in case of a charge of cavalry, to restrain the impetuosity of the men, and to prevent them from wasting their ammunition.[15]

Along with the Portuguese regiments of James Douglas's brigade, the Highlanders climbed the hill fighting and taking, and in some cases losing again, redoubt after redoubt. During the afternoon the 42nd and 79th captured the Colombette and Calvinet redoubts but were forced to evacuate them in French counterattacks, driven out with considerable losses. With the help of the 91st regiment, then in reserve, the redoubts were finally recovered and retained. At one stage the advance was halted to wait for Beresford's artillery to come up from where it had been left in order not to slow the advance across marshy land. When the guns arrived, Pack addressed the brigade again: 'I have just now been with General Clinton, and he has been pleased to grant my request, that in the charge which we are now to make upon the enemy's redoubts, the forty-second regiment shall have the honour of leading on the attack; the forty-second will advance.'[16]

The brigade suffered 739 casualties, some 35 per cent of the British and 16 per cent of all allied casualties at the battle.[17] Broken down further, the 42nd regiment lost 26 officers and 386 soldiers (killed and wounded), while the 79th lost 18 officers and 215 soldiers.[18] The 91st fared somewhat better, perhaps because it formed the reserve, losing 7 officers and 116 men.[19] Many of the dead were buried in the citadel of Toulouse.[20]

Marshal Soult acknowledged the role and suffering of the Highland brigade in his own post-battle report: 'les Ecossais y éprouverent une grande perte'.[21] Soult had fought a well-planned defensive action, and though the battle led to the capture of Toulouse, victory came at substantial cost. Almost inevitably figures vary, but Wellington's army lost over four thousand men killed and wounded as against some two thousand French casualties.[22]

At Toulouse the 6th division was once again commanded by Sir Henry Clinton. In his post-battle report to Beresford, the divisional commander praised both the Highland brigade and Denis Pack. Having given credit to the 2nd corps of the division (Major General John Lambert's) and the Portuguese brigade (Colonel James Douglas's), he referred to the 79th forming square when attacked by French cavalry, and the 'attacks made by the Highland Brigade upon the redoubts of the Mas des Augustins'. Four of the eight officers Clinton recommended to Wellington's 'favourable notice' for their conduct in the battle were members of the Highland brigade.[23] Not mentioned by Clinton was John Malcolm from the Orkney Islands, then a young lieutenant in the 42nd regiment. He had joined the 42nd in 1813, with his first taste of action being the siege of San Sebastian. At the battle of Toulouse he was wounded in the upper arm, splintering the bone, in the capture of one of the redoubts. Having fainted, he came to as the French were mounting their counterattack. He lay inert in the hope he would not be noticed, but was captured. He was taken into the city and there operated on and treated with great kindness by the inhabitants.[24] He became the editor of the *Edinburgh Observer* later in the 1820s and wrote both poetry and prose about the Peninsular War. His work included *Tales of Field and Flood*, published in 1829. While it is difficult to fact check these accounts, they bear the hallmarks of those who have witnessed the horrors of war, with their description of camps, marches, desertion, battlefields, death and destruction.[25]

In his own dispatch on the battle of Toulouse, Wellington referred to Pack's brigade carrying the two principal redoubts, as well as fortified houses in the enemy's centre.[26] He went on to say the French then made a desperate attempt to recover these but their onslaught was repulsed with considerable loss. In fact, the French counterattack by elements of Harispe's division was initially successful, with both the 42nd and 79th being forced to abandon the redoubts before recovering them again with the help of Lambert's brigade. Wellington singled out four regiments for mention for their performance at Toulouse, being the 36th, 42nd, 79th and 61st – significantly all part of the 6th division.[27]

Notwithstanding that they had borne the full force of the fighting at Toulouse, Wellington sent the 4th and 6th divisions under Beresford in pursuit of Soult, when the French marshal evacuated the city on the night of 11 April. Soult marched eastwards towards Carcassonne, closely shadowed by Beresford's force, resulting in a number of minor skirmishes before Soult formally agreed to a cessation of hostilities on 19 April. The battle of Toulouse had been unnecessary, for Napoleon had abdicated on 6 April. News of that demission had only reached Toulouse on 12 April, and when passed to Soult on 13 April he was disinclined to believe it. A few French towns continued to hold out until later in the month, but the war was now over. The 42nd, along with the 79th and 91st regiments, returned to Great Britain.

Pack himself led the light companies of the Highland brigade in the initial attack on Mont Rave and the Calvinet.[28] He reportedly set a fine example of undaunted bravery by sitting on his horse in the middle of the road with a placid smile upon his face during the assault.[29] Whether this act or some other was responsible, Pack was amongst the injured at Toulouse, but on this occasion he was able to remain in the field, and after the retaking of the Mas des Augustins and Colombette redoubts by the 79th regiment under Lieutenant Colonel James Dawes Douglas congratulated him in person.[30] Nonetheless the wound was serious enough that he needed time to recover. It is not known, though it seems unlikely, whether he participated in the pursuit of Soult. In mid-May he must have still been in the environs of Toulouse, though apparently he had formed the intention of returning home to recuperate.

Before the fact of and result of the battle of Toulouse was known (but in the knowledge of Napoleon's abdication which had reached London on 9 April), the British government had determined to send a substantial force of in excess of thirteen thousand to assist the campaign in North America, 'whenever circumstances may admit', and some of these soldiers were to be drawn from the Peninsular army.[31] This was to become the expeditionary force at first commanded by Major General Ross, and after his death by Sir Edward Pakenham. It was to be formed in two divisions under Sir Henry Clinton and Sir George Murray, if they were prepared to accept these appointments. Denis Pack was chosen by Horse Guards to command one of the brigades. It was not envisaged that the force would include the Highland brigade. Wellington wrote to Pack on 14 May to offer Pack this command. Pack clearly received and promptly accepted Wellington's offer to command a brigade but by the time his reply reached Wellington, the latter had appointed another officer to command the brigade in question.[32] The sequence of events is clear from Wellington's letters to Pack, even though the response has not been found. On 14 May Wellington wrote from Toulouse to Pack:

> I have been desired by the Commander in Chief and the Sec. of State to offer you the command of a brigade on the expedition about to be sent from Bordeaux, and I shall be very much obliged to you if you will let me know whether it will be agreeable to you to have it. Write to me at Gen. Colville's quarters, where I am going.[33]

Wellington then travelled to Madrid, from where he wrote to Pack on 26 May:

> I have received your letter of the 16th. After I had written to you from Toulouse, I understood that you had not recovered from your wound, and that you had gone to Bordeaux with the intention of returning to England for your recovery. Under these circumstances, as it was necessary to settle the expedition before I should quit France, I made the arrangements for the command of the brigades without you. I have only therefore to thank you on the part of the Commander in Chief and government for the readiness with which you consented to go, notwithstanding you were not quite recovered from your wound.[34]

Wellington left Toulouse for Spain on 17 April, so Pack's acceptance of the appointment presumably only just missed Wellington's departure, since Pack had responded to Wellington's letter of 14 May on the 16th. Wellington arrived in Madrid on 24 May and the correspondence must have caught up with him either on his journey, or shortly after arrival. Had Pack gone to the United States, would he have survived? Would he have been back in Europe in time to take a command at Waterloo? A further curiosity is that no thanks of parliament were voted for the battle of Toulouse, on the grounds that Great Britain was not at that time at war with the restored government of France. Had there been a vote of thanks it is highly likely Pack would have been named.

Pack largely recedes from view in the summer of 1814. He was still employed by the army and, having returned to England in early June, was appointed in September to the command of the Kent district, where he was based in Canterbury.[35] It is not known whether he revisited Ireland at this time. In 1813 he had been invested on the authority of Dom João, Prince Regent of Portugal, with the Ordem Militar da Torre e Espada (Order of the Tower and Sword), an ancient Portuguese military order revived in 1808 with a view to recognizing the services to the Portuguese crown by those not qualified by their religion to receive other Portuguese orders.[36] In January 1815 he was created Knight Commander of the Most Honourable Military Order of the Bath.[37] The ceremony was conducted by the Prince Regent on 12 April at Carlton House, where Pack was knighted, along with a number of others who had served in the Peninsula, including Major Generals William Ponsonby, Robert O'Callaghan, Lord Edward Somerset and Hussey Vivian. Pack's Peninsular Cross testified to his long and courageous service in Portugal, Spain and France. With four battles celebrated on the cross and seven clasps, he was honoured in a total of eleven battles. Only Wellington had more (thirteen), and Beresford was the only other staff officer with a similar number to Pack. In Pack's case the battles celebrated were Roliça/Vimiero (treated as a single battle honour), La Coruna, Bussaco, Ciudad Rodrigo, Salamanca, Vittoria, Pyrénées, Nivelle, Nive, Orthez and Toulouse.[38] Pack's service in the Iberian Peninsula was one of the most extensive of any officer. He had gone there with Wellington in 1808 and, apart from being absent at the recapture of Porto and the battle of Talavera in 1809, he had fought in every campaign. He had probably only missed the campaign of 1809 because the 71st was part of the British force targeting Antwerp and the Scheldt estuary, from which he, like thousands of others, returned sick. In Portugal, Spain and France he led both British and Portuguese troops with distinction. His independent Portuguese brigade performed well at Buçaco, Ciudad Rodrigo and Vitoria, as well as at a host of minor combats. One is left with the feeling that he was somewhat unfair to those troops for their precipitate retreat against a superior force at Salamanca, where they had to attempt to climb unarmed over a ledge in order to take on a well-organized and well-armed opponent. After he transferred back to the British army, his former Portuguese brigade continued to serve in such a manner as to receive the approval of Wellington and Beresford. As commander of the Highland brigade in the last ten months of the war Pack won further accolades, as did the men under him. He led from the front, as was attested on numerous occasions, and was reported to have suffered during that war eight wounds, six of them rather severe; he was frequently struck by shot, and had several horses killed or wounded under him.[39] He had proved himself a resolute soldier and talented leader of troops, a commander trusted by Wellington.

Chapter 11

The Waterloo Campaign, 1815

'A very forward & bold officer; one of those who says,
"Come, my lads, and do this", and who goes before you
to put his hand to the work.'[1]

Napoleon escaped from Elba on 26 February 1815, having spent just ten months there. Three days later he landed in France with about a thousand supporters, on what is now known as the Cote d'Azur.[2] He marched on Paris, gaining adherents at each major town, and entered the capital city on 20 March. Meanwhile, on 7 March news of his escape had reached Vienna, where the congress of that name was in session trying to establish agreed political entities and boundaries, as part of a post-war settlement. On 13 March Napoleon was declared an outlaw by the assembled heads of state and plenipotentiary ministers, including Wellington, who had replaced Castlereagh as Britain's emissary in February. The former coalition partners joined again to deploy their armed forces to move on France, with the object of ending once and for all the threat posed by Napoleon to European peace. British forces in the Low Countries were to be joined by Austrian, Prussian and Russian armies in a concerted campaign against Napoleon.

The nucleus of a British force was already in the Netherlands, placed there to ensure compliance with the Treaty of Paris. This treaty, sometimes referred to as the Peace of Paris, had restored France to her borders of 1792, together with other concessions designed to give the restored Bourbon monarchy stability and credibility. Thus, fifteen British battalions were based to the north of the French border. While the British government hastened to prepare additional troops for the Low Countries, Wellington sought to obtain from Portugal fifteen thousand Portuguese veterans of the Peninsular War, and hoped Beresford would come to lead them.[3] Notwithstanding Beresford's enthusiastic response, the Portuguese Regency maintained it could not release these men to serve outside Portugal without the consent of the crown, a stance that led to a distinct

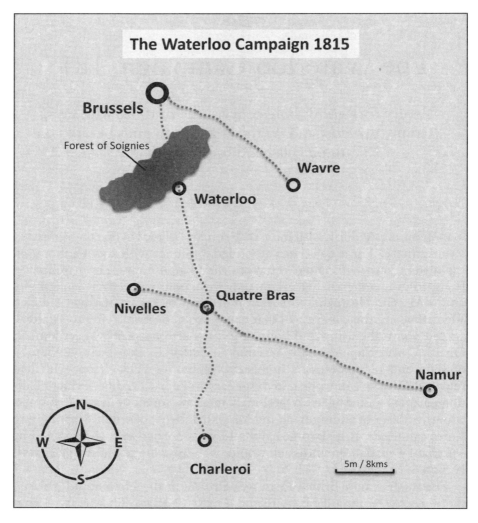

cooling of British support for Portugal, in the latter's efforts to secure reparations and the return of lands around Olivenza, lost to Spain in 1801.[4] Instead, Wellington's army was to be composed of Dutch and Belgian soldiers in addition to British and Hanoverian troops. Massive military support for Britain and Louis XVIII of France was to be supplied in the form of Austrian, Prussian and Russian armies, which would make their way westwards in late spring and early summer.

There are numerous contemporaneous and modern accounts of the campaign of 1815. This work will concentrate on the role of Lieutenant

General Sir Thomas Picton's division, and the performance of Major General Denis Pack's brigade, which served with the division.

In the summer of 1814 the Highland brigade, composed of the 42nd, 79th and 91st regiments, had sailed from Bordeaux to Ireland.[5] All three regiments were sent to the Low Countries in the spring of 1815, arriving at Ostend on various dates in May. Only the 42nd, however, was to form part of Pack's new brigade. Sir Thomas Picton was appointed to command Wellington's 5th division, made up of the 8th and 9th brigades under Major Generals Sir James Kempt and Sir Denis Pack respectively. Pack's new brigade still included two Highland regiments, the 42nd and 92nd. With these he had the third battalion of the 1st regiment (3/1) and the second battalion of the 44th regiment (2/44), the latter being one of those regiments which was already stationed in the Low Countries.[6] Notwithstanding that it was the most senior regiment in the British army, it is estimated that over 33 per cent of the third battalion of the 1st foot was made up of Irishmen at this time, and Irish numbers may well have exceeded 40 per cent, with one third being English, one fifth Scots and a scattering of foreigners.[7] The other regiments of Pack's brigade also had substantial representation by his fellow countrymen.[8]

Pack was perhaps fortunate to be given this command. There were a large number of major-generals senior to him on the army list.[9] Whether Wellington had any hand in his selection is unclear, but he was evidently delighted to have the experienced Pack as one of his brigade commanders. Henry Torrens, the military secretary to the commander-in-chief of the forces, advised Wellington on 16 April that four thousand infantry and three regiments of cavalry would be sent from Ireland to join Wellington, and that James Kempt and Pack would be among the major generals sent with them to the army.[10] The duke, by then in Brussels, responded that he would be very happy to have Kempt and Pack, and he would do his best for them.[11] Kempt had been created a major general in 1812. Senior to Pack, Kempt was given the 8th brigade and Pack the 9th brigade of the assembling force.

Throughout the spring and early summer allied forces gathered in what is now Belgium. The British garrisoned Antwerp and Ostend, while the Anglo-Dutch, Belgian, Brunswick and Hanoverian forces were stationed in an arc south of Brussels to protect that city. Wellington remained concerned at the size and quality of his army, which lacked sufficient experienced British troops, and in respect of which he did not know the extent to which he could rely on the Dutch and Belgians, some of whom had previously served Napoleon. Though the war had ended in America, many of the battle-hardened troops sent there had yet to return home. When they did so, expecting some rest, they were moved on quickly to the continent.[12] The well organized Prussians, moving expeditiously from their heartlands in northern Europe, occupied the territories east of Wellington. Thus, the Allies held the country between Tournai and Liege by early June. Pack's 9th brigade, all veteran regiments, was quartered in and adjacent to Brussels. There he inspected it on 1 June, seeming pleased with the appearance of the men.[13] Three days later the entire division was inspected by Wellington, 'who appeared highly delighted on seeing so many of his old friends again under his command'.[14]

Wellington's army now exceeded a hundred thousand men. He divided it into three corps, the 1st commanded by the young Prince of Orange, who had served with Wellington as his aide de camp in the Peninsula, the 2nd corps led by Rowland Hill, and the reserve, as so often commanded by Wellington himself.[15] Initially the 5th division, along with the 6th division, was part of that reserve based in and around Brussels.

Wellington's forward position in mid–June stretched from Genappe to Quatre Bras. When knowledge reached Wellington on 15 June that the French were moving towards his positions, orders were issued to assemble and be ready to move. It quickly became apparent that Napoleon was moving with his customary speed. That evening, news that the French were approaching Quatre Bras caused the Duchess of Richmond's ball to be interrupted by a requirement for officers to join their regiments. Pack, who was at the ball in the Richmond residence in the Rue de Blanchisserie, along with his brigade major Charles Smyth, assembled the 9th brigade and began the march south towards Quatre Bras as part of Wellington's reserve.[16] In the absence of a diary or correspondence from Pack, it is fortunate that so many men of the 9th brigade responded later to Captain William Siborne's efforts to collect information on the battles of Quatre Bras and Waterloo for the diorama he was creating of the latter battle.[17]

The brigade began to get under arms between 9 and 10pm on the evening of 15 June. It was assembled in the park, from where its departure was delayed by the late arrival of the 42nd regiment.[18] Eventually, at about 4am, the troops were marched south on the road to Waterloo, passing through the forest of Soignes outside Brussels.[19] The pipers of the Highland regiments played, and Sergeant James Anton of the 42nd referred to the high spirits that accompanied their departure from Brussels, but soberly observed: 'We passed through the ancient gate of the city, and hundreds left it in health and high spirits who before night were lifeless corpses on the field to which they were hastening.'[20] A march of some

38 kilometres brought Pack and his men to Quatre Bras about 2pm, having breakfasted at the small but otherwise then unremarkable village of Waterloo.[21]

During the afternoon of 16 June Ney attacked the allied positions at Quatre Bras, while Napoleon took on Blucher's forces at Ligny. The latter contest resulted in a Prussian retreat that night. At Quatre Bras, when Picton's division arrived, it went straight into action. Wellington ordered it to form a line on the Quatre Bras to Namur road. One of Pack's regiments, the 92nd, occupied the east end of Quatre Bras, with the other regiments spread out towards Namur.[22] To the left of the 9th brigade lay Kempt's 8th brigade. When the French broke through the Dutch, Belgian and Brunswick troops in the front line, Pack's brigade became heavily involved facing both a frontal attack and encirclement by cavalry coming from the right flank of the 92nd regiment. The 42nd and 44th, having advanced, faced Kellerman's heavy French cavalry and lancers, as well as destructive artillery fire which for a time caused considerable confusion. Reminiscent of Albuera in 1811, the British troops at first thought the cavalry behind them was their own, leading to losses before they could form square on being recognized as French. The fighting was intense, and

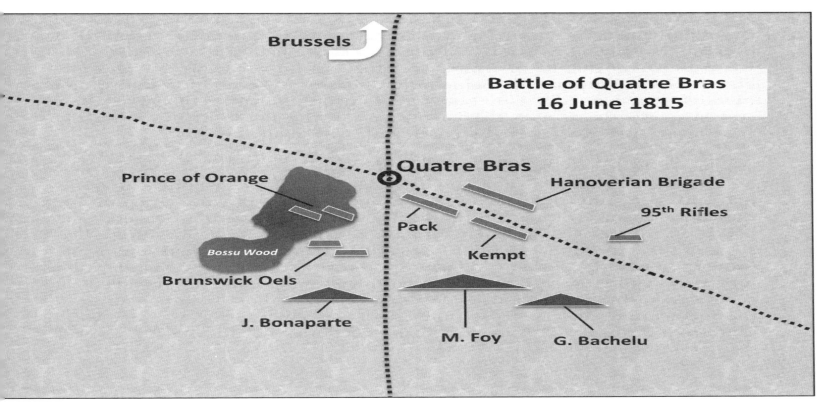

acts of individual bravery on both sides numerous. Sergeant James Anton of the 42nd testified that Pack was at their head when they were ordered to form square to oppose the cavalry.[23] At times Wellington was with Pack's regiments. Pack's troops began running dangerously short of ammunition, but the arrival of British reinforcements enabled Wellington to hold the hamlet until nightfall.[24] That night the Highlanders cooked their evening meal in the cuirasses of the Frenchmen they had killed a few hours before.[25] At Quatre Bras Pack's presence in different parts of the action was testified to by a number of correspondents.[26] Brevet Lieutenant Colonel George O'Malley of the 44th regiment, referring to the serious losses of the 42nd and 44th regiments, stated that both corps acted together as one regiment under Pack's immediate command.[27] The losses were indeed horrendous. While exact figures are difficult to tie down, one modern commentator has observed that the published statistics suggest the 42nd lost approximately 46 per cent of its rank and file, the 79th about 41 per cent, and the 92nd about 39 per cent, with the 1st regiment (third battalion) losing about 32 per cent. The nature of the onslaught Pack's brigade must have faced is fully demonstrated by the fact that these four regiments suffered the highest casualties of any engaged in the battle as a percentage of their strength.[28] James Archibald Hope, who was present at Quatre Bras with the 92nd regiment, gives an evocative description of the regimental piper trying to call together the regiment at 10pm that evening, but saying he could not produce above half of the regiment. He went on to say that of the thirty-six officers who went into action, only eleven escaped unhurt, six being killed, seventeen severely wounded and two lightly wounded.[29] Combined losses from the battles of Quatre Bras and Waterloo were such that at the end of the Battle of Waterloo the 79th regiment was reportedly commanded by a subaltern.[30]

One of those close to Pack who died on 18 June, from wounds received at Quatre Bras two days earlier, was Charles Smyth of the 95th rifles. Smyth was his brigade major, and had been to the Duchess of Richmond's ball with his commander. This gave rise to a heart-rending situation for the young Juana Dolores Smith. Born Juana de los Dolores de Léon, she had been trapped inside Badajoz in 1812, at the time of the third allied siege of that city. After the fall of Badajoz to the allies, she had sought the protection of Brigade Major Harry Smith of the 95th rifles. She married him a short time later. Thereafter, with few exceptions, she travelled on campaign with her husband. At Wellington's direction, in anticipation of the forthcoming battle, those other than soldiers and the baggage were sent from Brussels to Antwerp. Juana accompanied the fleeing crowd.

On 19 June in the afternoon the result of the battle of Waterloo became known in Antwerp. Having asked after her husband, she was told 'Major Smith' of the 95th had been killed. Grabbing her mare, Juana galloped back to Brussels and from there to the battlefield of Waterloo. Everywhere she looked she saw corpses waiting to be buried, burial mounds and wounded soldiers. Meeting with an old friend, Charlie Gore, aide de camp to Sir James Kempt, she was mightily relieved to hear that it was Charles Smyth who had had the misfortune to be killed, and not her darling 'Enrique'.[31] The confusion as to the identity of the deceased was understandable as both men served in the 95th regiment.

In his dispatch, written after the battle of Waterloo, Wellington acknowledged the contribution of Denis Pack, along with the 5th division, at Quatre Bras:

> We maintained our position, and completely defeated and repulsed all the enemy's attempts to get possession of it. The enemy repeatedly attacked us with a large body of cavalry and infantry, supported by a numerous and powerful artillery; he made several charges with the cavalry upon our infantry, but all were repulsed in the steadiest manner. In this affair, His Royal Highness the Prince of Orange, the Duke of Brunswick, and Lieut. General Sir Thomas Picton, and Major Generals Sir James Kempt and Sir Denis Pack, who were engaged from the commencement of the enemy's attack, highly distinguished themselves . . . The troops of the 5th Division and those of the Brunswick corps were long and severely engaged, and conducted themselves with the utmost gallantry. I must particularly mention the 28th, 42nd, 79th, and 92nd regiments and the battalion of Hanoverians.[32]

Pack, while obviously delighted with praise from Wellington, is reported to have taken a rather different view of the performance of the Dutch and Belgians on his front at Quatre Bras:

> A more distressingly anxious command I never had; the Dutch and Belgians were in headlong flight from the onslaught of the French. Our infantry, in particular the 79th Highlanders, did all in their power to stem the rout and charged repeatedly. The Brunswick Hussars (save the name!) were then ordered to charge to cover the retreat of the infantry, and so well did they perform their task that we had to kill a good number of them as they went to the right about and joined the French cavalry advancing on us. Had it not been for the

oft tried gallantry of our infantry, I know not how we should have fared.[33]

On 17 June Wellington began to withdraw to Mont St Jean and Waterloo, keeping his forces in contact with the retreating Prussians. The 92nd formed the rearguard of the infantry, with the cavalry covering the retreat. On 18 June Wellington drew up the army north of La Haye Sainte parallel to the route de Lion. His first line stretched from Hougmont to La Haye, and left of centre included the 1/95th, with Bylandt's Dutch-Belgian brigade further to the left. Beyond Bylandt's brigade was placed Best's Hanoverian brigade.[34] Kempt's and Pack's greatly reduced brigades, the 5th division, were placed initially in the second line with Vincke's and Best's Hanoverian brigades to their east.[35] Looking south, the 5th division was to the left of the Brussels road, with La Haye Sainte in front of them to the right of the road. The placement of the brigades of the 5th division was perhaps a recognition of the attritional fighting they had endured at Quatre Bras. The losses there had been so severe that by the end of the day Lieutenant Riddock noted that the 44th only possessed four small companies and the different regiments were reduced to mere skeletons.

Wellington's strongest divisions were on his right, west of the north–south route running from Brussels to Charleroi, where he seems to have anticipated the main French assault. The story of the battle has been well told on numerous occasions, with the heroic defence of Hougmont and La Haye Sainte noted. The battle began about 11.30 with Napoleon attacking the right of the allied line. It was about 1.30pm that D'Erlon's corps moved forward in an attempt to break through the Dutch first line and the 5th division behind it, with the objective of turning the allied left and forcing Wellington to retreat to the Channel ports. Dispensing with the traditional mode of attack utilized by French infantry in the Napoleonic wars, D'Erlon doubled the frontage of a number of battalions to give him additional firepower. Instead of bringing seventy muskets to bear with a long column, he employed 140 muskets. Beginning with an attack on La Haye Sainte, D'Erlon's men surrounded the farm and, having contained it, advanced on the first line of allied troops.

The French broke through Bylandt's brigade, part of the Netherlands 2nd division placed in the front line. This brigade had been heavily engaged at Quatre Bras and had suffered accordingly. Sir Thomas Picton had Kempt's and Pack's brigades on the reverse slope in classic Wellington style, and it was only as the French struggled to the top that Picton released his men. Fierce fighting developed. Both the 8th and 9th

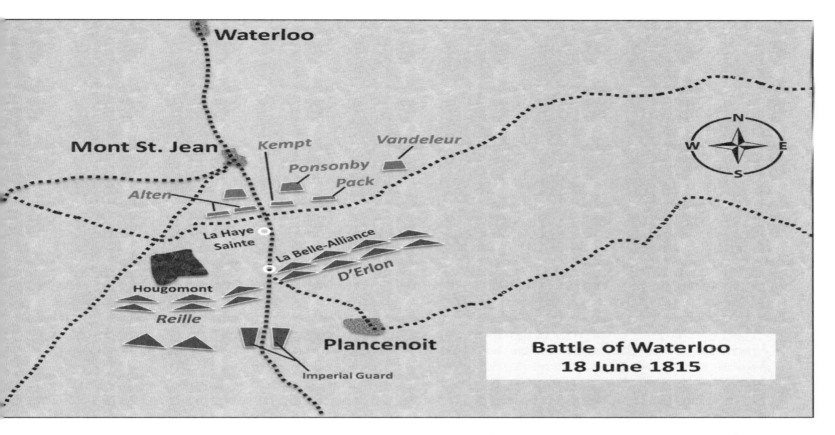

**Battle of Waterloo
18 June 1815**

brigades, heavily outnumbered and depleted, struggled to contain the French advance. The Black Watch, numbering only 330 men, was forced back. Turning to the 92nd, which retained less than three hundred men, Pack exhorted the regiment 'Ninety-second, you must charge, for all the troops on your right and left have given way.'[36] James Archibald Hope observed somewhat laconically in his *Reminiscences* 'To this not very encouraging address, the regiment responded with cheers, and then advanced to measure bayonets with their enemies.'[37] He would have us believe that it was just the 230 men of the 92nd who were involved in this advance, with the 3/1st and 2/44th having retired and the 42nd being posted on an 'important spot'. Others suggest the 3/1st, 42nd and 92nd advanced with the Union cavalry and assisted in taking a large number of prisoners, while the 2/44th was left on the hill as a reserve. Although the Union cavalry suffered heavy losses by overextending its charge, Napoleon had failed in his design to turn the left wing of the allied army. Allied control of this sector of the battlefield was only restored with the charge of the Union Brigade of cavalry under Sir William Ponsonby, though not without the loss of Picton, Ponsonby and many others who died in these exchanges. Frederick Cavendish Ponsonby, a cousin of William, himself a colonel in the 12th light dragoons employed to cover the retreat of the Union Brigade, was seriously wounded at Waterloo. Later he reported Pack to have said 'the greatest risk he run the whole day was in stopping his men, who were firing on me and my regiment, when we began to charge'.[38]

A false rumour reached Brussels that Pack had been killed and Wellington seriously wounded.[39] In fact, Pack had been wounded, although it cannot have been very serious, for he continued with his brigade.[40] One of those who lost their lives was Pack's aide de camp, Brevet Major Edmund L'Estrange, a young officer who had had the misfortune to be captured both in South America and Spain. Edmund's L'Estrange ancestors had emigrated from Norfolk to Ireland, where he had grown up in County Laois (then Queen's County). In 1804 he joined the 71st regiment, serving under Pack in the conquest of the Cape Colony (Cape of Good Hope) and the temporary capture and occupation of Buenos Aires in 1806. Made a prisoner on the surrender of Buenos Aires in August 1806, he was one of a number of officers, including Denis Pack, transported to the interior to forestall any British attempt to mount a rescue. Pack later escaped, but L'Estrange was less fortunate, only returning to Ireland at the end of 1807 on the release of all prisoners as part of the arrangement whereby all British forces would be withdrawn from the Rio de la Plata. Lieutenant L'Estrange was then captured a second time in the retreat to La Coruna in the winter of 1808/09. He was brought to Verdun in March 1809, where the fortress was utilized to house hundreds of British prisoners of war. There it was possible to live in the town, providing a prisoner gave his parole not to attempt escape. It was also possible to live a comfortable and relaxed life if one had the financial means to do so.[41] While at Verdun L'Estrange was accused by a tradesman of failing to pay a bill, which he maintained had already been discharged. Thrown into prison, he was released from his parole; he escaped and after months on the run, often in disguise as a female, he reached Rotterdam. He arranged for passage to England but was betrayed, recaptured and incarcerated in the notorious citadel of La Bitche in the Vosges mountains.[42] Here he was kept in an underground prison until, assisted by a French officer whom he had befriended, he effected his escape. Bizarrely, L'Estrange then made his way back to Verdun and then across France to Bordeaux dressed as a French soldier. This was made possible by Sir Stephen May, who organized the procurement of a forged French passport for L'Estrange. Sir Stephen may have acted as an agent to assist British prisoners in Verdun.[43] In Bordeaux L'Estrange was hidden by no lesser personages than the mayor, Jean-

Baptiste Lynch, and his wife, both of Irish descent. They procured a further passport for him and from Bordeaux L'Estrange obtained passage to Plymouth. He was interviewed by the commander-in-chief, the Duke of York, who was so impressed that he secured L'Estrange a captaincy in the 71st. L'Estrange then went back to Portugal, where he became aide de camp to his former commander, Denis Pack. He fought at Vitoria, where he was wounded, and then at Toulouse in the final battle of the war. Returning to Great Britain via Bordeaux in the summer of 1814, he was able to meet up in that city with the family who had assisted his earlier escape.[44] Sadly his leg was shattered by a cannonball at Waterloo. In spite of amputation, he died shortly afterwards.

In Picton's absence, it fell to Kempt as the senior surviving commander in the 5th division to prepare the post-battle report. He did so from his bivouac at Genappe on 19 June. Of Pack he wrote: 'Major-General Sir D. Pack displayed his usual judgment and gallantry in the command of the 9th British brigade, and I am much indebted to him for his advice and assistance after the command devolved on me.'[45] In his Waterloo dispatch Wellington noted that 'Generals Sir James Kempt and Sir Denis Pack who were engaged from the commencement of the enemy's attack, highly distinguished themselves'.[46] Denis Pack was one of many superior officers who received the thanks of both houses of parliament for their contribution to the victory.[47]

Many regiments had contributed to the success of the Waterloo campaign. The victory at Waterloo was hard won and the 5th division made a serious contribution to that triumph – an achievement which would have been unlikely without the dogged defence two days earlier at Quatre Bras. There the 5th division had suffered losses as serious as those incurred by the division at Waterloo, and it is important to realise that, but for the defence of Quatre Bras, the 'Waterloo campaign' might have been known by another name.

There was no comeback for Napoleon following the French defeat at Waterloo. Instead of trying to rally the army, he travelled to Paris, where, in the face of concerted opposition, he abdicated on 22 June in favour of his young son, Napoleon II.[48] He subsequently proceeded to Rochfort with the intention of sailing to the United States on a French frigate; frustrated in this objective by the appearance of a British fleet, he surrendered to Captain Maitland of HMS *Bellerophon*. He was taken first to England and then transported to St Helena, where he died in 1821.

Though the main French army retreated in disorder after Waterloo, the right wing under Marshal Emmanuel de Grouchy retired to France intact.

Grouchy had been charged with keeping Blucher from joining Wellington, but although he defeated the 3rd Prussian corps at Wavre, he failed to prevent the junction of the two allied forces and has been blamed by some for Napoleon's defeat at Waterloo. The 5th division, now commanded by Kempt, formed part of the allied forces that followed Grouchy's small army to Paris, where the French stood on the defensive.[49]

The efforts of the provisional French government to negotiate terms after Waterloo were rejected, and ultimately it was agreed to surrender Paris to the allies, with the French army retiring south of the river Loire.[50] The allies entered Paris on 7 July, and Louis XVIII re-entered his capital a day later. That was not the end of the matter, for the allies were now determined to ensure that once Louis XVIII was restored, there would be no repetition of the events of 1815 which had forced him into a sudden second exile. To this end the Treaty of Paris agreed in November 1815 provided for 150,000 allied troops under the overall command of the Duke of Wellington to occupy seven departments in northern France at the expense of the French government. Not surprisingly, the thirty thousand British troops provided as part of the army of occupation were stationed in the departments of Pas-de-Calais and the Nord, the two departments most adjacent to England. Wellington established his headquarters at Cambrai.[51] He was granted his request that the regiments and their commanders be mainly those with whom he had served in the Peninsula: a great comfort as he was able to have with him those he knew well and on whom he could place reliance. However, perhaps because of its suffering in the recent conflict, not all of the brigade with which Pack had served at Waterloo was to form part of the occupying forces. The fourth battalion of the Royals and the 42nd and 92nd regiments were sent home in December 1815 having marched from Montfort to Meulan and thence to Calais via Boulogne. In his brigade orders, given at Port Chartrain on 29 November 1815, Pack thanked the corps:

> Major-General, Sir Denis Pack, cannot allow these corps to pass thus from under his command, without expressing his regret at losing them. The conduct of the fourth battalion of the Royals, both in camp and quarters, has been like that of the third battalion; and that of the two regiments, 'orderly and soldier-like;' and he is confident, that from the high state of discipline the corps appears in, they would have imitated their comrades in the third battalion, had the same glorious opportunity been afforded them. The services rendered by the 92nd regiment, in the Duke of Wellington's campaigns in the

Peninsula, and his Grace's late short and triumphant one in Belgium, are so generally and so highly appreciated, as to make praise from him almost idle, nevertheless he cannot help adding his tribute of applause. And to the 42nd regiment, he really thinks he would seem ungrateful, as well as unmindful of the best feelings of a soldier, did he not, in taking leave, assure them that he will ever retain, with sentiments of admiration, the remembrance of the invincible valour displayed by the corps on so many memorable and trying occasions.[52]

Pack remained in France, where he was to play a substantial role in this army of occupation for the next three years until the troops were removed.

Chapter 12

The occupation of France, 1815–18

Denis Pack had now been on active military service for over twenty years. His duties had taken him to the Low Countries, France, Ireland, southern Africa, South America, Portugal, and Spain. In some of these he had served on multiple expeditions. Yet his correspondence after Waterloo shows no sign of weariness.

In April 1815 Pack had been made Knight Commander of the Bath (KCB). In the summer of 1815 he was the recipient of further awards. The Russian emperor, Alexander I, made Pack a member of the Order of St Wladamir in August, and a month later he was created a member of the Order of Maria Theresa at the behest of the Austrian emperor, Francis I.[1] Both Pack and Wellington's adjutant general, Sir Edward Barnes, were offered commands in the West Indies. Barnes declined because he liked his situation in France under Wellington. Pack also declined, but not before enquiring as to whether the value of the position offered would enable him to save part of his income.[2] As the son of a clergyman, without a large estate, Pack clearly did not have the independent means which would enable him to enjoy such an appointment. Having declined a West Indian command, Pack was immediately appointed to command the 4th brigade, part of the British contingent occupying northern France under the terms of the second Treaty of Paris.[3] That treaty provided not only for the payment of an indemnity by France of 50 million francs per annum, but for an occupation force of 150,000 troops. Great Britain, Austria, Prussia and Russia each contributed 30,000 men.[4] Bavaria contributed 10,000 troops, and Denmark, Hanover, Saxony and Wurtemberg each contributed a force of 5,000.[5] The occupation was to be for a minimum of three and a maximum of five years. Wellington was appointed on 22 October overall commander of arguably Europe's first multi-national peace-keeping force, and he established his headquarters at Cambrai.[6] From there he was able to supervise the building of the barrier fortresses agreed under the terms of the protocol to the Treaty of Paris, fortifications designed to protect the new kingdom of the United Netherlands.[7]

The British part of the occupation army was composed of three brigades of cavalry under Lord Combermere, and nine brigades of infantry, the entire under the command of Lord Hill. Wellington successfully lobbied for the inclusion in the occupation force of battle-hardened infantry who had served with him in the Peninsula. The 4th brigade under Denis Pack was made up of the 1/4th, 52nd and 79th regiments, all regiments that had fought in Portugal, Spain and southwest France.[8] From Paris they marched to their quarters at Cambrai as part of the 2nd division under Sir Henry Clinton. Before they left Paris, the 1/4th and the 79th regiments were inspected on 23 December by Sir Henry, who was complimentary about neither regiment. He criticized the officers of the 1/4th for their harshness to the men and their insubordination to each other, observing 'it will require some work of a capable commander of brigade to make this regiment what it is susceptible of becoming'. He wasn't much more complimentary about the 79th, noting that they were an uneven and different body of men. He acknowledged they were steady and well placed when under arms, but slovenly in appearance, though he found the highland dress becoming. Clinton observed that their commander, Lieutenant Colonel Neil Douglas, had too good an opinion of himself, lacking at that time what was required to become a useful battalion commander.[9]

The division's new headquarters were at St Pol. The other brigades in Clinton's division were commanded by Sir Thomas Bradford (6th) and Sir Robert O'Callaghan (3rd). Both Bradford and O'Callaghan had served alongside Pack in the Peninsula. The division was kept fresh by the conduct of repeated military exercises, mostly between Cambrai and Valenciennes. Clinton inspected Pack's brigade again on 13 February 1816 at their cantonments, but was no more impressed than on the occasion of his earlier inspection in December 1815.[10] An examination of his reports on the other brigades in the division would seem to suggest that the 4th brigade was neither better nor worse than any others. Further, Clinton had form, having shown himself a stickler for proper presentation on inspections he had made in the Low Countries during the build-up to the Waterloo campaign. Another inspection of Pack's brigade took place in April, when at least the 52nd regiment received a glowing report. Pack was not present for the inspections in February or April for he had travelled to England.[11] Wellington sought to have a strict discipline enforced and issued periodic orders in respect of cantonments, rations, desertion, pilfering, proper dress and a bar on marriage without the permission in writing of the field marshal himself. Battalion commanders were required to submit daily reports to brigade commanders.[12] Pack played his part in enforcing these orders, regularly attending reviews and exercises, and sitting on courts martial.[13] The military reviews were sometimes on a massive scale, designed no doubt to shock and awe the French establishment and those who might hearken after their former emperor. That at Denain (near Valenciennes) in October 1816 was held in fine weather, which was probably as well, as it was attended by fifty-four thousand men of whom twelve thousand were cavalry, and an immense train of artillery.[14] Pack was not always impressed with what he saw at these reviews. He bemoaned the lack of experienced officers and criticized those available for their lack of commitment to training. He did not hesitate to chastise senior officers if he felt they lacked commitment to training, notwithstanding their performance in battle.[15]

Those regiments not forming part of the army of occupation were returned home, in accordance with a general order issued by Wellington at the end of November 1815. Pack's duties appear to have involved more than the command of his own brigade, for in early 1816 he was involved in organizing the transport home of those regiments no longer required in France. January and February saw him in Calais, where on 8 January he advised Wellington there were forty-six vessels either full or ready to receive 3,736 men and 377 horses, leaving a further 5,500 men and 2,400 horses awaiting later embarkation. The departure of the convoy was delayed by weather.[16] On 1 February Pack was able to advise Wellington that the ongoing embarkation of troops was going so well that they were all likely to be embarked by the following day.

Life as an army officer in France was not all hardship. Apart from the reviews, which sometimes involved make-believe battles including replicas of the battle of Waterloo, there were numerous social events. Horse-racing took place at Valenciennes and St Omer in 1816 and 1817, and 'those who were fond of field sports indulged in them to their hearts' content'.[17] Indeed, Valenciennes became a social as well as a military milieu with one correspondent commenting: 'Some of the officers were walking with elegantly-dressed women, some were playing cricket , some were trotting their pretty ponies, and others exercising their dogs.'[18] There were concerts given by military bands and regular theatre performances. Several packs of hounds were brought out from England and, as one rifleman observed, 'the greater part of the army would willingly have protracted their stay a dozen years longer in those quarters'.[19]

The existence of an army of occupation in France, while irksome to some, bolstered the government of Louis XVIII. In particular, it enabled the allies to support the liberals against the extreme proposals of the ultras, the latter being those who opposed political reform and instead sought to maintain the absolutism of the ancient regime, with a traditional monarchy and hierarchy between classes. In early 1817 it was agreed between the occupation powers and France that the occupation force be reduced by 20 per cent. This enabled further British forces to be sent home, which Wellington effected by discontinuing the 3rd division and reallocating personnel.[20] This reorganization did not alter the composition or the command by Pack of the 4th brigade.[21]

In February 1816 Pack had sought and obtained leave to go to England.[22] It would seem that it was there, and probably in London, that he became engaged before mid-April to Lady Elizabeth Beresford, the sister of the 2nd Marquis of Waterford and of course also the half-sister of his good friend, Marshal William Carr Beresford. Born at Curraghmore, County Waterford in 1783, Elizabeth was the marshal's youngest sister. No evidence of how or when Denis and Elizabeth met has been found, but the marquis kept a house in London where members of his family spent part of the year. Elizabeth's mother, also Elizabeth (née Monck), had died in London in January 1816, but Pack did not attend her funeral back in Waterford as he was in France.[23] Pack was clearly not known to the marquis, who wrote on 14 April to Elizabeth to congratulate her, indicating he looked forward to making Pack's acquaintance.[24] However, Denis Pack was known to another senior member of the family, William Beresford, then Archbishop of Tuam. In early July William wrote 'I know Pack well and regard him much.'[25] The fact that Pack's father had been Dean of Ossory from 1784 to 1795 would have created plenty of opportunities for him and William to get to know each other as fellow clergymen. During most of the time Thomas Pack was Dean of Ossory, William Beresford was the Bishop of Ossory.[26]

Within weeks of his engagement, Pack was back in northern France undertaking his duties. The engaged couple were good correspondents, a feature that was to continue in their married life whenever they were apart.[27] He returned to Calais on 25 April, and proceeded south to Estruval, where his divisional commander, Sir Henry Clinton, was based. No sooner had Pack arrived there than Clinton sought leave of absence. Clinton left Estruval with his wife Susan on 11 May, but on their way to the ferry at Calais she suffered a strange accident from which she was lucky to emerge unscathed. The horses pulling the carriage bolted and went over the quayside. Fortunately, the carriage landed on one of the vessels in the harbour and Lady Susan was recovered unhurt.[28]

In late 1815 Pack had moved into a portion of a chateau at Roquetoire, some 60 kilometres from Estruval. He was back there by 8 May 1816. He wrote on several occasions to describe his quarters to Elizabeth. He thought she would like them. The château was owned by the De Rante family, whom he clearly came to like, although he described them initially as rich but stingy. The De Rante's main residence was in Aire sur la Lys, a small town 6 kilometres from Roquetoire. Pack's 'apartments' included a dining room, a saloon, two bedrooms and servants' quarters. In addition he had use of the *grand salon*. He had access to the gardens, which were well kept by Mrs De Rante, who he observed was a keen gardener.[29] Pack's Parisian chef, whom he described as excellent, was obviously somewhat overbearing, for Pack decided to part with him, whereupon peace and good order was restored to his household.[30]

With both other brigade commanders absent, Bradford in London and O'Callaghan also going on leave, Pack found himself the only general officer in the division and in command of it.[31] As such, for a short time it fell to Pack to organize exercises and the half yearly inspections. Perhaps luckily for him, Bradford and O'Callaghan returned before long, for Pack needed to obtain permission from Wellington to return to England for his impending marriage. Wellington notified Pack that he could make the trip when he pleased.[32]

In mid-June Pack reviewed the 79th regiment. Two days later he was invited to a 'very grand ball' in honour of the Duchess of Berri's nuptials, but he preferred to go out riding with General O'Callaghan. It was only towards the end of the month that he was able to get away and return to England. There, he and Elizabeth were married on 11 July in Marylebone church, London, by her brother Lord John Beresford, then Bishop of Raphoe.[33] Sir Denis and Lady Pack travelled in August to France, residing at Roquetoire. Marshal Beresford, writing in November from Portugal, to which he had then returned from Brazil, where he had gone to consult with Dom João who had recently succeeded his mother as ruler of the Portuguese empire, congratulated both of them, regretted that he had been unable to attend the wedding but indicated he hoped to visit them the following spring.[34] The visit did not take place, for unrest in Portugal meant Beresford could not leave that country. In any event, while it is not clear when the Packs left France, on 5 May 1817 Elizabeth gave birth in England to Arthur, the first of four children.[35]

Before leaving France for England in the spring of 1817 an event of some considerable importance to Denis Pack took place. Pack had commanded the 71st regiment of foot from 1800 to 1810. In doing so, he had served with the regiment in southern Africa, South America and Europe. With the 71st he had shared success, failure and even imprisonment. He had an extremely good relationship with the officers and men of the regiment, as is evidenced by the suggestion that he might rejoin it in Portugal in 1810, shortly after he had entered the Portuguese service. One of those who had served with Pack in the Peninsula, and at Waterloo, was Sir Thomas Reynell. In 1817 Reynell was lieutenant colonel of the 71st regiment. He was from a military family: his father had fought in the American War of Independence and was killed at Saratoga in 1777. Thomas joined the army in 1793. In the Peninsula the 71st under Lieutenant Colonels Cadogan and Reynell was cited by Wellington for its gallant conduct in repelling an attack on the Lines in October 1810.[36] When Cadogan was mortally injured at Vitoria in 1813, Reynell assumed command of the regiment, which subsequently fought at the battles in southwest France in late 1813 and early 1814. After fighting at Waterloo, where Reynell was injured, it formed part of the 6th brigade of the army of occupation of France from 1815 to 1818. The 6th brigade was commanded by Thomas Bradford and, along with Pack's 4th brigade, formed part of the 2nd division. It was based in Norrent-Fontes, not far from Pack in Roquetoire. Later, Reynell was to play an important role in the Pack family, but in December 1816 he wrote to Denis Pack requesting him to present the regiment's new colours, pursuant to the wishes of the entire corps, 'as our General of Division, but still more as our old and revered commanding officer'. Reynell even suggested that Lady Elizabeth might perform the ceremony, though he appreciated this was asking rather a lot in mid-winter.[37] In the event Pack made the presentation of the new colours in mid-January 1817, giving a stirring address in which he praised the regiment, applauding its esprit de corps. He noted that the regiment had mislaid its colours 'after a fete given in London to celebrate the Duke of Wellington's return, after his glorious termination of the Peninsular War' and he was therefore presenting the new colours supplied by the regimental colonel, General Francis Douglas.[38]

In September 1816, and the ensuing months, Pack sat as President of the court martial of Lieutenant Frederick Wood of the 11th dragoons, held at Blendecques (near St Omer). Wood's court martial was a strung-out affair, the charges relating to events which had occurred on 1 August 1816. The court had had to be adjourned on a number of occasions owing to various officers being absent because of divisional orders.[39] Wellington was later to direct that members could not go on leave of absence until the proceedings of the court were confirmed, but divisional business was another matter entirely.[40] Wood had been charged with disobeying orders and with unofficerlike and disorderly conduct, including an allegation of cowardice and a threat to blow out the brains of his commanding officer, Lieutenant Colonel Sleigh. He was sentenced to be cashiered, and the case was referred to the Duke of York as commander-in-chief for directions. These were received in February 1817. The decision was amended to provide that on the basis of the circumstances prevailing, and Wood's previous good conduct, he be placed on half pay.[41] The good conduct referred to may well have been at the Battle of Waterloo, where Wood had been severely injured. Wood's earlier career with the 11th light dragoons in the Peninsula had also involved some controversy, when he and his patrol of ten men were captured by the French in August 1811 while in a cherry orchard. Allegedly they were not security conscious and the regiment thereafter was known as 'the Cherry Pickers'. The price paid by Wood on that occasion was to have been kept a prisoner of war in Verdun until 1814.

Sir Denis returned to France after the birth of Arthur. He continued to reside at Roquetoire for the rest of the year and well into 1818. In 1817 a correspondent reporting in the *Evening Mail* stated that the 2nd division under Major General Pack were encamped in a very pleasant situation and appeared to be remarkably healthy.[42] On 7 July 1818 Elizabeth gave birth in England to a second son, Denis William, who in due course was to serve as a Royal Artillery officer. While in England, Pack solicited Wellington's help in attempting unsuccessfully to obtain the appointment as Governor of Mauritius. The duke supported him, but only to the extent that he did so while indicating he had already advised Lord Bathurst of the wish of Sir Alexander Campbell to obtain the post. Wellington's letter to Bathurst discloses his high opinion of Pack: 'no officer in the Service has been more zealous or more distinguished than himself upon all occasions'.[43] Whether Pack was motivated to apply by potential monetary gain, the likelihood that the occupation of France might soon end, or other circumstances is unclear. The application is interesting in the light of his having previously turned down a post in the West Indies. Perhaps marriage to Elizabeth had alleviated concerns of a financial nature. Those seeking the Mauritius appointment appear to have done so on foot of a rumour that the incumbent, Robert Farquhar, was about to resign, but in the event he chose not do so and therefore there was no place available.

Rumours that the allied occupation of northern France might be terminated abounded in the summer of 1818. In reality no party wished to prolong it, and once the question of reparations to be paid by France had been settled in April, the way was opened for the withdrawal of the forces. This was speedily agreed at the Congress of Aix-la-Chapelle in early October, and Wellington was to write to Bathurst on 5 October to suggest he lost no time in arranging to ship back to England soldiers, stores and horses.[44]

Notwithstanding the uncertainty governing the continuation of the allied occupation of France during the summer of 1818, Pack planned to return to Roquetoire with his wife before the middle of August.[45] In the event it was September before Sir Denis went back to France, alone, his wife and children moving into accommodation at Sandgate in Kent. In France the 2nd division was encamped near Valenciennes, where Lady Colville gave a ball in early October attended by Wellington and some of his young staff from Cambrai. Pack conversed during the evening with Wellington, and recounted to Elizabeth how the duke sent his respects to her and to their two young 'Pack-horses'. Pack thought this 'a rare turn of fun on his part', but it serves to illustrate the good relationship between the two military men.[46]

Pack was in little doubt now that the army was going home, but before it did so he advised Elizabeth there might be a review, although Wellington would not hold one unless the Emperors of Russia and Austria desired it.[47] Pack invited his brother in law, the Bishop of Raphoe, to attend the review, noting that Marshal Beresford and Admiral Sir John Poo Beresford would do so.[48] In addition Pack had invited his old friend James Butler, Lord Ormonde, to attend the review. Ultimately Butler did not attend. His failure to do so upset Pack, who had corresponded with Butler during the Napoleonic wars. He viewed this invitation as a means of paying his old friend back for 'his unceasing hospitality to me through life'.[49]

The Russian troops were reviewed on 22 October, with the review of the British troops at Valenciennes taking place before the Emperor of Russia and the King of Prussia on 23 October.[50] These reviews were followed by a further review of the Austrian and Prussian troops some days later. These showcases were accompanied by a series of dinners, plays and balls, the highlight of which would have been the grand fête thrown by the Duke of Wellington at his Cambrai headquarters. While all this was going on, Pack was preparing the route for the march of the 4th and 5th brigades to Calais, from where they would embark for England. The day following the review at Valenciennes Pack's 4th brigade marched for Calais. Pack followed the regiment via Douai and Lens, but before doing so returned to Roquetoire. At the château on 26 October Pack arranged for the disposal of many items acquired during his sojourn there, from furniture to pigs. He managed to sell the pianoforte to Mrs De Rante for 40 Napoleons, and he also sold her carpets and lumber.[51]

Before leaving France, Pack wrote to Wellington from Calais a letter of thanks and appreciation for serving under him, a letter that shows real appreciation for a good relationship:

> Although I could not venture to trespass on your Grace's time in order to take leave at Valenciennes, still I cannot resist my inclination to write these few farewell lines before I embark for England, and am removed from your Grace's command.
>
> I believe there is scarcely an individual in the army who has had the honour of serving under your Grace with more good fortune than myself, for, with the exception of the Talavera campaign, when I was at Walcheren, I do not recollect to have lost, by sickness or accident, any one service in the field from the first landing of our army in Portugal to the present moment.
>
> When I call to mind the confidence and delight with which I have always met your Grace, and reflect that in this long and eventful period I have never seen you discomposed, or heard a harsh expression from you to anyone under your command, I am beyond all bounds impressed with feelings of admiration for your Grace's character, and with deep regret for the separation that has just taken place. I beg that your Grace will accept my best acknowledgements for the kind attentions that I have ever experienced from you, and the best wishes of my heart that you may enjoy many years of honour and happiness.[52]

Major General Sir Manley Power was now directed to Calais to oversee this final evacuation of British troops.[53] On 1 November Wellington issued the order to move the military chest to Calais.[54] By the end of November the British army of occupation had left France.

Pack's departure from France brought to an end his foreign service. Henceforth he was to be based in the British Isles.

Chapter 13

A peacetime appointment and a social life ends all too soon, 1819–23

On 12 August 1819 Denis Pack was appointed Lieutenant Governor of Plymouth and general officer commanding the Western District, in succession to Major General Gore Browne.[1] He took up his post with immediate effect, moving himself and his family to Plymouth before the end of the month. Temporarily leaving Elizabeth and the children at Weymouth, Pack travelled in advance via Dorchester and Exeter, arriving at Plymouth on the morning of 22 August. Within hours, he was called on by Edward Pellew, 1st Viscount Exmouth, the renowned naval officer of the French revolutionary and Napoleonic wars, who himself was commander-in-chief of the navy at Plymouth at this time.[2] In turn, Pack called on numerous members of the nobility and gentry over the next few weeks, including Lord Edgcumbe and Lady Hardy. The latter was about to move abroad in the absence of Sir Thomas, and offered Pack her Irish maid who coincidentally came from Kilkenny, Pack's own birthplace, though he apparently declined the offer.[3] Instead, Pack told his wife he was looking for a good cook and housekeeper.[4]

The Packs initially moved into the lieutenant governor's house in the Plymouth citadel. On 13 April 1820 Elizabeth gave birth to their third child, Anne Elizabeth ,and in December 1821 to another daughter, Elizabeth Catherine.[5] In 1820 the family moved from the lieutenant governor's house to that of the governor by permission of the Duke of Wellington, who was appointed Governor of Plymouth in late 1819.[6] The lieutenant governor's house was redecorated following the departure of the previous incumbent. This meant that Pack was able to lease that house to his brigade major for £50 per annum. By all accounts, the lieutenant governor's house was not a very comfortable establishment. The next lieutenant governor after Pack referred to it in the following terms: 'the citadel is a barrack and unsuitable for a general officer'.[7] In addition to permitting him the use of the governor's house, the duke allowed Pack to collect various rents and port dues to which the governor was entitled, amounting to £300 per annum.[8] In October 1819 the duke visited Plymouth as part of a tour of the west of England, arriving at the Royal Hotel in Plymouth about 10.30pm on 2 October. The following day, escorted by a guard from the 55th regiment, Wellington attended on Pack in the citadel and in the latter's company inspected the defences. That evening the two officers dined together before attending a ball given in the duke's honour.[9] Wellington's appointment as governor led to considerable correspondence between Pack and the duke on military matters, including the maintenance of the extensive fortress, a breach in the harbour basin and ordnance.[10] In 1820 they corresponded on parliamentary elections held in Devon and Cornwall.[11] Pack remained on good terms with the duke and the correspondence reveals their meeting from time to time in London, where they sometimes dined.[12] When in London, Pack frequently stayed at a Beresford family house, 29 Upper Harley Street, and socialized with many of his wife's relatives, including Louisa Hope, Archbishop Lord John George Beresford, Lord George Thomas Beresford and Admiral Sir John Poo Beresford.[13] Pack certainly had one aide de camp and may have had more. In 1819 he was joined by Anthony Pierce Pack, a young relative, the grandson of Denis's uncle Richard. Anthony had joined Denis Pack's old regiment, the 71st Highland Light Infantry, in 1813, serving with that regiment in the Peninsular War. He fought at Vitoria in June, and in the battle of the Pyrénées at the end of July 1813. In the latter battle he was wounded, as of course was Denis himself. His Peninsular War medal had no further clasps, so his injuries suffered in the Pyrénées or another cause would seem to have prevented involvement in the major battles in southwest France. The 71st regiment formed part of the third brigade at Waterloo, but Anthony Pack is not listed as an officer serving there on the Waterloo Roll Call.[14] In March 1820 he transferred as a lieutenant to the 55th, and in December 1821 to the 84th regiment, all the while remaining the general's aide de camp.[15]

Pack's life in Plymouth involved an extensive round of military and social appointments. In late April 1820 and again in April 1821 he reviewed the troops of the Plymouth garrison to mark the king's official birthday.[16] Further reviews were held on other occasions.[17] A serious soldier, Pack was reported as expressing his disapprobation when an officer, for a wager, dressed as a woman and 'vagabondised' Plymouth for a fortnight in 1821.[18]

The year 1820 was a momentous one in Great Britain. George IV finally succeeded his father as king on 29 January, having served as Regent since 1811. Engaged in a bitter struggle with his wife, Caroline of Brunswick, the coronation set for 1 August was postponed to 1821. In May 1820 Pack was in London to attend a levée with George IV. Perhaps because of the birth of Anne Elizabeth less than four weeks before, Pack was not accompanied to London by his wife. He went to the levée with one of his wife's relatives, probably Admiral Sir John Poo Beresford. The levée required a new outfit with decorations placed carefully on the coat. Pack thought the king looked well and was charmed by the reception he received from him, but the crush was tremendous. Pack remarked humorously to his wife that thankfully he had emerged 'without loss of leg or arm, or anything whatsoever'.[19] While in London, Pack participated in the social whirl, including a party at the Hopes and dinner with General Sir Henry Fane, a colleague with whom he had served at length during the Peninsular War. Another evening saw him visiting with Lord and Lady Liverpool.[20] Liverpool was then the prime minister, so this was no doubt a most welcome invitation. Pack met Wellington on a number of occasions and had dinner with the duke on Thursday, 11 May. During this visit Pack was witness to the frenzied gossip concerning King George IV and his wife, the attempted dissolution of their marriage which had to be abandoned by the king, and the king's affair with Lady Conyngham, leading to a threat by her own father to disinherit her.[21] At the end of May Pack returned to Plymouth. He was taken seriously ill that autumn, but before the end of the year he was able to resume his duties.[22] The illness served to show his popularity amongst his peers, with Lord Exmouth assuring him from London that Wellington, Lords Combermere, Hill and Howard, as well as hundreds of others asked after him on a daily basis.[23]

His correspondence when away from Plymouth reveals Pack the family man, clearly missing both his wife and children. On one occasion in 1820 he received a letter from the three-year-old Arthur.[24] He and Elizabeth were regular correspondents, and she kept him informed of the doings of other members of her extended family. Marshal Beresford observed to Elizabeth (he always addressed her as 'Bess' in correspondence) on one occasion in rather old-fashioned language, 'I am glad my friend Pack is as I always prognosticated he would be so kind a master (that word you will say probably is as it should be not as it is) to you, he leaves madame to her own figaries as to the journey to town'.[25] Elizabeth was clearly close to her half-brother, the marshal, letting him know in late 1819 that there was a 'fair lady' in her neighbourhood, with whom he might be united. The marshal thanked her politely for the suggestion but observed on 1 January 1820 'it is too late for me to think of such things'.[26]

The coronation was rescheduled for 19 July 1821. Pack travelled to London for the event without Elizabeth, who remained in Plymouth now carrying their fourth child. He travelled from Plymouth to Portsmouth under sail before continuing the journey to the capital by coach. At Portsmouth he inspected the king's yacht, *Royal George*, which was shortly to be used for the royal visit to Ireland. While in Portsmouth Pack had a conversation with Captain William Crokat, who had brought the news of 'poor Bonaparte's death' to England just a few days earlier. While Crokat had seen Bonaparte's body after it was opened up, Pack does not relate the conclusions that were formed from this event.[27]

On this occasion Pack stayed initially at his London club, Arthur's.[28] Later he moved into George Beresford's London home in Harley Street, where a fellow guest was Marshal Beresford. Pack became immersed in a series of meetings and social events.[29] The coronation was to be an occasion of considerable expense, funded by a government grant and a portion of the war reparations paid by France under the terms of the Treaty of Paris.[30] Nevertheless, there were to be restrictions on the numbers attending, which caused much social anguish. Pack faced no such dilemma for while it was reported that KCBs were to receive two tickets each for the Abbey and the Hall, Lord George Beresford as a privy councillor and comptroller was reported to have at least fifteen tickets to give away.[31] In the event, Pack thought the coronation passed off 'as well as the best friend of the King could desire', notwithstanding the refusal of entry to Westminster of Queen Caroline. He remarked on the king favouring members of the opposition over the government. He wished Elizabeth could have been there, though it was 'a great undertaking for ladies'. The many guests included Elizabeth's cousin, Mrs Thomas Hope, 'by far the richest dressed person I saw, except Prince Esterhazy'.[32]

The only disappointment for Pack was that he did not make the cut in the round of military appointments made at that time. Hoping to be made up to lieutenant general, he observed to Elizabeth that they would have to wait for the next 'brevet' as the present one merely took in all the major generals of 1812.[33] Pack of course had only been promoted a major general in the summer of 1813.

King George IV embarked on a visit to Ireland soon after his coronation. His chosen method of conveyance was HMY *The Royal George*, a three-masted schooner launched in 1817, which the king joined at Portsmouth after a levée attended by Pack on 25 July. Pack rushed back to

Plymouth by land, so as to be there should the king call in on his way to Ireland, though he told Elizabeth that only a contrary wind would take George IV into Plymouth.[34] Pack was clearly puzzled that the king had not requested the presence of Wellington or Lord George Beresford in Ireland, given their knowledge of the island, remarking that the selection of aides de camp for the visit appeared curious.[35] Pack travelled via Southampton and Exeter, arriving back in Plymouth on Monday, 30 July, just in time to welcome the king when the royal yacht put in on 1 August. George IV did not spend long there but proceeded to Holyhead, from where he intended to cross to Ireland. In the event adverse weather caused the king to transfer from the royal yacht to the steam packet *Lightning*, which carried him from Holyhead to Howth, where he landed in Ireland on 12 August.[36] Three weeks later the king returned on the royal yacht from Dun Laoghaire, renamed Kingstown in his honour.[37] In Ireland a public subscription was taken up to erect a memorial to commemorate the royal visit, to which Pack subscribed the sum of £5 13*s* 9*d*, a generous sum but by no means the most substantial amount contributed.[38]

A paucity of information surrounds Pack's movements during the remainder of 1821. On 8 December 1821 a second daughter was born to the couple, Elizabeth Catherine.[39] In May 1822 Marshal Beresford visited the Packs in Plymouth, and at the end of the month Sir Denis and the marshal travelled to London together.[40] There, along with a number of other former Peninsula officers, they attended a levée held by the Duke of York at Horse Guards on 28 May.[41] Pack spent several weeks in June 1822 at Leamington Spa, taking the waters with Marshal Beresford. They stayed at the Bedford Hotel, a fine four-storey, eight-bay Georgian building, though Pack remarked that he believed the recently opened Regent Hotel was preferable.[42] Pack does not seem to have appreciated the restorative process of attending the spa, writing of taking 'large potations' of disagreeable water.[43] Indeed, he advised his wife that he had begun drinking the waters on 7 June, 'and I do not mean to give them one day longer than is absolutely required'.[44] However, he noted that the waters seemed to be having a good effect on the marshal, reporting that his brother-in-law felt 'better in health and spirits than he has done for two or three years past'.[45] The treatment was combined with long walks with his brother-in-law, of which Pack approved. Otherwise the pair rode out to see Coventry, and Warwick castle, as well as to visit others in the locality. Pack remarked that the weather was hot and his wife found this to be the case at Plymouth as well, reflecting the fact that temperatures were above average that summer.[46] While at Leamington Pack lost a tooth, which caused a great gap in his mouth, but which he happily noted did not impair his speech. He gently chided his wife for failing to mention their daughter Anne in correspondence.[47]

A topic of correspondence for Pack with his wife was her forthcoming dinner party to celebrate the outcome of the battle of Waterloo, a celebration that was mirrored elsewhere throughout the British Isles.[48] From 1822 onwards Wellington hosted his own annual banquet each year until his death in 1852, inviting those who had served with him at the battle to dinner in Apsley House. Pack did not attend the 1822 dinner for he was at Leamington.[49] Rather more prosaically, Pack wondered who would attend his wife's dinner, given that the Royals (1st dragoons) who had served at Waterloo would have left Plymouth before 18 June.

There were other matters which preoccupied Pack while at the spa town. Surprising but welcome news of a knighthood for his brother-in-law John William Brydges, and the advancement of another brother-in-law Archbishop John George Beresford to the Primacy of Armagh, was offset by his own at this stage unsuccessful wish to secure a colonelcy of a regiment.[50] Pack had previously been colonel of the York Chasseurs, a regiment disbanded in 1819. Advised by Wellington to bide his time rather than apply for a regiment on the basis that his merit spoke for itself, Pack was rewarded in September with the colonelcy of the 84th regiment of foot.[51]

When he left Leamington, Pack went with Marshal Beresford to Malvern, another spa town which the marshal felt resembled Sintra, where he had spent time while in Portugal. In Worcester, en route, they looked at the china being produced there, and in July, having returned to London, the marshal purchased a dessert service for Elizabeth.[52] Meanwhile, Pack had returned to Plymouth at the end of June. In August he reviewed Lord Rolle's cavalry in Exeter.[53] In September he was looking for details of the circumstances whereby Plymouth Hoe had been ceded to the corporation.[54]

That November the Packs went to Ireland. In his absence the command of the Plymouth garrison devolved on Colonel Vinicombe. During the winter of 1822/23 the Packs visited Elizabeth's brother, the Primate, in Armagh. They also spent time in Waterford and Dublin, before returning to Plymouth in February 1823.[55]

In July 1823 Sir Denis and Lady Elizabeth travelled to London. It appears that initially Elizabeth had not intended to travel there, but she was persuaded to do so by Marshal Beresford, who had written to tell her '*la maison est a votre disposition*'.[56] It was while visiting Marshal Beresford at home in Wimpole Street on 23 July that Pack collapsed and died, having suffered a ruptured blood vessel.[57] Beresford had been on the verge of returning to Portugal, with a view to assisting the beleaguered King João VI, but postponed his departure.[58] Wellington wrote a personal note of condolence to Lady Pack, saying 'it will give me great satisfaction for your sake and that of my poor friend to contribute in any manner to your comfort. I shall always be happy to manifest my respect and affection for his memory by my regard for those whom he has left behind him.' Lady Elizabeth was most appreciative.[59] When the news of Pack's death reached Plymouth, flags both on shore and on the vessels in the harbour were lowered to half-mast. His remains were conveyed by sea to Dublin and just over two weeks later, on Saturday, 9 August, Major General Denis Pack KCB was laid to rest in the family vault in the north transept of Kilkenny Cathedral.[60] The cortège was accompanied from Dublin by Lord Combermere and Major General Sir Colquhoun Grant. Combermere had served (as Stapleton Cotton) with Pack in the Peninsula and at Waterloo as a cavalry commander. Grant had also served in the same theatres of war and in 1823 was serving on the army staff in Ireland. The cortège must have travelled overnight from Dublin for at 7am it was reported to have reached Carlow, accompanied by two coaches and a further four carrying family and friends. Shortly after 8am the convoy left for Kilkenny. Outside Kilkenny the procession was met by the mayor and members of the corporation and the military garrison, watched by many of the inhabitants.[61]

Elizabeth was left with four children, all under the age of six. In the autumn of 1823 the family vacated their lodgings in Plymouth and moved to Marshal Beresford's London house.[62] The Packs were not wealthy, but were certainly not without means. Elizabeth had property of her own in Ireland that had been settled on her at the time of marriage. There were death duties to be paid on Pack's own property, which the marshal administered as his friend's executor. The marshal, in addition, drafted a petition for Elizabeth to send to the king seeking a pension.[63] Elizabeth also elicited the help of both Wellington and the Primate of All Ireland to secure a pension from the government of Lord Liverpool. Matters moved quickly and on 20 September the marshal was able to tell her that he had been to Windsor to attend a council meeting and to take leave of the king (before going to Portugal), and that the king had told the marshal he had given Elizabeth's memorial to Lord Liverpool 'with the desire that your little ones should be pensioned'. The marshal went on to confirm he had himself spoken to Liverpool, who had said he would attend to the matter at an early opportunity. In early 1825 a pension of just over £400 per annum was awarded by the government.[64] The marshal advised her to direct that the annuity be paid to the four children in equal shares, with provision that if any of them should die, the others would benefit proportionally. This was done and each of the four children was awarded an annual sum of £100 13*s* 5*d*.[65] Trustees were named to administer the children's pension fund during their minority, being Lady Pack, the Archbishop of Armagh (her brother) and the marshal.[66]

While Elizabeth was not entirely satisfied with the sum awarded, Wellington and Beresford felt this to be the best that could be achieved. Indeed, the marshal was critical of Elizabeth's letters to both Liverpool and the Duke of York on the subject, explaining to her that these were very different times from those pertaining during the late war when pensions were lavished for all sorts of wounds. Instead he pointed out

> our dear friend was neither killed in battle or died during the campaigns, and the very giving of this pension under the circumstances is a great tribute to his merit and services, for those alone at the time it is done, could have procured any consideration whatsoever. How many General Officers die now and their widows have only the ordinary pension & nothing to their children.[67]

Pack's sister Anna Catherine Pack also applied for a pension on the basis that Pack had supported her during his lifetime. She was granted a pension on the Irish Civil List of £43 18*s* 4*d* in 1826, and lived until she was seventy-six, dying in 1844.[68] At the time of the grant Richard, Marquess Wellesley, the duke's brother, was the lord lieutenant of Ireland.

Determined that Denis should be suitably honoured, Elizabeth at considerable cost engaged the well-known sculptor Sir Francis Chantrey to design a monument surmounted by a bust of her late husband.[69] This magnificent memorial was installed in Kilkenny Cathedral in the summer of 1829, at a total cost of £593 15*s*, a striking sum well in excess of the annual pension granted on Pack's demise. To mark the occasion there was a procession through the streets of Kilkenny by a crowd, which included survivors of the battle of Waterloo then stationed in the city, and the tomb was decorated with laurel.[70] The monument contains a lengthy inscription reflecting the life and career of Denis Pack.[71] On 19 May 1837 new colours were presented to the 71st regiment in Phoenix Park in Dublin. The date was significant in that it was the anniversary of the regiment's participation in the destruction of a bridge held by the French at Almaraz in 1812. The lord lieutenant of Ireland in his speech at the presentation referred to the old colours: 'those relics of your former glory will be placed over the grave of one who often led you to victory, as a curtain to shade the honoured remains of a departed warrior'.[72] The old colours were then taken to Kilkenny Cathedral, and placed over the memorial to Denis Pack, where they hung for many years.[73]

In February 1831 Lady Elizabeth remarried. Her second husband was Denis Pack's old friend and successor as commanding officer of the 71st regiment, Sir Thomas Reynell.[74] The two officers had fought alongside each other in the Peninsular War and at Waterloo, and had both been involved with the occupation of France after Napoleon's final defeat. They were regular correspondents. Writing to Elizabeth in 1821, Pack referred to having dined with his old friend General Reynell, and they clearly enjoyed a harmonious relationship.[75] Reynell must have left for India shortly after that dinner, for he commanded the Meerut division of the Bengal army from 1821 to 1828. There he served under Lord Combermere at the siege of Bharatpore in the winter of 1825/26. Curiously, notwithstanding the friendship between Pack and Reynell, the marshal and perhaps others seemed uncomfortable with Elizabeth's decision to marry Thomas Reynell. He did not explain the reasons, but did counsel her to burn a letter from Lord Howden on the subject, which he enclosed with his own.[76] No explanation has been found as to why some might have held an adverse opinion of Reynell. He came from a long line of successful politicians and soldiers, had a distinguished military career of his own, and had been a good friend of Denis Pack. Furthermore, Marshal Beresford clearly held Thomas Reynell in high regard, for he made him one of the parties to his own marriage settlement with Louisa in 1831, and left Elizabeth monies under his will out of regard for both her and Thomas.[77] There is no suggestion that the marriage of Elizabeth and Thomas was other than happy. They had no children, but Denis Pack's eldest son Arthur adopted the Reynell name to become Reynell-Pack on the death of his stepfather.[78] Denis's second son, Denis William, assumed the name Beresford, as a precondition to succession to the marshal's Irish estates in County Carlow on the death of his godfather, Marshal Beresford, in 1854.[79] The Reynells lived at Avisford Park, Sussex. Thomas died in 1848 and when Elizabeth died in 1856 she was buried alongside Thomas at St Mary's, Walberton, in Sussex.

Had he lived beyond the age of forty-eight Denis Pack would, in the normal course of events, have advanced further in the army. It is likely he would also have been offered postings of a similar nature to those achieved by his contemporaries in the armed forces. General Sir James Kempt later became Governor of Nova Scotia and then Governor General of Canada. General Sir Henry Fane became commander-in-chief in India. General Sir Colin Halkett became Lieutenant Governor of Jersey. Pack's reputation as a dashing and courageous commander of troops was built on and enhanced by his performance in two campaigns in South America (1806 and 1807), in the Peninsula at Vimiero, La Coruna, Buçaco, Ciudad Rodrigo and Salamanca, and in France particularly at Toulouse, Quatre Bras and Waterloo. Sir Henry Hardinge, who had served with Pack in the Iberian Peninsula and was later to go on to become Commander in Chief of the army, was, even allowing for potential bias in favour of a former comrade, most complimentary in his appraisal of Pack in 1834, eleven years after the latter's death. At that time Hardinge wrote to Elizabeth to tell her the engraving of Denis Pack she had sent him would hang in his office next to the Duke of Wellington and other celebrated officers of the Peninsular War 'amongst whom no one was more eminent for his military heroism or excelled in those amicable qualities which numbered him so universally the most popular officer in the army'.[80] His performance as a leader of men has led to a modern reference to Denis Pack as 'possibly the best battalion and brigade commander in the British Army'.[81]

Pack was, like many others, festooned with honours. What makes him different is that his battle honours in the Peninsula were only exceeded amongst field officers by Wellington and only equalled by Beresford. His Peninsular Gold Medal contained the cross with seven clasps (eleven battles and sieges) and perhaps not surprisingly when his medals were auctioned at the beginning of the twenty-first century they fetched £115,000.[82] In addition, Pack received the Portuguese Commander's Cross, a gold star out of which the rays reflect battles in which he fought. Pack's Portuguese cross contained eleven rays, with only Marshal Beresford's twelve rays exceeding that number. Pack's other honours included further foreign awards, and in Ireland he was awarded the freedom of the cities of Kilkenny (1811), Cork (1814) and Waterford (1817). The eloquent address by the Corporation of Kilkenny is dated 7 May 1811, so it was clearly made in Pack's absence (when he was engaged in the blockade of Almeida). Inter alia it read:

> We follow you with mingled emotions of pride and admiration, from your early and voluntary service on the Continent, to the shores of the East, and thence to the Southerly regions of the New World, from which, as well as from the recent laurels acquired in Portugal,

your countrymen would borrow a reflected credit, without robbing the object of their pride.

The freedom of the city of Waterford was awarded in 1817, but Pack only collected it in person when he visited the city in January 1823, six months before his demise.[83]

Knighted by George III for his services in the Peninsula, Pack's coat of arms included a representation of the gold cross and clasps awarded on account of his major encounters with the enemy there, pendent from a crimson ribbon bordered blue, being the colour of the Peninsular ribbon. As a motto he chose *fidus confido*.[84]

* * *

Pack was an ever-present officer, leading from the front, whether in northern Europe, South America or the Iberian Peninsula. His fellow officers regarded Pack as not just competent, but eminently suited to command. Five times he received the thanks of parliament for his military services. His example at Buenos Aires, Salamanca and Toulouse, to name a few battles, is evidence of a dashing and courageous commander. Benjamin D'Urban, himself a soldier of note, credited Pack with sound judgement, and he showed repeatedly his tactical nous and ability, not least at the assault of Ciudad Rodrigo in 1812. Wellington thought highly of Pack, praising him for converting a false attack into a real one at Ciudad Rodrigo. At Toulouse Pack's name was mentioned as one of the officers 'whose ability and conduct he [Wellington] cannot sufficiently applaud'.[85] Wellington showed delight when Pack was assigned to his army in 1815 and Pack's good judgement and gallantry were again mentioned in Kempt's Waterloo report to Wellington. Pack was indeed one of 'the heroes of Waterloo'.[86]

Pack's legacy as a brigade and regimental commander lived on beyond his death. At a court martial held in 1835 the standing orders of the 71st regiment compiled by Pack were cited as being founded on 'the best principles' by 'an officer who was remarkable during his long services for a most profound and thorough knowledge of the duties of a regiment in all its branches'.[87] At the same time, Pack had a clear regard for the men serving under him. Though said by some to be of uneven temper, as evidenced by the couplet allegedly chalked on a barn in South America after his escape from captivity and return to the army:

'The Devil break the Gaoler's back
That let thee loose sweet Denis Pack'

he was well liked by those who served under him and developed a particular rapport with the men of the Highland regiments.[88] They looked after him when he required assistance or sustenance, and he in turn took care of them. Some of the reported examples have been referred to already, but it is worth noting his attention to securing shelter for his men on the difficult retreat to La Coruna, and on the same long march his ordering an officer off the back of one of the men when fording an icy river. Later, at the battle of St Pierre, he intervened to prevent troops, some of them wearing kilts, having to march through fields of furze, thorns and brambles, quickly finding an alternative route.[89] After Waterloo a number of hungry soldiers of the 42nd raided the vegetable gardens and fruit orchards of residents on the march to Paris. Arrested by an officer, they were delighted to be released on the orders of the passing General Pack.[90] He recognized the achievements of those serving under him, such as those of John Fraser of the 71st regiment. Fraser's bravery had been recognized when he had been the sole survivor of a party that stormed a battery at the taking of the Cape of Good Hope. He showed that courage again at Buenos Aires, where he was publicly complimented by Pack for his gallantry.[91]

Sergeant James Anton of the 42nd foot summed up Pack:

> Major-General Sir Denis Pack, a brave officer, under whom our regiment obtained the honorary distinction of bearing on its colours and other insignia, 'PYRENEES, NIVELLE, NEVE (sic), ORTHEZ, TOULOUSE, QUATRE BRAS, WATERLOO.' At each of these places he himself was personally distinguished, not by a forward unnecessary daring, but by attending to the proceedings of each of the corps in his brigade, and directing its movements so as to secure the success of the whole.[92]

In modern parlance a perfect team player.

Wellington's memorandum to Pack, 20 October 1812

MEMORANDUM

For General Pack, for the Blockade of Burgos
Villa Toro, 20th October, 1812.

1. While the enemy shall be in force in front of the army, Brig. General Pack will take charge of the blockade of Burgos, keeping possession of the ground which has been acquired during the siege. He will have under his command, besides his own brigade, the 24th and 58th regiments, Colonel Brown's battalion of caçadores, the 11th, 53rd and 61st regiments, and the Spanish battalions of Asturias and Guadalaxara, which are in the town of Burgos.

2. The guns, howitzers, and ammunition now in the trenches are to be brought down this night, for which purpose a working party of 200 men must be ordered for this evening at 5 p.m.

3. Orders will be sent to Colonel Robe regarding the disposal of the artillery and ammunition.

4. Orders will be likewise be sent for the 11th, 53rd, and 61st regiments to go round and occupy the bivouac lately occupied by the brigade of Guards.

5. Brig. General Pack, and all the troops under his command, will be in readiness to march at a moment's notice, with the exception of 500 men, in their due proportions of English and Portuguese troops, to relieve the trenches at the hour of the next relief, and Colonel Brown's battalion of caçadores, and two battalions of Spanish infantry. The officer who shall take General Pack his orders will show him the road he is to march.

6. When General Pack shall move, he is to give charge of the blockade to Colonel Brown, who will concert his measures with Lieut. Colonel Burgoyne to preserve all the ground gained.

7. General Pack will settle with the Commandant of the Spanish troops, to take some of the duties in the town, now taken by the caçadores.

8. All the avenues from the town to the castle should be barricaded.

9. One of the French guns and a howitzer might be left in the right hand battery, in order to give the enemy a shot occasionally, and to check sorties. An officer and artillerymen of the reserve must remain for this purpose.

10. The Engineer officer must load the mines in the horn work, and these mines must be sprung, if by any accident it should be necessary to withdraw from the trenches.

WELLINGTON.

From *The Dispatches of Field Marshal the Duke of Wellington*, vol. 6, 130–1.

Inscription on the memorial to Sir Denis Pack, St Canice's Cathedral, Kilkenny

The memorial in St Canice's Cathedral, Kilkenny by Sir Francis Chantrey is of white marble. Erected in 1829, it consists of just two blocks of marble and weighs over 2 tons. The memorial is surmounted by a bust of Major General Sir Denis Pack. The inscription reads:

Near this place are interred the mortal remains of Major-General Sir Denis Pack, Knight Commander of the most Honorable Military Order of the Bath, and of the Portuguese Military Order of the Tower and Sword, Knight of the Imperial Russian Order of Wladimir, and of the Imperial Austrian Order of Maria Theresa; Colonel of the 84th Regiment of Foot, and Lieutenant-Governor of Plymouth, who terminated a life devoted to the service of his King and Country on the 24th day of July 1823, aged forty-eight years. The name of this distinguished officer is associated with almost every brilliant achievement of the British Army during the eventful period of Continental warfare between the year 1791, in which he entered his Majesty's service, and the year 1823, in which he ended his honourable career. Throughout the campaigns in Flanders in 1794 and 1795, he served in the 14th Regiment of Light Dragoons. At the capture of the Cape of Good Hope in 1806, and in the arduous and active campaign which immediately followed in South America, he commanded the 71st Regiment of Highlanders in a manner which reflected the highest credit on his military skill and valour.

At the head of the same corps in 1808, he acquired fresh reputation in the battles of Roleia and Vimiera, and in the following year at the Battle of Corunna. In 1809 he accompanied the expedition to Walcheren, and signalized himself by his zeal and intrepidity at the siege of Flushing.

He was subsequently engaged at the head either of a brigade or a division of the army in every general action and remarkable siege which took place during the successful war in the Peninsula, under the conduct of the great Duke of Wellington. He finally commanded a brigade in the action at Quatre Bras, and again in the ever memorable and decisive battle of Waterloo.

For these important services, in which he was nine times severely wounded, he obtained, at the recommendation of his illustrious chief, from the foreign potentates in alliance with Great Britain, the honourable titles of distinction above mentioned, and from his own sovereign, besides the Order of the Bath, and a medal in commemoration of the Battle of Waterloo, a gold cross with seven clasps on which are inscribed the following names of the battles and sieges wherein he bore a conspicuous part, viz.:- Roleia, Vimiera, Corunna, Busaco, Ciudad Rodrigo, Salamanca, Vittoria, Pyrénées, Nivelle, Nive, Orthes, Toulouse.

Upon five different occasions he had also the honour to receive the thanks of both Houses of Parliament:-

> On the 3rd of February, 1813, for his conduct at Salamanca; on 10th February, 1813, for his conduct at Ciudad Rodrigo; on 8th November, 1813, for his conduct at Vittoria; on the 24th March, 1814, for his conduct at Orthes; on the 23rd June, 1815, for his conduct at Waterloo.

Whilst these, his merits as an officer, ensure for him a place in the records of his grateful country amongst those heroes who have bravely fought her battles and advanced her military glory, his virtues as a man, which were securely founded upon Christian piety, are attested by the esteem of his companions in arms, and by the love of all who were intimately connected with him.

This monument is erected by his widow, the Lady Elizabeth Pack, daughter of George de la Poer, Marquess of Waterford, as a just tribute of respect to the memory of one of His Majesty's most deserving soldiers and subjects, and in testimony of her own affection.

Notes

Abbreviations

AHM: Arquivo Historico Militar, Lisbon

BL: British Library

General Orders: Wellington, *General Orders, Spain and Portugal*, 4 vols, 1809–12 (London 1811–13)

NA: National Archives, Kew, London

NAI: National Archives Ireland

NAM: National Army Museum, London

NLI: National Library of Ireland

PRONI: Public Record Office of Northern Ireland

TCD: Trinity College Dublin Library

TT: Torre do Tombo, Portuguese National Archives

WD: *The Dispatches of Field Marshal the Duke of Wellington* (London 1844), 8 vols. References are to the digitally printed version published by Cambridge University Press 2010

WP: Wellington Papers, Hartley Library, University of Southampton

WSD: *Supplementary Despatches, Correspondence and Memoranda of Field Marshal Arthur, Duke of Wellington, KG* (London 1858–72), 15 vols

Introduction

1. Major General Sir William Erskine was one officer about whom Wellington had reservations both before and during his appointment in the Peninsula. Neither did Wellington object when Major General Robert Ballard Long was recalled to London in 1813. Mindful of his political connections, Wellington moved slowly, but ultimately effectively, when Sir Robert Wilson objected to the integration of the Loyal Lusitanian Legion into the Portuguese army under Marshal William Carr Beresford. In 1813 he ensured that Beresford removed Major General Sir George Allen Madden from the command of an infantry brigade, sending him back to Lisbon.

2. Wellington to Lieutenant Colonel Torrens (Horse Guards), 29 August 1810: *WSD*, vol. 6, 582. This letter is highly illustrative of Wellington's frustrations with officers imposed on him.

3. Wellington to Bathurst, 18 June 1818: *WSD*, vol. 12, 578.

4. *London Gazette*, Issue 16291, 22 August 1809.

Chapter 1: Early life

1. The other children were Thomas, Catherine and Anne. Denis R. Pack-Beresford, *A Memoir of Major-General Sir Denis Pack* (Dublin 1908), 1, states the year of birth as 1775. Hereafter *Memoir*.

2. For a history of the college see Howard Terence Welch, *A history of Kilkenny College, 1538–1903* (Trinity College Dublin, PhD thesis 2002). The college was in fact re-established in 1666 by James Butler, 1st Duke of Ormonde, following the restoration of Charles II.

3. Denis Sullivan had served in Bragg's regiment, which became the 28th (North Gloucestershire) when the regiments were numbered in 1734. A cornet was the lowest rank in a British cavalry troop, equivalent to the modern-day rank of a second lieutenant. Pack's commission appeared in the *London Gazette*, 14–17 January 1792, 25. It is not stated whether he purchased this commission.

4. *Memoir*, 2, quotes an entry in the Pack family Bible then (1908) in the possession of Arthur Reynell Pack to the effect that Denis Pack was 'dismissed from the Army for some breach of discipline'. Subsequently having served as a volunteer his rank was restored to him. Further, the *History of the Cathedral Church of St Canice* by the Revd James Graves & August John Prim (Dublin 1857), 336, quoted a gentleman still living in Kilkenny as confirming that Pack had been cashiered in 1792 or 1793 for having struck Captain George Dunbar, while the 14th light dragoons were stationed in Castlecomer (County Kilkenny). The informant, who was elderly when the *History* was written, claimed to have been present at the promulgation of the sentence following the trial at Kilkenny courthouse.

5. Later, during the Peninsular War, insubordination (sometimes provoked) was the largest class of offences which brought officers to court martial. Sentences varied from being cashiered to suspension of pay to the almost more humiliating public reprimand in front of the regiment (see the case of Colonel Basil Cochrane, chapter 6). See Charles Oman, 'Courts Martial of the Peninsular War, 1809–14', *Royal United Services Institution Journal*, 1912, 56 (418), 1699–1716.

6. *Naval & Military Gazette and Weekly Chronicle of the United Service*, 5 April 1834, 5.

7. Sir George Dunbar was promoted to Major on 1 September 1795. On 15 October 1799, however, he took his own life at Norwich following a violent dispute with fellow officers of the regiment in the mess the previous evening: *Annual Register of World Events*, 1799, 107.

8. A gentleman volunteer served as a private but messed with the officers. It was an opportunity to serve while waiting for a commission to become available.

9. Bremen is in Hanover. The electorate and subsequently kingdom of Hanover was in personal union with Great Britain (Great Britain & Ireland 1801) from 1714 to 1837.

10. *London Gazette*, 21–24 March 1795, 262.

11. The French royalists were led by Count Joseph de Puisaye. His second in command was Count d'Hervilly and from the outset the operation was bedevilled by disputes over tactics and strategy.

12. A curious footnote to this episode involves the discovery of a Waterford regiment uniform button on the sands of Quiberon. This regiment (the 124th) was only raised in 1794 and was merged with the 88th regiment (Connaught Rangers) in 1795, whereupon the 124th regiment ceased to exist. Perhaps the uniform continued to be used, though the presence of the button at Quiberon is difficult to explain given the 88th regiment did not serve there. Had some of the marines landed at Quiberon served briefly in the 124th regiment?

13. William Pitt to George III, 13 July 1795: Aspinall (ed.), *Later correspondence of George III* (Cambridge 1963), vol. 2, 357.

14. Welbore Ellis Doyle was the younger brother of General John Doyle. Welbore died at the age of thirty-nine in Sri Lanka in 1797.
15. Doyle and elements of the 12th, 78th, 80th and 90th regiments only arrived after the evacuation of Quiberon. They participated in the plan to capture Noirmoutier which did not proceed and the capture of Ile d'Yeu.
16. A small number of dragoons sailed with the expedition. Welbore Ellis Doyle refers to these (he gives their identity as the 4th light dragoons rather than the 14th light dragoons) in a letter to the Duke of Portland of 17 July 1795 quoted in Arthur Doyle, *A Hundred Years of Conflict being Some Records of the Services of Six Generals of the Doyle Family, 1756–1856* (London 1911), 58. Because of a lack of forage on Ile d'Yeu some of the cavalry was sent home before the island was finally abandoned. Doyle to Henry Dundas, 22 October 1795: Doyle, *A Hundred Years of Conflict*, 70. Of the 1,400 horses sent home, Fortescue reported 400 perished on the journey and were disposed of at sea: J.W. Fortescue, *The British Army and the Peninsular War* (reprint Leonaur 2016).
17. Appointment 27 February 1796.
18. Major General Sir William Ponsonby succeeded to Le Marchant's command on the latter's death at Salamanca. Ponsonby himself was killed at the battle of Waterloo.
19. Thomas Bartlett & Keith Jeffery, *A Military History of Ireland* (Cambridge 1996), 269.
20. The 5th dragoon guards fought at every major engagement in the 1798 rebellion, including Arklow, Vinegar Hill and Ballinamuck.
21. Cornwallis was appointed on 13 June 1798 and held office until 17 March 1801. He supported the policy of a union between England and Ireland but advocated it be accompanied by Catholic emancipation, a desire that it proved impossible to advance, not least because of George III's opposition.
22. General Jean Joseph Amable Humbert. He had been involved in the expedition of 1796 and had reached Bantry on that occasion. Humbert was rumoured to have had an affair with Napoleon's sister Pauline Leclerc, fell out of favour with Napoleon and ended his life in New Orleans, where he was involved in a number of plots involving Mexican independence.
23. The regimental history of the 5th dragoon guards suggests that Captain William Ponsonby commanded this escort, but even though Pack had been appointed Major in the 4th Royal Irish dragoon guards on 25 August there seems little doubt that he was with the escort: *Historical Record of the Fifth or Princess Charlotte of Wales's Regiment of dragoon guards* (London 1839). Ponsonby was also at Ballinamuck.
24. The French were taken to Tullamore, whence they were shipped to Dublin by barge with thousands watching their progress along the Grand Canal: *Dublin Evening Post*, 20 September 1798.
25. The court martial of Wolfe Tone took place in Dublin on 10 November 1798. The President was General William Loftus. Those serving on the court martial in addition to Loftus were Colonels Daly, Vandeleur and Wolfe, Major Armstrong and Captain Corry. Wolfe Tone died on 19 November 1798.
26. He is listed as Captain Pack, notwithstanding his majority having been gazetted on 25 August. For details of the trial see T.W. Moody, R.B. McDowell & C.J. Woods (eds), *The Writings of Theobald Wolfe Tone, 1763–98*, vol. 3 (Oxford 2007).
27. Bart Teeling, who had travelled with him from France, was executed on the same day as Mathew Tone.

28. The fighting at Tuberneering (today known as Toberanierin), south of Gorey in County Wexford, was a serious reversal for the Crown forces, involving the death of the commander, Lieutenant Colonel Lambert Walpole, and a hundred men. Other battles during the rebellion involving the 4th Royal Irish dragoons included Naas (24 May 1798), Prosperous (25 May 1798) and Vinegar Hill (21 June). For an account of Walpole's bravery see Kevin Whelan & Thomas Bartlett (eds), *Memoirs of Miles Byrne – 1798 in County Wexford* (Dublin 1998).

29. The 71st regiment went through a number of name changes during the period in question. In 1808 it became the 71st (Glasgow Highland) Regiment of Foot, and in 1809 was converted to a light infantry regiment, becoming the 71st (Highland) Regiment of Foot (Light Infantry).

30. The purchase of rank by commission was part of British military practice until abolished by the Cardwell reforms of 1871. It was practised in other armies (though not the Prussian) to a certain extent. Its raison d'etre was that it ensured the officer class had a vested interest in maintaining political and social stability and it maintained to a degree social exclusivity. In addition, unless cashiered for misconduct, the officer could sell his rank on advancing in the army or on retirement. Regulations existed requiring an officer to hold a rank for a certain period before advancing further but the Commander-in-Chief could allow exemptions. It was also possible to advance where an officer was killed in action or appointed to the staff. Positions above lieutenant colonel could not be purchased but were based on seniority. The argument against the ability to purchase promotion was that it allowed the rich incompetent to succeed at the expense of competent but poor officers. Nevertheless, Wellington, who had a number of officers of dubious ability inflicted on him in the Peninsular War, supported the system.

31. Robert Burnham & Ron McGuigan, *The British Army against Napoleon, Facts, lists and trivia 1805–1815* (Barnsley 2010), 152. Hereafter *British Army, facts*.

32. The six accounts mentioned are:
    (1) *Journal of a soldier of the Seventy-First or Glasgow Regiment Highland Light Infantry from 1806–1815* (Edinburgh 1819) (hereafter *A Soldier*). A new edition edited and introduced by Stuart Reid (Barnsley 2010) enabled him to identify the author as Joseph Sinclair. John Howell had published the 1819 edition and he later confirmed that material had been sourced with information from two other soldiers, James Todd and Archibald Gavin.
    (2) Anon., *Vicissitudes in the life of a Scottish soldier written by himself* (London 1827) (hereafter *Vicissitudes*), remains an anonymous work but one which is clearly written by a man serving in the ranks. The author of *Vicissitudes* only joined the 71st regiment in 1807, having previously served with other regiments. He was clearly aware of the existence of 'A soldier of the Seventy-First'.
    (3) 'A short sketch of the campaigns of Balfour Kermack, 71st regiment Highlanders (Light Infantry) from 1806 to 1814', *Highland Light Infantry Chronicle*, vol. 14, 128 et seq., quarterly January, April, July and October (hereafter *Kermack*).
    (4) Major Eric Robson (ed.), 'Peninsula Private', *Journal of the Society for Army Historical Research*, 1954, 32 (129), 4–14 (hereafter *Peninsula Private*). Macfarlane only joined the 71st regiment in 1807 and was not at Buenos Aires.
    (5) Gareth Glover (ed.), *The Diary of William Gavin, Ensign and Quartermaster of the 71st Highland Regiment 1806–1815; being his daily notes of his campaigns in South*

Africa, South America, Portugal, Spain, southern France and Flanders under Sir David Baird, Sir William Beresford, Sir John Moore and The Duke of Wellington (Hunting-don 2013) (hereafter *Gavin*). William Gavin was an Irishman who in 1806 was Quartermaster Sergeant with the 71st regiment. He later became an officer without purchase and survived the war.

(6) Andrew Bamford (edited and introduced), *With Wellington's Outposts, The Peninsula and Waterloo Letters of John Vandeleur* (Barnsley 2015) (hereafter *Vandeleur*). Note Vandeleur served with the 71st from 1809 to 1811. John Vandeleur was a cousin of Major General John Ormsby Vandeleur who served in the Iberian Peninsula and at Waterloo.

33. The regiment received a substantial injection of manpower with the transfer to the 71st of 600 men from the Scotch Fencible Corps, then serving in Ireland. See L.B. Oatts, *Proud Heritage, The story of the Highland Light Infantry* (London 1952), vol. 1, 51. See also J.T. Hildyard, *Historical Record of the 71st regiment Highland Light Infantry, from its formation in 1777, under the title of the 73rd, or McLeod's Highlanders, up to the year 1876* (London 1876), 50.

34. In 1800 the 71st regiment was sent from Scotland to Ireland, being based that year in Dundalk. At the beginning of January 1801 it moved to Dublin with Denis Pack being promoted lieutenant colonel of the regiment on 6 December 1800. In 1802, following the Peace of Amiens, the regiment was quartered in County Wicklow and in 1803 marched to Loughrea in County Galway. In 1804 it moved to County Limerick with its headquarters at Rathkeale.

35. Lord George Thomas Beresford (1781–1839) was a soldier and Tory politician. He served with William Carr Beresford in the 124th and 88th regiments. Ultimately he became a major general in 1814. From 1802 until 1831, with the exception of 1826–30, he was a member of parliament and served as Comptroller of the Household from 1812–30.

Chapter 2: The Cape Colony and Rio de la Plata, 1806–07

1. For a further account of this expedition see Marcus de la Poer Beresford, *Marshal William Carr Beresford, 'the ablest man I have yet seen with the army'* (Newbridge 2019). Hereafter *Marshal Beresford*.

2. Sir Ronald Craufurd Ferguson (1773–1841), soldier and Whig politician. He served throughout the French revolutionary and Napoleonic wars, though his contribution was on occasion ended by ill-health, such as required him in 1806 to return from the Cape Colony to Great Britain.

3. Maggs Bros Ltd Catalogue, June 2005, item 30.

4. Ferguson to Baird, 19 January 1806, quoted in full in *Memoir*, 7–8.

5. Peter Carew, 'A Gallant Pack', *Blackwood's Magazine*, 1946, vol. 260, 391–401. Carew knew and was a neighbour of Pack's grandson (probably Denis Robert Pack-Beresford OBE, who had died in 1942, as in the 1946 article he is referred to in the past tense). A great-grandson of Denis Pack clearly made papers available to Carew. This may have been Commander Denis John Pack-Beresford who died in 1986. In the quoted article Carew refers to a journal of Denis Pack, 394.

6. Pack to James Butler, 24 March 1806: *Memoir*, 9. James Butler (1774–1838), 1st Marquess of Ormonde (later 19th Earl of Ormonde). Butler was a firm friend of Denis Pack, with whom he corresponded on a regular basis.

7. In 1804 Popham, together with the Venezuelan general Francisco Miranda, had drawn up plans for a three-pronged attack on the Spanish colonies in South America. These were Venezuela, the Rio de la Plata and the Pacific coast. E.A. Kirkpatrick, *A History of the Argentine Republic* (Cambridge 1931), 47–8.

8. Pack to James Butler, 6 July 1806: *Memoir*, 11.

9. Hilarion de la Quintana (1774–1843), a full-time soldier who later in life fought for Argentine independence and in the civil war that followed it. He also served with San Martin in the Army of the Andes that helped secure Chilean independence.

10. Pack refers to the frigate *Narcissus* being grounded not once but twice. If that was happening to a frigate, it is not surprising that the ships of the line stayed out to sea. It appears that Beresford was on the *Narcissus* for Pack refers to the fog and sending out boats to look for him. At the same time Pack was in suspense as if Beresford were not found, Pack would have had to lead the invasion force. *Memoir*, 11–13.

11. Pack estimated 4,000 but other sources quote 2,000–3,000.

12. Riachuelo means small river. It is sometimes known as Rio de la Matanza.

13. Pack to James Butler, 6 July 1806: *Memoir*, 12.

14. See *Marshal Beresford*, 13.

15. The 71st lost two officers and twenty-four rank and file killed in the defence of Buenos Aires, with two officers also wounded, along with sixty-seven rank and file. The killed officers were Lieutenant Mitchell and Ensign Lucas. The injured officers were Denis Pack and Ensign Murray.

16. See *Marshal Beresford*, 15–17.

17. *Gavin*, 32.

18. The Bethlehemite Brothers, a Hospitaller order, were founded by Pedro de Betancourt in 1653 and suppressed in Argentina in 1820. Five men from the 71st died in the hospital notwithstanding the ministrations of the Brothers. *Gavin*, 31.

19. Pack to Sir John Cradock, _ August (the postscript is 28 August) 1806: *Memoir*, 16–17.

20. The officers sent to Lujan are listed in Oscar Tavani Perez Colman, *Martinez de Fontez y la fuga del General Beresford* (Buenos Aires 2005), 76. As well as Beresford and Pack, they were Robert William Patrick, Alexander Forbes, Robert Arbuthnot, Alexander MacDonald, Edward L'Estrange and Santiago Evans. Patrick, Forbes, Arbuthnot, MacDonald and L'Estrange later served in the Iberian Peninsula, some with Beresford on secondment to the Portuguese army. Santiago Evans may be the James Evans of the 71st; if so, he too served in the Peninsula.

21. De Liniers is reported to have supplied Beresford with 240 ounces of gold so that the officers might purchase necessaries: Colman, *Martinez de Fontes*, 76.

22. James Ogilvie had previously been injured when defending Buenos Aires in August 1806.

23. On 25 August 1807 Pack wrote an account of this murder, which is quoted in *The Annual Biography and Obituary for the Year 1824*, 350–5. Pack refers to the assault as taking place on 27 November 1806.

24. De Liniers to Beresford, ? January 1807: *Memoir*, 19–20.

25. Saturnino Rodriguez Pena (1765–1819), soldier and politician, was interested in Argentine independence from an early stage. In 1807 he left Buenos Aires and went to Rio de Janeiro, where he lived for a number of years, becoming involved in a plot to install the infanta Carlota Joaquina de Borbon as Regent of the Rio de la Plata. With the commencement of the war of independence he was able to return to Argentina.

Although a lieutenant colonel in the artillery, he fell out with those in power and retired to Rio de Janeiro. Manuel Aniceto Padilla (1770–c.1840), lawyer, diplomat and newspaperman. He had supported Beresford at the time of the 1806 invasion, but subsequently distanced himself from this stance. Beresford on his return to England obtained pensions for Pena, Padilla and two others who had assisted his escape. Two other officers from Beresford's force later escaped. These were Major Henry Dunbar Tolley (1784–1837) and Lieutenant Peter Adamson. Both were attached to the 71st regiment and escaped from San Ignacio. Tolley went on to become lieutenant colonel of the 16th regiment and ultimately a major general. Adamson later served in the Portuguese army under Beresford before returning to the 71st as a major in 1814. *London Gazette*, 1814, part 2, 2553. Wounded at Salamanca. Awarded Torre e Espada by the Portuguese Crown.

26. It was argued that not only had the Spaniards broken the terms of surrender, but that the parole was given on the basis of the officers remaining in or adjacent to Buenos Aires. Their removal to Lujan and then a further projected exile to Catamarca in the foothills of the Andes was seen as a further breach of the parole terms by their captors. Anon., *Notes on the Viceroyalty of La Plata, in South America: with a sketch of the manners and character of the inhabitants, collected during a residence in the city of Monte Video, by a gentleman recently returned from it: to which is added, a history of the operations of the British troops in that country, and biographical and military anecdotes of the principal officers employed in the different expeditions* (London 1808), 272.

27. Court of Audienza to Admiral Stirling and Sir Samuel Auchmuty, 2 March 1807: *Proceedings of a General Court Martial held at Chelsea Hospital on Thursday January 28, 1808 and continued, by adjournment, till Tuesday March 15, for the Trial of Lieutenant-General Whitelocke, late Commander-in-Chief of the forces in South America*, 2 vols (London 1808), vol. 2, 770–72. Hereafter *Proceedings*.

28. Auchmuty to William Windham (secretary of state for war and the colonies, 1806–07), 6 March 1807, quoted in *Proceedings*, vol. 2, 766–9.

29. Ernestina Costa, *English Invasion of the River Plate* (Buenos Aires 1937), 37.

30. Francisco Xavier de Elio (1767–1822), soldier and last Spanish-appointed governor of the Rio de la Plata (1810–12). Returning to Spain, he participated in the war against the French, commanding the Spanish Second army (Valencia & Murcia). An ardent supporter of absolutism, he was executed following the liberal revolution of 1820. The reward (4,000 pesos) for Pack's capture is quoted in Enrique Williams Alzaga, *Martin de Alzaga en la Reconquista y en la Defensa de Buenos Aires (1806–1807)* (Buenos Aires, 1971), 128–9.

31. General Leveson Gower listed the troops with Pack in Colonia as a small detachment of artillery, a few mounted dragoons, the light companies of the 38th, 40th, 47th and 87th, together with four or five companies of the 40th regiment. *Proceedings*, vol. 1, 54.

32. Pack to Whitelocke, 8 June 1807; Whitelocke to Horse Guards, 12 June 1807; and Whitelocke to Pack, 10 June 1807: *Memoir*, 25–7.

33. Denis Pack to Charles Stewart, 29 March 1809, and Stewart to Pack, 30 March 1809; quoted in *Annual Biography and Obituary for the Year 1824* (London 1824), 350–1.

34. General Leveson Gower said in evidence that he had gone to Colonia in the gun brig *Rolla* to collect the garrison and they rejoined the fleet on 26 June, with the landing taking place on 28 June. *Proceedings*, vol. 1, 15–16.

35. Colonel Richard Bourke, chief officer in the Quartermaster General's department in South America, had surveyed the shoreline either side of Buenos Aires and determined that Ensenada de Barragan was the only place where men could be landed from ships of war. Beresford had landed at Quilmes, a lot nearer Buenos Aires, but Bourke confirmed that even in a brig the nearest he could get to Quilmes was 1.5 miles offshore. *Proceedings*, vol. 1, 80.

36. Robert 'Black Bob' Craufurd later commanded the Light Division in the Peninsula under Wellington. He died at the siege of Ciudad Rodrigo, 1812. In 1807 Craufurd's force (the 5th, 36th, 45th and 88th, together with companies from the 95th regiment, artillery and the 6th dragoons) had originally been designated to undertake an invasion of Chile. While revictualling at Capetown, his orders had been amended, requiring him to join Whitelocke.

37. Ben Hughes, *The British Invasion of the River Plate 1806–1807* (Barnsley 2013), 192. Richard Vandeleur served later in the Peninsula under Wellington and with Beresford but died at Campo Maior on 17 October 1809, where the 88th regiment was stationed following the retreat from Talavera.

38. In his official dispatch on the battle Whitelocke refers to this as the Jesuit College. Whitelocke to William Windham, 10 July 1807: *Proceedings*, vol. 1, apps xv–xix. San Ignacio church is on the corner of Catedral and San Carlos, beside the San Carlos Royal School. San Francisco church is on the corner of San Francisco and San Martin.

39. Henry Cadogan was from Ireland and had previously served in the 18th (Royal Irish) regiment and as an ADC to Sir Arthur Wellesley. He was well connected, and his sisters Charlotte and Emily Mary married Henry and Gerald Wellesley respectively. Cadogan was mortally wounded at the Battle of Vitoria, 1813.

40. *Proceedings*, vol. 2, 523.

41. Evidence of Brigadier General Craufurd, *Proceedings*, vol. 2, 519. The other field officers included Colonel William Guard of the 45th regiment and Major Norman MacLeod of the Rifles.

42. Stuart Reid (ed.), [Joseph Sinclair], *A soldier of the 71st: From de la Plata to the Battle of Waterloo* (Barnsley 2010), 34. Originally published Edinburgh 1819.

43. *Proceedings*, vol. 2, 569.

44. Captain John Randal Forster said at the court martial that Pack was escorted to Whitelocke's headquarters. *Proceedings*, vol. 2, 644.

45. *Proceedings*. Hathi Trust reprint.

46. The charges are set out in the Appendix to volume 1 of the *Proceedings*.

47. Whitelocke to William Windham, 10 July 1807: *Proceedings*, vol. 1, xxi. The breakdown given by Whitelocke was 316 killed, 674 wounded and 208 missing. He had no return for the light company of the 71st regiment, though he understood it to have suffered severely. Hughes, *British Invasion of the River Plate*, gives the total of killed, wounded, prisoners and missing as 2,824, appendix I.

48. *Proceedings*, vol. 1, 554.

49. Auchmuty to William Windham, 6 March 1807: *Proceedings*, vol. 2, 766.

50. Denis Pack's testimony is contained in *Proceedings*, vol. 2, 545–50.

51. *Proceedings*, vol. 1, 196.

52. *Proceedings*, vol. 2, 553. The Judge Advocate observed, however, that this remark could not be used as evidence against Whitelocke as it involved a conversation between Pack and Craufurd.

53. *Proceedings*, vol. 1, 174 et seq.

54. *Proceedings*, vol. 2, 552–7.

55. *Kermack*, 128 et seq.

56. *Gavin*, 441–3, recounts that they shipped home on different vessels, one of which, *Princesa*, a Spanish galleon, sank on the way home, luckily not before everyone was taken off the vessel.

57. *A Soldier*, says 25 December 1808. He was with the light company of the 71st, so may have been on a different vessel from others. On arrival the men were transferred to the barracks at Middleton.

58. See Chapter 1. In 1804, before being sent to the Cape, the 71st had been based in the west of Ireland with headquarters at Rathkeale and detachments at Newcastle and Askeaton in County Limerick, and Tarbert in County Kerry.

59. See *Marshal Beresford*, ch. 2, note 77.

60. The Paseo de la Alameda was a walk laid out on the instructions of Viceroy Vertiz in the 1780s. It is currently named Avenida Leandro N. Alem.

61. Bandas Militares: www.revisionistas.com.ar

62. Amongst others, Major Alexander Gillespie testified to the kindness of the Bethlehemite Brothers. See *Gleanings and remarks collected during many months of residence in Buenos Ayres, and within the upper country* (Leeds 1818).

63. The inscription on the front of the clock in English and Spanish reads 'Presented by the 71st Regiment as a slight testimony of gratitude to the Bethlemite Fathers [sic] for their great kindness towards the soldiers of this and other British Regiments at Buenos Aires. London April 3rd 1809.' The inscription on the side is in Latin and records the thanks of the 71st regiment for the medical assistance rendered by the Brothers at Buenos Aires. A similar inscription to that on the side of the grandfather clock is on the base of one of the sphinxes supporting the over-mantel clock.

64. Pack to Sr Don Luis Chorroarin, Superior of the Convent of Santo Domingo. 16 July 1809 (University of Southampton Library, MS 296 Pack Papers 296/1/2). The surname appears as 'Sphohonoaring' in *Memoirs*, 38, a spelling which is understandable as It is not easily decipherable on the letter itself. Chorroarin was one of the founders of the Public Library of Buenos Aires and served as Director for some time. Information supplied by Robert Elissalde and Maria Laura Maciel, Argentina.

Chapter 3: The Portuguese and Spanish campaigns, 1808–09

1. In contrast, the army under General Sir Ralph Abercromby had defeated the French in Egypt in 1801.

2. Napoleon Bonaparte, *Correspondence Générale*, Vol. 3 Pacifications 1800–1802 (Paris 2006), 438.

3. See *Marshal Beresford*, ch. 3.

4. Lieutenant General Sir John Floyd (1748–1818). He held various commands in Ireland between 1803 and 1812, including command of the Cork Division (1808–12). The 71st had served under him in India in the 1790s so he knew the regiment from that time.

5. Extract from address of Lieutenant General Floyd quoted in Hildyard, *Historical record of the 71st regiment Highland light infantry*.

6. Wellesley's force was made up of battalions from the 5th, 9th, 38th, 40th, 60th, 71st, 91st, 95th and 4th Royal Veterans. To these were shortly added battalions from the 36th and 45th regiments. See *WD*, vol. 3, 16 and 21.

7. *WD*, vol. 3, 18.

8. After the Battle of Vimeiro Major General William Carr Beresford joined the army in Portugal from Madeira with the 3rd Foot.

9. *Vicissitudes*, 2–3. A recent version has been edited by Paul Cowan (Barnsley 2015).

10. *Vicissitudes*, 6, refers to the fleet of seventy transports, two men of war and a gun brig.

11. *WD*, vol. 3, 27.

12. The disembarkation of the army took place over a number of days. *A Soldier*, ch. 2, suggests from 1 to 5 August. Spencer's force disembarked on 7 and 8 August. Wellesley to Castlereagh, 8 August 1808: *WD*, vol. 3, 56.

13. *Gavin*, 47.

14. In some cases the soldiers of the 71st were also offered wine as well as fruits. *Peninsula Private*, 5.

15. The French were commanded by General Henri Laborde. Heavily outnumbered, Laborde's division conducted an orderly retreat following resistance for much of the day.

16. See *Marshal Beresford*, ch. 3, for an account of the negotiation and outcome of the Convention of Cintra.

17. Wellesley to Lieutenant General Sir H. Burrard, 21 August 1808: *WD*, vol. 3, 90–3.

18. *Vicissitudes*, 26; *Peninsular Private*, 7.

19. Tales of bravery included the continued playing of the pipes by Pipe Major George (John) Clark, wounded in the groin by a musket ball. *A Soldier*, ch. 2; *Kermack*, 159.

20. Antoine-François Brenier de Montmorand (1767–1832). Following capture in 1808, he was exchanged in 1809 for Lieutenant General John Abercromby (son of Sir Ralph Abercromby), who had been held in France since 1803. The following year Brenier served with Marshal Masséna in the third French invasion of Portugal. Governor of Almeida following its capture in 1810, he was to cross paths again with Pack in 1811 when Brenier organized a brilliant night escape from the fortress. See below, ch. 6.

21. *Vicissitudes*, 20.

22. *Kermack*, 160, and *Vicissitudes*, 20, both credit an Irishman with the capture of Brenier. This was clearly not William Gavin, who was a quartermaster sergeant at this stage in his career. In fact William Gavin does not mention his namesake in his diary. There was an Irish soldier in the regiment, John Gavin, who died during the Walcheren campaign of 1809. See Paul Cowan (ed.), *With Wellington in the Peninsula: The adventures of a Highland soldier 1808–1814* (Barnsley 2015), 29.

23. *Kermack*, 160.

24. Probably the park attached to the Paco da Rainha ('Queen's Palace', now the Academia Militar). In 1808 this would have been on the outskirts of the city. It was the palace to which Catherine of Braganza retired as a widow following the death of her husband Charles II. In addition, João VI of Portugal lived there from his return from Brazil in 1821 until his death in 1826. Information courtesy of Major General (retd.) Rui Moura.

25. *Vicissitudes*, 29.

26. *Peninsula Private*, 7; *Vicissitudes*, 30.

27. *A Soldier*, 61.

28. *Vicissitudes*, 31.
29. The 71st was brigaded with the 36th and 98th under Brigadier Catlin Craufurd.
30. *A Soldier*, 75.
31. *A Soldier*, 53.
32. *Gavin*, 57. He does not say whether Mrs Cahill or the boy survived, but perhaps they did do so, as one would have expected comment in the alternative.
33. *A Soldier*, 55.
34. The regiment lost ninety-three men to weakness, sickness and fatigue on this march: *Historical Record of the 71st regiment*, 68.
35. *Vicissitudes*, 54 and 56.
36. *Ibid.*, 68.
37. William Gavin was somewhat critical of Pack when Gavin loaned him his mule to carry Pack to the next village on 1 January 1809, reporting that 'all he got for his humanity was to have his mule tied to a tree in the village, and after searching till one o'clock next morning found him by a miracle': *Gavin*, 58.
38. *Ibid*.
39. It is often difficult to obtain precise figures for losses in a campaign, particularly where it results in a retreat under pressure. Thus, the figures for those who returned to England from northern Spain may not be reliable because of the inability to place entire regiments together on vessels, which resulted in their returning to different ports. Further, it is clear that of those who became detached from their regiments on retreating to La Coruna, a considerable number eventually turned up in Portugal. Steve Brown has undertaken an in-depth study which is most helpful. It suggests that a comparison of regimental strength for 1 November 1808 and those lost in Portugal and Spain as of 6 May 1809 produces a loss of 15.2 per cent of other ranks in the 71st regiment for the period. Compare this with the two extremes: the regiments in Beresford's brigade, which suffered losses of between 26 per cent and 44 per cent, and those in the brigade of Robert Craufurd, which lost between 7 per cent and 10 per cent of other ranks. However, Craufurd's brigade marched to Vigo, not La Coruna, and was not pursued by the French, so did not suffer in combat to the extent of other brigades. See Steve Brown, 'British losses in the Corunna Campaign', *Napoleon Series*, October 2015.
40. Baird to Pack, 30 January 1809; the vote is recited in letters to Baird dated 25 and 27 January 1809 of the House of Commons and House of Lords respectively: Baird Archive.
41. Order issued by Horse Guards, 9 September 1810: *Cobbett's Weekly Political Register*, 1810, vol. 18, 723–4.
42. Kermack in his account of his career does not explain how he became detached, but it must have been before La Coruna as he makes no claim to have fought there. He was one of the very few men of the 71st who fought both at Porto and Talavera in 1809. He was entitled to the Peninsular War Medal and eight clasps (but not 'Corunna'). Died 1862.
43. 20 March 1809.

Chapter 4: Walcheren Fever' . . ., 1809

1. In the event Austria was knocked out of the war before the British force even sailed for the Low Countries, following the French victory at Wagram on 5–6 July 1809.

2. Henry Cadogan served in the army from 1797 to 1813 with distinction. He exchanged into the 71st regiment in 1808 and served with Wellesley as ADC in 1808–09 before rejoining the 71st on its return to Portugal in 1810. He commanded a brigade including the 71st at Arroyo dos Molinos in 1811 and again at Vitoria on 21 June 1813, where he was mortally wounded.

3. Gerald Wellesley married Emily Mary Cadogan. Henry Wellesley married Charlotte Cadogan, who later married William Paget.

4. Later Sir William Payne-Gallwey, Governor of the Leeward Islands. Payne was a major general in the British army in 1809. He fought at the Second Battle of Porto and the Battle of Talavera in 1809 before returning to England in 1810. He died in 1831.

5. Jacqueline Reiter, 'Day after day adds to our miseriese: The Private Diary of a staff officer on the Walcheren Expedition, 1809: Part 1', *Journal of the Society for Army Historical Research*, Autumn 2018, vol. 96 (386), 131–51, at 144. Some fine detective work has enabled Ms Reiter to establish with high probability that this is the diary of Lieutenant Colonel Thomas Walsh, Assistant Adjutant General to General Sir Eyre Coote.

6. Called Ter Veer in English accounts. *Gavin*, 66. Previously Pack and part of the 71st had occupied the fort of Ten Haak on 30 July.

7. The assault party included detachments from the 36th, 71st and the King's German Legion (KGL).

8. *Historical Record*, 74.

9. *Gavin*, 71.

10. *London Gazette*, 25 July 1810, 1096.

11. *Historical Record*, 75–6. The full regimental order to this effect is reprinted in *The Highland Light Infantry Chronicle*, July 1905, 108.

12. Peacocke had been Commandant of Lisbon in succession to Beresford in 1808.

13. *Vandeleur*, 40. Erskine suffered from bouts of mental illness and Wellington thought him mad, but could not dismiss him because of his political connections. Ultimately his conduct became so erratic that he was ordered to leave the service and in 1813 he killed himself jumping from a window in Lisbon. In 1810–11 Erskine commanded a brigade in the 1st Division made up of the 50th, 71st and 92nd regiments. By the time of Fuentes de Oñoro (3–5 May 1811) Erskine was in command of the 5th Division, so no longer with the 71st regiment.

Chapter 5: Seguindo as ordens de Beresford, 1810

1. Beresford's brigade was initially composed of the 1/9th, 2/43rd and 2/52nd. It was part of Lieutenant General Alexander Mackenzie Fraser's 2nd division.

2. See *Marshal Beresford*, esp. chs 6–8.

3. Beresford to Forjaz, 21 September 1809 (AHM, 1–14, CX 162, f. 43).

4. *Instruccoes para a formatura, exercicio e movimentos dos regimentos de infanteria. Por Ordem de Guilherme Carr Beresford, Marechal e Commandante em Chefe dos exercitos de Sua Alteza Real o Principe Regente de Portugal* (Lisbon 1809).

5. The first twenty-four officers to serve with Beresford in Portugal obtained a double step in promotion in the Portuguese service and a single step up in the British service as an inducement. Thus a captain became a lieutenant colonel and a lieutenant became a major. The first wave of British officers to come out with Beresford were commissioned into the Portuguese army in March and April 1809. Only one British colonel,

Richard Blunt, and one British lieutenant colonel, William Cox, joined Beresford at that time. Later in the year one British major general, John Hamilton, and a number of British lieutenant colonels sign up to serve with the Portuguese army. In contrast, at least eleven British officers became captains in the Portuguese army in March and April 1809. Even larger numbers of British junior officers took up positions in the Portuguese army during the remainder of 1809 and early 1810. *Ordens do Dia do Illustrissimo e Excellentissimo Senhor Guilherme Carr Beresford, 1809* (Lisbon). Lionel S. Challis, 'Roll of British officers serving in the Portuguese army, 1809–1814', *Journal of the Society for Army Historical Research*, Summer 1949, vol. 27 (110), 50–60.

6. See *Marshal Beresford*, ch. 8. Sir Arthur Wellesley had been created Viscount Welling-ton of Talavera on 26 August 1809 following the battle of Talavera on 27 July that year.
7. *WSD*, vol. 6, 477.
8. The other independent Portuguese brigades at the time of Hill's arrival were the 5th brigade of Alexander Campbell (the 6th and 18th line, 6th caçadores) and the 6th brigade of Francis Coleman (7th and 19th line, 2nd caçadores).
9. Portuguese brigades were numbered in accordance with the seniority of the senior line regiment in the brigade. The 1st brigade was commanded by Pack until he reverted to British service on 19 July 1813 (see S.G.P Ward, 'The Portuguese Infantry Brigades 1809–1814', *Journal of the Society for Army Historical Research*, 1975, vol. 53, 103–12). His successor was John Wilson, until he was wounded at the Battle of Nivelle in 1813.
10. The theoretical strength of the Portuguese army was 52,000 (infantry 37,200, caçadores 3,768, cavalry 7,128 and artillery 4,800). Throughout the war, however, regiments were frequently understrength. In addition, there existed the militia and the ordenança (*levée en masse*). See *Marshal Beresford*, 56–71.
11. Benjamin D'Urban, *The Peninsular Journal 1808–1817* (reprint London 1990), 124.
12. Trancoso was Beresford's headquarters (Quartel General) from 25 June until 27 July 1810: *Ordens do Dia* (1810).
13. D'Urban, *Peninsular Journal*, 124.
14. *Ordens do Dia*, 4 July 1810.
15. *Ordens do Dia*, 15 June 1811. Four of the eight soldiers named to be executed by shooting were from the 1st and 16th regiments: José Marques Lourical (1st), Manoel de Oliveira (1st), Manoel da Costa (16th) and Joaquim Antonio (16th).
16. Wellington to Cotton, 16 and 19 August 1810: *WD*, vol. 4, 230 and 233, stating that on 17 August Pack will go to Trancoso and placing cavalry at Trancoso under Pack's orders. This observation would seem to suggest Pack had been somewhere else in the intervening period but his brigade was there on 17 August 1810. D'Urban, *Peninsular Journal*, 132.
17. Wellington to Beresford, 24 and 26 July 1810; TT, MNE CX 204.
18. Synge's notebook is entitled 'Private Memorandum Book Capt. Charles Synge Prince of Wales Own' (hereafter 'Synge Memorandum'). The reference to 'Prince of Wales Own' is to the 10th Hussars of which Synge was a member. I am greatly indebted to Mrs Jane Tottenham for access to the Synge Memorandum and other family papers ('Synge papers'). Mrs Tottenham's late husband Robert E. Tottenham was the great-great-grandson of Charles Synge.
19. Synge does not mention any action with the French on 19 September, but refers to skirmishing at Santa Comba Dao on 21 September and more skirmishing on

22 September before they crossed the river Criz and destroyed the bridge: *Synge Memorandum*.

20. Wellington to Liverpool, 30 September 1810: *WD*, vol. 4, 305.
21. Carew, 'A Gallant Pack', 394.
22. The battle order of the allied army is set out in D'Urban, *Peninsular Journal*, 147–8.
23. While the Portuguese militia regiment of Tomar quickly panicked and gave way, it must be remembered this was only a militia regiment not trained for high intensity fighting of this nature. It was unusual for militia to be used in such a tactical situation, though of course militia were used extensively in the Lines of Torres Vedras. At Buçaco they were with Spry's Portuguese brigade, part of Leith's 5th division, and were probably very unfortunate to be in the path of the French attack hitting home at the juncture of the 3rd and 5th divisions.
24. D'Urban explains exactly where Pack's brigade was situated: 'On his [Spencer's] left the Brigade of Genl. Pack, its left upon the Convent Garden Wall, in the prolongation of the Eastern Front of which and extending beyond the high road of Vit to the front of the Chapel of Santa Anna dos Alvas.' D'Urban, *Peninsular Journal*, 147.
25. *Synge Memorandum*. Lieutenant Colonel Thomas Noel Hill, a brother of Rowland Hill, commanded the 1st Portuguese regiment, part of Pack's brigade.
26. Wellington to Liverpool, 30 September 1810: *WD*, vol. 4, 304–8, at 307. In the same letter he gives Beresford the exclusive credit for having raised, formed, disciplined and equipped the Portuguese army. See *Marshal Beresford*, ch. 9.
27. Willoughby Verner, *History and Campaigns of the Rifle Brigade 1800–1813* (London), vol. 2, 150. The letter quoted is an undated letter by Jonathan Leach, then a captain in the 95th (Rifles) regiment.
28. *Ordens do Dia*, 6 November 1810.
29. *WD*, vol.4, 304-8, at 307.
30. Royal Welch Fusiliers Museum, Acc. 3335, Hamilton to father, 27 October 1810, quoted in Donald E. Graves, *Dragon Rampant, the Royal Welch Fusiliers at War, 1793–1815* (Barnsley 2010), 122.
31. Anthony Hamilton, *Hamilton's campaigns with Moore & Wellington during the Peninsular War* (Troy, New York 1847), 88.
32. Charles Synge. References to this Notebook are courtesy of Mrs Jane Tottenham.
33. Synge gives the route of Pack's brigade on this retreat via Fornos, Condeixa, Pombal, Boa Vista, Batalha, Candeira, Alcantara and Alenquer: *Synge Memorandum*.
34. There was also a third line of fortifications surrounding Sao Juliao da Barra so as to enable the army to embark should it be necessary to do so. A fourth line was also built south of the Tagus in the area of Almada to guard against any attempt to approach the Tagus and Lisbon from the south.
35. *Synge Memorandum*, 10 October 1810.
36. At Coimbra, for instance, the young French officer Jean-Baptiste Barrés reported that the soldiers found plenty of rice, stockfish, coffee, sugar, tea and chocolate, and at Leiria plenty of corn, as well as wine, sugar and cinnamon for mulled wine, and wood to dry out the troops subjected to rain. M. Barrés (ed.), *Memoires of a French Napoleonic Officer: Jean-Baptiste Barrés* (London 1925), 144.
37. Jean-Baptiste-Frederic Koch & Antonio Ventura (eds), *Memorias de Masséna: Campanha de 1810 e 1811 em Portugal* (Lisbon 2007), 101.

38. Maria Antonia Lopes, *Na Rota da 3a invasao francesa: o concelho de Mangualde e as suas vitimas* (Mangualde 2009), 31.
39. Work number 11 was the windmill above the Arruda road intended for a garrison of 300. Number 12 was a rocky bluff above the Arruda road with provision for a garrison of 120. Number 13 was the Fort de Canara, on the paved road to Bucellas, with a garrison quota of 120. See John Grehan, *The Lines of Torres Vedras, the cornerstone of Wellington's strategy in the Peninsular War 1809–12* (Barnsley 2015), 193–4.
40. Wellington to Hill, 15 October 1810: *WD*, vol. 4, 333. Synge refers to the occupation of battery no. 14 on Monte Agraco: *Synge Memorandum*.
41. Wellington to Pack, 12 October 1810: *WD*, vol. 4, 328–9.
42. Synge refers to the investment and a fête at Mafra but it is unclear as to whether he was there: *Synge Memorandum*, 7 November 1810.
43. *Memoir*, 49. See also Beresford to Pack, 1 June 1811 (*Memoir*, 58) in which Beresford writes 'You must have mistaken the tenor of my letter relative to your returning to the British service. I had not the least intention of finding fault with your intention or decision, but really wrote to you in confidence as I thought on the subject, and I think it cannot be long, if you continue in the same mind, before you will have the opportunity, as I think you will soon be circumstanced so as to ask for a British Brigadiership, and you are not likely to be refused.'
44. Brigaded with the 50th and 92nd regiments. The 71st was quartered at Sobreira: *Gavin*, 80.
45. *Gavin*, 78. Note Gavin suggests the encounter with the French grenadier was on 16 October.
46. *Ibid.*, 80.
47. The IX corps consisting of over 8,000 men under the Count d'Erlon reached Masséna's army in December.
48. Synge papers; undated letter to Colonel William Napier following publication of Napier's *History of the War in the Peninsula and in the south of France from the year 1807 to the year 1814* (London 1831), 3 vols. Napier, vol. 3, 384, refers merely to Wellington being 'not quite satisfied with the appearance of his adversary's force, after three hours demonstrations, ordered the troops to retire to their former ground'. Synge in his letter makes the point that this was on Pack's initiative.
49. Wellington to Hill, 19 November 1810: *WD*, vol. 4, 424.
50. D'Urban, *Peninsular Journal*, 20 November 1810, 163.
51. Synge to William Napier, undated letter: Synge papers.
52. D'Urban, *Peninsular Journal*, 22 November 1810, 164.
53. Pack to James Butler, 21 March 1811: *Memoir*, 51.
54. Wellington to Liverpool, 14 March 1811: *WD*, vol. 4, 661–70 at 668.
55. Edward Costello, *The adventures of a soldier; or memoirs of Edward Costello, KSF* (London 1841), 89.
56. Pack to James Butler, 21 March 1811: *Memoir*, 51. The position was dire, notwithstanding Beresford's efforts. Whole regiments were short of men because they were ill from lack of food or forage and in the forthcoming battle at Fuentes de Oñoro, the Portuguese artillery ran out of ammunition, leaving Wellington having to resort to the gathering of French expended shot and recycling it. Wellington to Liverpool, 8 May 1811: *WD*, vol. 4, 791, and Wellington to Beresford, 11 May 1811: *WD*, vol. 5, 5.

57. Wellington to Stuart, 26 February 1811: *WD*, vol. 4, 637.
58. Wellington to Liverpool, 16 March 1811: *WD*, vol. 4, 677.
59. Wellington to Beresford, 25 March 1811 and Wellington to Beresford 27 March 1811: *WD*, vol. 4, 695 and 704.
60. Wellington to Stuart, 30 March 1811: *WD*, vol. 4, 712.
61. Wellington to Stuart, 11 April 1811: *WD*, vol. 4, 743.

Chapter 6: Fuentes de Oñoro and the escape of . . ., 1811

1. John Colville, *The Portrait of a General* (Salisbury 1980), 55.
2. Wellington told his brother William that 'If Boney had been there, we should have been beaten.' Wellington to William Wellesley Pole, 2 July 1811: *WSD*, vol. 7, 176.
3. Wellington to Beresford, 12 May 1811: *WD*, vol. 5, 6.
4. Antoine François Brenier de Montmorand (1767–1832), governor of Almeida from 28 August 1810 to 10 May 1811.
5. Memorandum of arrangements respecting the blockade of Almeida, 14 April 1811: Murray Papers, 85, 99–101.
6. Brigade Order, 17 April 1811: *WD*, vol. 5, 16.
7. Notes by Brigadier General Pack respecting Almeida (hereafter Notes). These were enclosed with a letter from Pack to James Butler, 22 May 1811, reproduced in *Memoir*, 54–7.
8. In fact Brenier was active even before Campbell's division was moved to join Wellington in Fuentes de Oñoro. In his own report on his escape Brenier refers to a sortie on 28 April during which a number of English were killed and four captured. He then refers to another undated sortie against the Portuguese during which he took three prisoners. Report, Brenier to Marechal Marmont, 17 May 1811: *WD*, vol. 5, 768. Wellington himself suggests the picquets were attacked on 7 May, but the source of his information is not clear. Wellington to Liverpool, 15 May 1811: *WD*, vol. 5, 19.
9. Pack to Murray, half past seven, 8 May 1811: *Murray Papers*, 35, 199–200.
10. The Napoleonic franc was a silver coin weighing 5g. A multiplier of four would produce an approximate sterling value today.
11. The reference to Bayard is probably a reference to the Chevalier Bayard, a hero of the sixteenth-century Italian wars, whose relics were used by Napoleon to stimulate and glorify France. Bayard, 'le bon chevalier', was considered the epitome of chivalry 'sans peur et sans reproche'.
12. *Memoir*, 54–7.
13. Baron Eben's Portuguese brigade was at or near Junca to the southeast of Almeida.
14. Wellington to Torrens, 29 August 1810, and Torrens to Wellington, 19 September 1810: *WP* 1/312 and 315. Torrens was military secretary to the Duke of York, commander-in-chief, 1809–14.
15. Wellington to Major General J.O. Vandeleur, 26 April 1813: *WD*, vol. 7, 450–1.
16. Wellington to Beresford, 24 April 1811: *WD*, vol. 4, 770–1.
17. *Gentleman's Magazine*, 1813, vol. 1, 595. His death was reported as 'throwing himself out of a window in a fit of delirium, which caused instant death'.
18. Both the notes and the post-engagement report are contained in *Memoir*, 54–7 and 179–81. The notes were enclosed with a letter of 22 May 1811 to James Butler. The post-engagement report is dated 12 May 1811.

19. Major Thomas Francis Dursbach originally served with the Loyal Lusitanian Legion and subsequently with the 1st Portuguese Regiment. Promoted lieutenant colonel, he commanded the 11th caçadores from 6 June 1811, and distinguished himself at Vitoria.

20. Pack says the French did not fire a shot until daylight: *Memoir*, 56.

21. J.-B. Antoine Marcelin Marbot, *Mémoires du général baron de Marbot* (Paris 1891–2), 3 vols, vol. 3, 471. Heudelet's division was part of Reynier's 2nd corps. In fact Marbot was not correct, for the French briefly invaded Portugal again in 1812.

22. Notes: *Memoir*, 56.

23. Brenier to Marmont, 17 May 1811: *WD*, vol. 5, 770.

24. The promotion was dated 26 May 1811. This means the news of his escape must have reached Napoleon very quickly or the promotion was backdated. Arnauld Divry, *Les noms gravés sur l'Arc de Triomphe* (Paris 2003), 147.

25. The 8th Portuguese regiment led by James Dawes Douglas was part of a Portuguese brigade commanded by Baron Eben (8th and 12th), itself part of Campbell's 6th division.

26. Wellington to Beresford, 11 May 1811: *WD*, vol. 5, 4–5.

27. Wellington to William Wellesley Pole, 15 May 1811: *WSD*, vol. 7, 123–4. Campbell of course did not have 13,000 men at his disposal. He had some 6,000, and Erskine's task was not to watch Almeida.

28. James Tomkinson (ed.), *Diary of a cavalry officer in the Peninsular and Waterloo campaigns 1809–15* (London 1840), 102. Wellington repeated Erskine's assertion of the 4th regiment missing the road in his official report to Liverpool; Wellington to Liverpool, 15 May 1811: *WD*, vol. 5, 18.

29. Campbell was later appointed military governor of Mauritius and finally commander-in-chief of the Madras army. He died in Madras in 1824.

30. Wellington to Major General Alexander Campbell, 15 May 1811: WP 1/332. Wellington remarked to his brother William 'there is nothing on earth so stupid as a gallant officer'. Wellington to William Wellesley Pole, 15 May 1811: *WSD*, vol. 7, 123.

31. *General Orders*, vol. 4, 1812, 173–6.

32. Philip Henry Stanhope, *Notes of conversations with the Duke of Wellington* (London 1888), 89.

33. Wellington to William Wellesley-Pole, 2 July 1811: *WSD*, vol. 7, 175–7.

34. Wellington to Beresford, 4 April 1811: *WD*, vol. 4, 723.

35. Wellington had a personal grievance against Brenier as well. He had lent the Frenchman £500 when the latter was a prisoner in 1809, to be repaid on his return to France. It was not repaid then and allegedly was never repaid.

36. Rory Muir, *Wellington, the path to victory, 1769–1814* (Yale 2013), 425–6.

37. Henry Cadogan to Pack, 9 June 1811: Southampton University Archive, MS 296.

38. Wellington to Masséna, 11 May 1811: *WD*, vol. 5, 3. Note there are two short letters.

39. Wellington to Liverpool, 15 May 1811: *WD*, vol. 5, 18–22.

40. Notes: *Memoir*, 55–7.

41. One witness noted that on the north side of the fortifications a mine with 300 barrels of gunpowder had failed. Thomas Downman, 'Diary of Major Thomas Downman R.H.A. in the Peninsula from 30 April 1811 to 17 August 1812', *Journal of the Society for Army Historical Research*, October–December 1926, vol. 5 (22), 180.

42. Wellington to Beresford, 12 May 1811: *WD*, vol. 5, 6.
43. Wellington to Brent Spencer, 15 May 1811: *WD*, vol. 5, 22. In addition Pack was allocated one regiment of Barbacena's cavalry. Wellington to Spencer, 1 June 1811: *WD*, vol. 5, 63.
44. Wellington to Beresford, 6 April 1811: *WD*, vol. 4, 725.
45. Wellington's correspondence with Beresford in May and June 1811 clearly displays their anxiety regarding desertion. See *WD*, vol. 5. While Beresford's health suffered after, and probably because of the trauma of, Albuera both he and Wellington felt he needed to be in Lisbon to galvanize the Regency.
46. Beresford to Pack, 1 June 1811: *Memoir*, 58–9.
47. Presumably Lieutenant Trench. See Wellington to Stuart, 13 May 1811: *WD*, vol. 5, 9.
48. Beresford to Pack, 1 June 1811: *Memoir*, 58–9. It is noteworthy that Pack's letter from Almeida of 30 May had reached Beresford in Elvas by 1 June.
49. Wellington to Spencer, 29 May 1811: *WD*, vol. 5, 55.
50. Wellington to Spencer, 24 and 29 May 1811: *WD*, vol. 5, 45 and 55.
51. Wellington to Spencer, 10 June 1811: *WD*, vol. 5, 79.
52. Wellington to Beresford, 7 July 1811: *WD*, vol. 5, 141–2.
53. Wellington to Beresford, 7 August 1811: *WD*, vol. 5, 206–7.
54. General Order, 7 October 1811: *WSD*, vol. 7, 227–8.
55. General Order, 16 November 1811, *WSD*, vol. 7, 239.

Chapter 7: Ciudad Rodrigo to Salamanca, 1812

1. General Order, 18 December 1811, Freneda; *General Orders*, vol. 3, 280. Additional payments were made to the men who made the fascines, gabions and piquets.
2. Wellington used reconnaissance officers extensively, most famously perhaps George Scovell, who became proficient at breaking French codes. In 1811 and 1812 one of his most useful spies was Patrick Curtis, an Irish seminarian who was a professor and rector at the Irish College in Salamanca. He ran a spy ring with his seminarians. He was arrested by the French in 1811, but subsequently released. He was imprisoned again as Wellington approached the city in 1812 but rescued by British forces on the taking of the city. His cover was by then completely blown and he had to go into hiding when the French recaptured the city later that year. He later became Archbishop of Armagh: *WD*, vol. 5, 324. Ambrose MacAuley, 'The appointments of Patrick Curtis and Thomas Kelly as Archbishop and Coadjutor Archbishop of Armagh', *Seanchas Ardmacha, Journal of the Armagh Diocesan Historical Society*, 1982, vol. 10, 331–65.
3. Wellington to J. Bissett, Commissary General, 3 January 1812: *WD*, vol. 5, 456.
4. Wellington to Charles Stuart, 8 December 1811, and Wellington to Charles Stuart, 28 March 1812: *WD*, vol. 5, 397–8 and 563–5. 'Subscription for the relief of the UNFORTUNATE SUFFERERS in Portugal, who have been plundered and treated by the French Armies with the most unexampled Savage Barbarity.' See BL X.708, 2695. The administration of the fund proved extremely difficult for Wellington. He appointed a priest, Mr Briscall, to administer it, but Briscall fell ill before being able to do so. Further, both rich and poor Portuguese claimed the right to receive monies and the curates of villages dared not refuse the rich and powerful, a situation that irritated Wellington. As a result, following discussions with the Bishop of Pinhel, Wellington

purchased 276 bullocks to be distributed to the villages in the district, recognizing that those to whom they were given might sell them to the better off, but would thereby still benefit.

5. Lieutenant Colonel Bryan O'Toole. See AHM/DIV/1/14/057/06. O'Toole served with the British army until 1810, when he went with the 39th regiment to Portugal. There he became a major and later lieutenant colonel in the Portuguese service. He lost an arm at Pamplona on 27 July 1813, for which he received a temporary pension of £300. He died at Wexford in 1825.

6. Arrangements for the Assault of Ciudad Rodrigo, 19 January 1812: *WSD*, vol. 7, 253–5.

7. Journal of Caroline Synge, 8 (sic) January 1839, 16. Synge papers.

8. Wellington to Liverpool, 20 January 1812: *WD*, vol. 5, 472–8.

9. *Ibid.*, 475.

10. *Annual Biography and Obituary for the Year 1824*, 345 et seq.

11. Henry Torrens was military secretary to the Duke of York, commander-in-chief. In due course Alten was promoted to lead the Light Division and Clinton the 6th division.

12. Wellington to Torrens, 28 January 1812: *WD*, vol. 5, 486–7.

13. The brigade seems to have been quartered over quite a large area after the capture of Ciudad Rodrigo. Apart from Freixo, it was at Campillo and Ituero (presumably Ituero de Azaba, southwest of Ciudad Rodrigo, adjacent to El Bodon). Oman, *A History of the Peninsular War*, vol. 5, 218.

14. Warre to father, 18 March 1812: William Warre, *Letters from the Peninsula 1808–1812*, 151. Wellington to Hill, 16 March 1812: *WD*, vol. 5, 551.

15. Sir Colin Campbell, 1776–1847. He served with Wellington in India and the Peninsula. Campbell's Peninsular Gold Cross and six clasps did include Badajoz.

16. Synge Papers: Synge to Wellington, 8 June 1847, and Wellington to Synge, 16 June 1847, together with extracts from Synge's notes of the siege.

17. Oman, *A History of the Peninsular War*, vol. 5, 599 and 603, gives the figures for the allied and French armies at Salamanca respectively as 51,939 and 49,646 (officers and men).

18. Wellington to Bathurst, 24 July 1812: *WD*, vol. 5, 754. It should be noted the 4th caçadores sustained serious losses during the day, with sixty-five men killed, injured or missing: AHM /DIV/1/14/057/06. Antonio Mendo Castro Henriques, *Salamanca, Companheiros de Honra* (Lisbon 2004), 75, lists a greater loss with 8 dead, 87 injured and 49 prisoners. The injured included Lieutenant Colonel Keynton Williams and Captain Alexander McGregor, the latter receiving a pension of £100 for his wounds: *Accounts and Papers of the House of Commons*, vol. 13, 220–1.

19. AHM-DIV-1-14-243 -0056.

20. Tomkinson, James (ed.), *Diary of a cavalry officer*, 188. Wellington later confirmed to Marmont in conversation that he had intended to attack at that point in the day, but that Beresford had dissuaded him, pointing out the strength of the French. *Mémoires du Marechal Marmont, Duc de Raguse* (3rd edition, Paris 1857), vol. 5, bk xv, 87. 'J'ai su depuis, par le duc de Wellington, qu'effectivement l'attaque allait avoir lieu quand lord Beresford vint a lui et dit qu'il venait de reconnaitre avec soin et en detail l'armée francaise, qu'elle lui paraissait si bien postée, qu'il serait imprudent de l'attaquer.'

Synge (see below) also implied Beresford dissuaded Wellington from launching an attack at this time.

21. Tomkinson was gazetted a captain in the 16th light dragoons on 3 June 1812.
22. There are a number of good accounts of the battle of Salamanca, historically Oman, *History of the Peninsular War*, vol. 5, and more recently Rory Muir, *Salamanca 1812* (Yale 2001); Mendo Castro Henriques, *Salamanca* (Lisbon 2004); Peter Edwards, *Salamanca 1812. Wellington's year of victories* (Barnsley 2013).
23. Spry's brigade was the 3rd Portuguese brigade. It was made up of the 3rd and 15th line and the 8th caçadores. William Spry, like Pack, had served in the disastrous Walcheren expedition of 1809. He was promoted brevet colonel in 1810 and joined the Portuguese service at the same time as Pack, being appointed a brigadier on 16 August 1810. Spry received the thanks of parliament for his performance at Salamanca.
24. See *Marshal Beresford*, ch. 12.
25. Pack's report is lodged in AHM-Div-1-243-m0056-59. In fact there are two reports by Pack. A printed copy of these has been made by Pedro de Brito, who kindly supplied it to the author. Pedro de Brito has also authored 'Os Anglo-Irlandeses e o fiasco de Denis Pack em Salamanca (1812)' in *XX Colloquio de Historia Militar – A Guerra Peninsular em Portugal (1810–1812)-Derrota e Perseguicao* (Lisbon 2011), vol. II, 1291–1313. Charles Synge's account of the battle was reproduced as 'Captain Synge's experiences at Salamanca, a war memory of a 10th hussar' in *The Nineteenth Century* (July 1912), 54–68. The assistance of Pedro de Brito is gratefully acknowledged here.
26. Battle of Grijo, 10/11 May 1809.
27. Colonel Stubbs to Manoel de Brito Mozinho, adjutant general of the Portuguese army, 9 August 1812: AHM/DIV/1/14/243-m0029. See also Colonel Wade to Lord Grantham, 24 July 1812: *Memoirs: Sir Lowry Cole*, 85–6. Wade wrote: 'our Portuguese Brigade was outflanked and their left obliged to give way. However, they soon recovered.' This would seem to be a reference to Stubbs' Portuguese brigade which formed part of Cole's division, rather than a reference to Pack's independent brigade.
28. Wellington to Bathurst, 24 July 1812: *WD*, vol. 5, 754.
29. *The Nineteenth Century*, 58.
30. AHM-DIV-1-14-243-m0056-60. The reports are dated 2 (Rio Pega) and 25 August 1812. The 243 series also contains the brigade reports on the battle, mostly dated from sometime in August 1812. Many of the reports commend particular officers.
31. Charles Oman (*History of the Peninsular War*, vol. 5, 599) puts the strength of Pack's brigade at Salamanca at 2,605 (85 officers and 2,520 men). It was stated to comprise 2,751 on 5 January 1813, at which stage replacements had been found for the losses sustained in 1812: *WSD*, vol. 7, 521.
32. José Antonio Vidigal. His early career was spent with the 15th regiment before transferring to the 16th regiment. Francisco Quevedo Pizarro was at Salamanca but serving with the 12th regiment. He later commanded the 16th regiment, which may be the reason for Synge's confusion.
33. *The Nineteenth Century*, 59–61. Some men must have been able to load their weapons for Pack refers to the advanced companies firing too soon: AHM-DIV-1-14-243-0056-60.
34. *The Nineteenth Century*, 60.
35. Sir Augustus West (1788–1868). When he retired he went to live in Portugal, before dying in France.

36. Synge's home for recovery was in the Calle de Zamora, where Marshal Beresford was also recuperating at no. 42: *The Nineteenth Century*, 67.
37. Charles Synge was initially a 10th Hussar. He became one of the most decorated Peninsular War veterans, with nine clasps.
38. Carew, 'A Gallant Pack', 391–401.
39. See the reports in AHM-DIV-1-14-243-m0056-60. Pack also praised individual caçadores for their performance at the chapel.
40. William Grattan, *Adventures with the Connaught Rangers, 1809–1814* (London 1902), 251.
41. Mendo Castro Henriques, *Salamanca*, 104–5.
42. Wellington to Bathurst, 24 July 1812: *WD*, vol. 5, 757.
43. Tomkinson (ed.), *Diary of a cavalry officer*, 186.
44. W.F.K. Thompson (ed.), *An Ensign in the Peninsular War, The Letters of John Aitchison* (London 1981), 176. These remarks are extracted from Aitchison's diary.
45. Curiously Pack's name, along with a number of others serving in the Portuguese army, was omitted from the initial resolution passed by the House of Lords. That was later remedied. *Journal of the House of Lords*, vol. 49, 59. See also *Thanks voted by both Houses of Parliament to the Army and Navy with the Replies of those Officers who were addressed in their places, 1801 to 1843* (London 1843), 187.
46. De Brito, *Os Anglo-Irlandeses e o fiasco de Denis Pack em Salamanca*, 11. Fearon, however, did serve as a caçador both before and after 1812.
47. See the reports referred to at n. 27 above.
48. Maurice Girod de l'Ain, *Vie Militaire du General Foy* (Paris 1900). I have used Oman's translation: *History of the Peninsular War*, vol. 5, 472. Foy had been involved in all three French invasions of Portugal, under Junot (1807–08), Soult (1809) and Massena (1810–11).

Chapter 8: The siege of Burgos and the retreat to . . ., 1812

1. Wellington to Stuart, 31 October 1812: *WD*, vol. 6, 141.
2. William Wheeler, *The letters of a soldier of the 51st Light Infantry during the Peninsular War & at Waterloo. 'Vivi Wellington, vivi les Angolese, vivi Les Ilandos and ten thousand other Vivis I cannot think on'*, 91. It is interesting, but not surprising given the long Spanish association with Ireland, that the Madrilenos distinguished between the English and Irish.
3. Wellington to Hill, 8 September 1812: *WD*, vol. 6, 59–60.
4. Wellington to Henry Wellesley, 9 September 1812: *WD*, vol. 6, 66–7.
5. Wellington to Cotton, 9 September 1812: *WD*, vol. 6, 64.
6. For a full account of the siege of Burgos, see Carole Divall, *Wellington's Worst Scrape, the Burgos Campaign, 1812* (Barnsley 2012).
7. James Stanhope, *Eyewitness to the Peninsular War and the Battle of Waterloo, The letters and Journals of Lieutenant Colonel James Stanhope* (Barnsley 2011), 91. Napier refers to a combined total of twenty-six guns and howitzers in the fortress.
8. Brigadier General Dubreton commanded Burgos fortress. He had 9-, 12- and 16-pounders with mortars and howitzers.
9. Napier, *History of the Peninsular War*, vol. 5, 263–4.
10. Instructions for the Attack of the Hornwork, 19 September 1812: *WSD*, vol. 14, 119–20.

11. Tomkinson (ed.), *Diary of a cavalry officer*, 206.
12. Lieutenant Colonels Noel Hill, Neil Campbell and Major Keynton Williams, the latter having recovered from his wounds sustained at Salamanca. Wellington to Torrens, 21 September 1812: *WSD*, vol. 7, 425.
13. Wellington to Beresford, 22 September 1812: *WD*, vol. 6, 87–8. Wellington to Popham, 2 October 1812: *WD*, vol. 6, 101.
14. Wellington to Liverpool, 23 November 1812: *WD*, vol. 6, 174.
15. Wellington to Bathurst, 27 September 1812, Wellington to Hill, 2 October 1812, Wellington to Beresford, 5 October 1812: *WD*, vol. 6, 95, 100 and 104–5.
16. Wellington to Beresford, 5 October 1812: *WD*, vol. 6, 104–5.
17. Wellington to Bathurst, 26 October 1812: *WD*, vol. 6, 133–7. The governor was General Jean Louis Dubreton.
18. George Brown (aka Gustavus Braun) joined the Portuguese army from the 60th regiment in April 1810. He commanded the 9th caçadores at Salamanca, the Pyrénées, the Nivelle and the Nive, where he was badly wounded. See Lewis Butler, *Annals of the King's Royal Rifle Corps*, vol. 2, 112. The 9th caçadores behaved with conspicuous bravery in the assault on the walls of Burgos on 18 October, capturing an outwork before being forced to retreat through lack of support.
19. Memorandum for General Pack, for the blockade of Burgos, 20 October 1812: *WD*, vol. 6, 130–1. See Appendix I.
20. Wellington to Pack, 21 October 1812, 1.30pm: *WD*, vol. 6, 132.
21. Thompson (ed.), *An Ensign in the Peninsular War*, 216.
22. George Burrows, 1st Dragoons, *A Narrative of the Retreat of the British Army from Burgos* (1814), quoted in Edwards, *Salamanca 1812*, 308.
23. Two of the three 18-pounders were abandoned at Villa Toro. Souham to Ministre de la Guerre, 1 November 1812: *WD*, vol. 6, 770, Appendix VI. Oman says all three were found abandoned: *A History of the Peninsular War*, vol. 6, 68.
24. Alexander Dickson, *Journal*, vol. 4, 712, entry for 23 October 1812.
25. Grattan, *Adventures with the Connaught Rangers*, 291–4.
26. Wellington to Beresford, 31 October 1812: *WD*, vol. 6, 140.
27. Hippolyte D'Espinchal, *Souvenirs Militaires 1792–1814* (Paris 1901), vol. 2, refers to his cavalry on crossing the river Tormes surprising two hundred Portuguese, and cutting up 'sabré' almost the entire in revenge for insults they had previously hurled at the French. Since D'Espinchal (5th hussars) was with Soult's army pursuing Hill, and Hill was retiring from Alba, this was presumably a loss suffered by one of the Portuguese regiments with Hill, rather than either Pack's or Bradford's brigade. Hamilton's Portuguese brigade (2nd, 4th, 10th and 14th line) were the reserve behind Alba de Tormes, and this is likely a reference to Portuguese piquets surprised on the crossing of the Tormes on 14 November.
28. Oman, *A History of the Peninsular War*, vol. 6, appendix IV, 747. According to Oman, Portuguese losses on the retreat mirrored British losses (2,374:2,368). He suggests the worst affected was Bradford's Portuguese brigade, which lost 514 men out of 1,645.
29. *Ibid.*, vol. 6, appendix I, 741.
30. Wellington to Liverpool, 23 November 1812: *WD*, vol. 6, 172–5.
31. Wellington to Bathurst, 19 November 1812: *WD*, vol. 6, 164–7.

Chapter 9: Spain and the Pyrénées – an ambition realized, 1813

1. John Malcolm, from 'The Campaign' in *Scenes of War and other poems* (Edinburgh 1828).
2. Wellington to Beresford, 3 October 1809: TT, MNE CX 204.
3. Alexander Henry Craufurd, *General Craufurd and his light division, with many anecdotes, a paper and letters by Sir John Moore, and also letters from the Right Hon. W. Windham, the Duke of Wellington, Lord Londonderry and others* (London 1891), 169.
4. Wellington to Robert Craufurd, 28 January 1811: *WD*, vol. 4, 558.
5. Craufurd, *General Craufurd and his light division*, 173.
6. Correspondence Miller and Beresford, 15 and 27 November 1809, 27 December 1809: TT, MNE CX 206 f. 226 and CX 207, ff. 92 and 152.
7. Denis Pack's memorial in Kilkenny Cathedral refers to him having been 'nine times severely wounded' (see image). There may be some licence in this description, but he was certainly wounded at the battles of Blaauwberg, Buenos Aires (1807 wounded twice), Sorauren, Toulouse and Waterloo.
8. *Gavin*, 88. Pack's lodgings were in Bury Street, London.
9. Wellington to Torrens, 20 December 1812: *WD*, vol. 6, 217.
10. Wellington to Beresford, 29 December 1812: *WD*, vol. 6, 226.
11. Pack to Wellington, 26 April, 1813: *WSD*, vol. 7, 612–13.
12. *Ibid*.
13. Wellington to Pack, 29 April 1813: *Memoir*, 67.
14. Wellington to Pack, 1 May 1813: *WD*, vol. 6, 456–7. Thomas Fermor, later 4th Earl of Pomfret.
15. Pack received royal assent to accept and wear the insignia of an Honorary Knight Grand Cross of the Order of the Tower and Sword on 11 March 1813: *London Gazette*, pt 1, 531.
16. Sir Thomas Graham led the 1st and 5th Divisions and Pack's independent brigade, together with Anson's and Bock's cavalry brigades. In due course he was joined by a Spanish division under Colonel Francisco Longa.
17. Wellington, Memorandum to Sir Robert Kennedy, 5 June 1813: *WD*, vol. 6, 514.
18. See Oman, *History of the Peninsular War*, vol. 6, appendix XI. According to Oman, Pack's brigade suffered 75 losses (killed, wounded or missing) out of a total 921 Portuguese lost at the battle of Vitoria. He calculated British losses at 3,675 and Spanish losses at 562.
19. Graham to Wellington, 23 June 1813: *WSD*, vol. 8, 7–9.
20. Wellington to Bathurst, 22 June 1813: *WD*, vol. 6, 539–43.
21. Beresford's General Orders of 1 July 1813 were published in full in the English newspapers: *The Sun*, 5 August 1813, 4.
22. Carew, 'A Gallant Pack', 395.
23. Pack to Mozinho, AHM/DIV/1/14/256/0082. Major General Edmund Keynton Williams later commanded the 14th Portuguese line before reverting to the British service, in which he later served in Madras.
24. Graham took with him the 1st division, Pack's and Bradford's Portuguese brigades and Anson's cavalry.
25. Pack to Mozinho, 26 June 1813, AHM/1/14/ 243/14/002.
26. Torrens to Wellington, 3 June 1813: *WSD*, vol. 7, 626–7.

27. The departure of Denis Pack and his ADC Charles Synge from the Portuguese service was noted in the Ordens do Dia of 19 July and 22 August 1813, when replacements were promoted. They are referred to respectively as Diniz Pack and Carlos Synge: *Ordens do Dia 1813*, 137 and 159.

28. Katie Louise McCullough, *Building the Highland Empire: The Highland Society of London and the Formation of Charitable Networks in Great Britain and Canada, 1778–1857* (PhD thesis, University of Guelph, 2014), appendix list of members 1817.

29. The Highland brigade had formerly been commanded by Lieutenant Colonel James Stirling of the 42nd regiment. He returned to Scotland in the autumn of 1813.

30. Clinton returned to England, and clearly Dr McGrigor certified this illness. Wellington to Clinton, 22 July 1813: *WD*, vol. 6, 619; Pakenham to Pack, 6 July 1813: Pack correspondence held by the author.

31. Santesteban/Doneztebe: San Estevan in Napier's *History*, vol. 6, 104.

32. Instructions for Major General Pack, Olague, 27 July 1813: *WSD*, vol. 8, 122.

33. Wellington to Bathurst, 1 August 1813: *WD*, vol. 6, 636–44 at 639.

34. Madden's brigade was made up of the 8th and 12th line and the 9th caçadores.

35. The 91st reportedly lost 1 sergeant and 11 men killed, with 6 officers and 97 rank and file wounded on 28 July. *Historical records of the 91st regiment*, 49.

36. *The Royal Military Calendar, or Army service and commission book*, 1820, vol. 4, 298.

37. *Vandeleur*, 112.

38. *Ibid.* The village of Errenteria/Renteria was used to house sick and wounded for the rest of the year.

39. Wellington to Bathurst, 1 August 1813: *WD*, vol. 6, 636–44 at 642.

40. Ordem do Dia, 11 August 1813.

41. Madden had been appointed a brigadier general in the Portuguese army on 13 September 1809. Pack was appointed to a similar rank on 7 July 1810.

42. For an account of Madden's life and career see Mark Thompson (ed.), *The Services of Sir George Allen Madden* (Sunderland 2014). In the course of his career he had been court-martialled when he made allegations of perjury against a fellow officer. He was sentenced to be dismissed from the army, but was allowed to resign. Having rejoined, he was appointed a brigadier general in the Portuguese army in June 1809 (he had served in Portugal with a British force in the 1790s). Early success as a cavalry officer following this appointment had not been sustained, and for not wholly explained reasons Madden's cavalry had failed to join Beresford before Albuera. The difficulties finding remounts for the Portuguese cavalry had led Beresford to reduce that force in effectives in 1812, whereupon Madden had been moved to command an infantry brigade.

43. Subsequent to Pack being injured, the advance on 30 July of the 6th division had been led by Edward Pakenham. Colville was Pack's senior and had already commanded the 3rd division in Picton's absence in 1812. On Picton's return to the Peninsula, Colville had reverted to being a brigade commander and fought in that capacity at Vitoria.

44. Pakenham to Colville, 14 August 1813: quoted in *The Royal Military Calendar or Army Service & Commission Book containing the services and progress of promotion of the generals, lieutenant-generals, major-generals, colonels, lieutenant-colonels, and majors of the army, according to seniority*, 5 vols (London 1820), vol. iv, 115.

45. Madden to Wellington, 19 August 1813: *Royal Military Calendar, 1820*, vol. 4, 115.

46. Wellington to Beresford, 19 August 1813: *WD*, vol. 6, 691. The names are omitted from the published version.
47. Manoel de Brito Mozinho, adjutant general of the Portuguese army, to Madden, 22 August 1813: *Royal Military Calendar, 1820*, vol. 4, 116.
48. *Ibid*.
49. Wellington to Liverpool, 4 August 1813: *WD*, vol. 6, 649.
50. Wellington to Bathurst, 19 August 1813: *WD*, vol. 6, 695.
51. Wellington to Colonel Bunbury, 19 September 1813: *WD*, vol. 11, 121–2.
52. Charles Colville to his father John, 8th Lord Colville, 6 August 1813: Colville, *Portrait of a General*, 136.
53. Pack to Sir J.W. Gordon, 30 October 1813: BL, Add. MS 49507. Gordon was a favourite of the Duke of York and had previously served as the duke's military secretary.
54. Carew, 'A Gallant Pack', 395.
55. Robert Blakeney, *A Boy in the Peninsular War, The Services, Adventures and Experiences of Robert Blakeney, subaltern in the 28th regiment*, ed. J. Sturgis (London 1899), 316.
56. Soult lost fifty-two guns in the retreat from the Nivelle, many of them abandoned in the redoubts. While this figure represents only one third of the number of guns lost at Vitoria, this was a serious setback for Soult.
57. James Dawes Douglas, one of the original twenty-four British officers to go to Portugal in 1809 with Beresford.
58. Clinton to Hill: *WSD*, vol. 8, 358–9.
59. Wellington to Clinton, 16 November 1813: *WD*, vol. 7, 295–6.
60. Wellington to Bathurst, 13 November 1813: *WD*, vol. 7, 131–5. Ainhoué is the old spelling of Ainhoa.
61. Charles J.F. Bunbury (ed.), *Memoir and literary remains of Lieutenant-General Sir Henry Edward Bunbury, bart.* (London 1868), 295.
62. Rue Mazarin.
63. *The Annual Biography and Obituary for the year 1824*, vol. 8, 365.
64. Wellington to Bathurst, 14 December 1813: *WD*, vol. 7, 194–7.
65. Beresford was fulsome in his praise for Hill's actions at St Pierre. Beresford to Lady Anne Beresford, 15 December 1813: Beresford family papers. See *Marshal Beresford*, 197.
66. All three regiments of the brigade, the 42nd, 79th and 91st, have the Battle of the Nive as a battle honour. They crossed the Nive by way of the repaired bridge at Villefranque, probably about 1pm.
67. Sir Robert Macara was criticized for unnecessarily exposing the men to heavy fire at Toulouse by causing them to perform unnecessary manoevres while advancing on Mont Rave: Donald Maclean (ed.), 'A Highland Soldier's Manuscript', *Celtic Review*, June 1916, vol. 10 (40), 289–311. Macara was killed while leading his regiment at Quatre Bras on 16 June 1815.
68. James Anton, *Retrospect on a military life during the most eventful periods of the last war* (Edinburgh 1841), 96–7. He suggested 14 officers, 8 sergeants and 163 rank and file of the regiment were killed at St Pierre.
69. *Ibid*., 56.
70. *Ibid*., 98.

71. George Larpent (ed.), *The Private Journal of F.S. Larpent, Judge Advocate General of the British Forces in the Peninsula* (London 1853), vol. 2, 125.

72. British army officers serving with the Portuguese army were also entitled to the award. It was subject to recommendation by the commanding officer and also subject to the officer in question having fulfilled the requirement that the corps to which he belonged must have been involved in musketry in the engagement in question.

73. *London Gazette*, 7 October 1813. Interestingly Pack is still listed there under 'Portuguese troops', even though he had transferred back to the British army in July 1813. Perhaps this was intended to reflect the latest reward, which was for Vitoria where he still commanded an independent Portuguese brigade.

Chapter 10: Bonaparte's building must now fall . . ., 1814

1. Beresford to Lady Anne Beresford, 5 December 1813: Beresford family papers.

2. Though victorious at Brienne (Blucher), Champaubert (Ossufiev), Château-Thierry (Yorck von Wartenburg) and Montereau (Schwarzenberg) and a number of other engagements in January and February 1814, Napoleon was forced to retreat after each battle.

3. Beresford's force included the 4th, 6th and 7th divisions. Hill had command of the 2nd and Portuguese divisions as well as Morillo's Spaniards, and was supported by Cotton and part of the cavalry. According to Sergeant James Anton, the Highland brigade was located in and around Villefranque from 14 December 1813 until 21 February 1814: Anton, *Retrospect on a military life*, 93. The latter date, if correct, means the march speed was impressive as Villefranque to Laas, where the brigade was reported to be on 24 February, is at least 75 kilometres and armies rarely marched more than 20 kilometres per day in this war.

4. The 6th division's route to join Hill was via Hasparren and St Palais. Movement Orders, 20 and 23 February 1814, quoted in F.C. Beatson, *Wellington, the crossing of the Gaves and the battle of Orthez* (London 1925), 162 and 169.

5. Morillo's Spanish division was now engaged with the siege of Navarrenx, a small fortified town on the Gave d'Oleron 20 kilometres south of Orthez.

6. The bridge over the Gave de Pau at Berenx had been destroyed by Taupin in his retreat to Orthez.

7. Beresford to Lady Anne Beresford, 2 March 1814: Beresford family papers.

8. Maclean, 'A Highland Soldier's Manuscript', 289–311.

9. *Ibid.*, 305.

10. Wellington to Hope, 28 February 2014: *WD*, vol. 7, 335–6.

11. *WSD*, vol. 8, 692 and 695. Pack was named with all the other major generals at the battle so this was a pro forma nomination.

12. Anton, *Retrospect on a military life*, 120.

13. *Ibid.*, 126.

14. Fortescue says that Pack's brigade was in the first line on the right of Beresford's attack on the heights: *The British Army and the Peninsular War*, vol. 6, 229.

15. G.L. Goff, *Historical Records of the 91st Argyllshire Highlanders* (London 1891), 61–2.

16. Richard Cannon, *Historical Record of the 42nd or the Royal Highland Regiment of Foot* (London 1845), 137.

17. British casualties 2,124, Spanish casualties 1,928 and Portuguese casualties 607. These figures reflect killed, wounded and a few missing. This gives an allied total loss of

4659; Wellington to Bathurst 12 April 1814: *WD*, vol. 7, 431. French losses estimated at 3236.

18. The names of the officers lost are given in the regimental histories of the 42nd and 79th regiments. The dead included Captains John Swanson and John Henderson, together with Lieutenants William Gordon, James Watson and Donald Farquharson.

19. Fortescue, *The British Army and the Peninsular War*, vol. 6, 238. A list of the officers lost by the 91st regiment is in *Historical Records of the 91st Argyllshire Highlanders*, 64.

20. Thomas Arthur McKenzie et al. (eds), *Historical Records of the 79th Queen's Own Cameron Highlanders* (London 1877), 52.

21. Soult to Ministre de la Guerre, 11 April 1814: *United Service Magazine*, 1838, vol. 28, 161–3.

22. Wellington to Bathurst, 12 April 1814, Return of killed, wounded and missing: *WD*, vol. 7, 431.

23. Clinton to Beresford, 11 April 1814: *WSD*, vol. 8, 742. Captains Walker and J. Campbell (42nd), Major Cameron (79th) and Captain Walsh (91st).

24. John Malcolm, 'Reminiscences of a campaign in the Pyrénées and the south of France in 1814', *Constable's Miscellany, Memorials of the late war*, 2 vols (Edinburgh 1827). In hospital he was visited by French ladies who supplied him with soups, oranges and sponge cakes. Others supplied him with wine. Initially treated by a French surgeon, he was later looked after by an English surgeon, long-time resident of Toulouse.

25. John Malcolm, *Tales of Field and Flood; with sketches of life at home* (Edinburgh 1829). These tales include some of romantic liaisons, evidence that these were a far from unusual occurrence.

26. Fortescue states that the 42nd advanced on the Mas des Augustins and the 79th on the Calvinet Redoubt with the 91st and the 12th Portuguese in support. Fortescue, *The British Army and the Peninsular War*, vol. 6, 233.

27. Wellington to Bathurst, 12 April 1814: *WD*, vol. 7, 425–31.

28. McKenzie et al., *Historical Records*, 49.

29. Malcolm, 'Reminiscences', vol. 2, 294.

30. McKenzie et al., *Historical Records*, 50. Douglas himself lost a leg at Toulouse. See also Wellington to Bathurst, 12 April 1814: *WD*, vol. 7, 427.

31. Duke of York to Wellington, 14 April 1814: *WSD*, vol. 9, 82–4.

32. Part of a force of 12,000 infantry, together with cavalry and artillery, which sailed from Bordeaux to the United States under Major General Robert Ross.

33. Wellington to Pack, 14 May 1814: *WD*, vol. 7, 479. That is the extent of the letter as recorded in the *Dispatches*, though the full letter quoted in *Blackwood's Magazine* suggests that Wellington stated he hoped Pack would not accept the offer to serve in the American expedition. Carew, 'A Gallant Pack', 395.

34. Wellington to Pack, 26 May 1814: *WD*, vol. 7, 495–6. Given that Pack replied to Wellington's letter of 14 May on 16 May, he cannot have yet gone to Bordeaux. The journey by boat took three to four days normally and by horse longer.

35. Kent along with Sussex comprised the Southern Military District, created along with other military districts in 1793. The Kent district commanded by Pack was 'Kent east of the river Cray and Holwood Hill'. His aide de camp was Brevet Major Edmund L'Estrange and his brigade major was Brevet Major Napier: *Army List for May 1815*, 77.

36. Like other such orders it evolved into hierarchical categories. Wellington, Beresford, Sir John Hamilton, Sir Robert Arbuthnot and Admiral Sir Sidney Smith were Grand Cross. Pack was a Commander of the Order.

37. Appointment as Knight Commander of the Bath (KCB) made 2 January 1815 and reported 15 January 1815: *European Magazine and London Review*, vol. 67, 165. Ceremony reported in the *London Gazette*, 18 April 1815, no. 17004, 726.

38. Pack did not receive a clasp for the siege and capture of Badajoz in 1812, presumably as his brigade was part of the screening force and not involved in the siege itself. Some years later his ADC Charles Synge claimed this right from the Duke of Wellington. See ch. 7 above.

39. *Annual Biography and Obituary 1824*, vol. 8, 366. Presumably the ninth wound recorded on his memorial was that received at Waterloo. See image and text in Appendix II.

Chapter 11: The Waterloo campaign, 1815

1. This is a reference to Denis Pack that appears in Anon., *The personal narrative of a private soldier who served in the 42nd Highlanders for twelve years during the late war* (London 1821), 200–1.

2. The supporters were troops he had been allowed to keep for his own security on Elba. They comprised some 600 of the Old Guard, 300 Corsicans and 100 dismounted Polish Lancers.

3. Wellington to Beresford, 24 March 1815: PRONI, D3030/4464.

4. Perhaps Great Britain's desire to mollify Spain for its loss of Trinidad played a part in her failure to support Portugal's recovery of the area around Olivenza.

5. In Ireland the 42nd was stationed in Kilkenny, while the 79th and 91st were posted to bases in and around Cork city. In each case these regiments recruited Irishmen during Napoleon's Elba interlude.

6. The 1/3rd foot commanded by Major C. Campbell; 1/42nd commanded by Lieutenant Colonel Sir Robert Macara; 2/44th led by Lieutenant Colonel J.M. Hamerton; 1/92nd led by Lieutenant Colonel J.Cameron.

7. Peter Molloy, 'Ireland and the Waterloo campaign of 1815', *Journal of Military History and Defence Studies*, January 2020, vol.1 (1), 69–119. Molloy identifies 224 confirmed Irish personnel out of a total strength of 604 in the 3/1st foot, or 37.08 per cent. See also Philip Haythornthwaite, *Picton's Division at Waterloo* (Barnsley 2016), 52.

8. These included Lieutenant Colonel John Millet Hammerton and Major George O'Malley, commander and second in command of the 2/44th.

9. The Army List for 1814 shows some 250 major generals senior to Denis Pack. Many of these would have been on half pay. Even in 1816 there were still some 200 major generals listed senior to Pack: *A list of all the officers of the army and royal marines on full and half pay with an Index and a succession of colonels 1814 and 1816*, 14.

10. Torrens to Wellington, 16 April 1815: *WSD*, vol. 10, 83–4.

11. Wellington to Torrens, 21 April 1815: *WD*, vol. 8, 38.

12. For instance the 40th regiment arrived back at Spithead from North America on 15 May 1815. After hurriedly taking on supplies, it sailed immediately to Ostend, arriving on 19 May. Marcus de la Poer Beresford, 'The Peninsular romance of Lieutenant Waldron Kelly and Ana Ludovina de Aguilar', *Irish Sword*, vol. 32 (2020), 299–315.

13. James Hope, *Letters from Portugal, Spain and France during the Memorable Campaigns of 1811, 1812 and 1813 and from Belgium and France in the year 1815* (Edinburgh 1819), 218.

14. *Ibid.*

15. See Wellington to Torrens, 21 April 1815: *WD*, vol. 8, 38, in which he wrote 'I must, besides, mention that in the Peninsula I always kept three or four divisions under my own immediate command, which, in fact, was the working part of the army, thrown, as necessary, upon one flank or the other.'

16. Wellington's residence was in the Montague de Parc, near the Richmond home.

17. Captain William Siborne (1797–1849). As well as building two dioramas of the battle of Waterloo, William Siborne was the author of *History of the War in France and Belgium in 1815* (London 1844). One of his sons, Major General H.T. Siborne, later published a selection of the letters elicited by his father: *Waterloo Letters. A collection of accounts from survivors of the campaign of 1815* (London 1891).

18. Anton, *Retrospect on a military life*, 188. Anton refers to Pack waiting impatiently for the 42nd and chiding its commanding officer, the unfortunate Lieutenant Colonel Robert Macara, on his arrival.

19. The park may have been what is now the Parc de Bruxelles, or the Place Royale, or both. Robert Winchester, then a lieutenant in the 92nd Highlanders, refers to 'the park': Winchester to Siborne, 27 February 1837. Charlotte Waldie, a Scots tourist, refers specifically to the 42nd and 92nd regiments marching through the Place Royale: C.A. Eaton, *Waterloo Days, the narrative of an Englishwoman resident at Brussels, June 1815* (London 1888), 22–5.

20. Anton, *Retrospect on a military life*, 188. This is a reference to the Namur gate: see Hope, *Letters*, 226.

21. Robert Winchester to W. Siborne, 27 February 1837: Siborne, *Waterloo Letters*, 385.

22. The 3/1st regiment was moved from Pack's command early in the battle and fought with Kempt's brigade under the overall command of Picton.

23. Anton, *Retrospect on a military life*, 194.

24. The savage nature of this often close combat is all too apparent in the letters to William Siborne. Captain R. MacDonald (1st regiment) to W. Siborne, 14 February 1839; Colonel J. Campbell (42nd regiment) to W. Siborne, 15 March 1838; Lieutenant A. Riddock to W. Siborne, 11 April 1837; and R. Winchester (92nd regiment), 27 February 1837: all in Siborne, *Waterloo Letters*, 373, 376, 380 and 385.

25. Winchester to W. Siborne, 27 February 1837: Siborne, *Waterloo Letters*, 387.

26. Riddock to W. Siborne, 11 April 1837 and Winchester to W. Siborne, 24 November 1834: Siborne, *Waterloo Letters*, 381–3.

27. O'Malley to W. Siborne, 10 May 1837: Siborne, *Waterloo Letters*, 379.

28. Haythornthwaite, *Picton's Division*, 113. See also *British Army, facts*, 224. The enormity of the losses suffered by the 42nd regiment is apparent when one considers that it had suffered similarly at Toulouse a year earlier. In effect an entire regiment had been killed or wounded in the fighting in April 1814 and June 1815.

29. Hope, *Letters*, 233.

30. *The Globe*, Saturday, 8 July 1815, 3.

31. Henry George Wakelyn Smith, *The autobiography of Lieutenant-General Sir Harry Smith* (London 1903), ch. 25. Captain Charles Gore of the 43rd regiment became

ADC to Kempt in 1813 while in Spain, having previously served General Andrew Barnard in the same capacity.

32. Wellington to Bathurst, 19 June 1815: *WD*, vol. 8, 146–51.

33. Carew, 'A Gallant Pack', 396. The language used here by Pack is reminiscent of his words when given command of the blockade of Almeida; see ch. 6 above.

34. In 1815 the Netherlands consisted of the modern-day Netherlands, Belgium and Luxembourg.

35. Report of Major General Sir James Kempt to Wellington, 19 June 1815: *WSD*, vol. 10, 535–7.

36. *Memoir*, 86, reportedly taken from War Office records. Siborne puts the quote slightly differently. Instead of referring to troops having given way on the right and left, which would imply *British* troops had given way, Siborne says '92nd, you must charge – all in front of you have given way!', which could be a reference to the Dutch-Belgian troops. Siborne, *History of the War in France and Belgium*, 261. Siborne's source may have been Lieutenant James Hope of the 92nd (Highland) regiment, whose *Letters* had first been published in Edinburgh in 1819 (revised edition, Heathfield 2000), 253. Hope, *Letters*, 247, also mentions 'the troops in front have given way!'.

37. Hope, *Letters*, 247.

38. *The Royal Military Calendar or Army service and commission book, 1820*, vol. 4, 243.

39. Charlotte Anne Eaton & Jane Waldie Watts, *Narrative of a Residence in Belgium During the Campaign of 1815: And of a Visit to the Field of Waterloo* (London 1817), 142. See also Eaton, *Waterloo Days*, 69.

40. Two of Denis Pack's first cousins served in the British army in a medical capacity. Richard and Percy were both sons of the Revd Richard Pack, brother of Denis's father, the Revd Thomas Pack. Richard's son Thomas was also a doctor. Percy served as a surgeon with the 40th regiment and Thomas was an assistant-surgeon with the 21st regiment. The 40th regiment was at Waterloo but the 21st was not there. A distant cousin, Major Robert Packe, Royal Horse Guards, was killed at Waterloo.

41. John Goldworth Alger, *Napoleon's British visitors and captives 1801–1815* (London 1904), 196–7. At Verdun there was an English club and an Irish club; gaming was rife and led to debts, insolvency and imprisonment in the debtor's prison for some. Other entertainments included dancing, singing, amateur theatricals, horse races and cock-fights.

42. For an account of the sufferings of prisoners in La Bitche see Joshua Done, 'Narrative of the Imprisonment and adventures of Joshua Done in various parts of France', *London Magazine*, January 1826, vol. 4, 26–37.

43. Lloyds Patriotic Fund and the Committee for the Relief of British Prisoners of War in France both sought to alleviate hardship and facilitate making monies available to prisoners through banking contacts. Sir Stephen May was the illegitimate son of Sir James Edward May. Both represented the borough of Belfast in parliament. Stephen May is not listed as either an agent or a member of the Charitable Committee at Verdun. See Elodie Duché, 'Charitable Connections, Trans national financial networks and relief for British prisoners of war in Napoleonic France, 1803–1814', *Napoleonica, La Revue*, 2014/3 (no. 21), 74–117.

44. George B. L'Estrange, *Recollections of Sir George B. L'Estrange* (London 1874), 70, 73. Edmund's cousin, Guy Carleton L'Estrange , a major in the 31st foot, was also

captured in the Peninsula and interned in 1809 at Verdun: Steven Brown, 'Register of British Officers held at Verdun 1804–13', *Napoleon Series* (March 2013).

45. Report of Major General Sir James Kempt to Wellington, 19 June 1815: *WSD*, vol. 10, 537.

46. *London Gazette*, 22 June 1815, 1,214, reprint of the dispatch dated 19 June 1815.

47. *The Battle of Waterloo, containing the accounts published by authority Britain & Foreign and other relative documents with circumstantial details, previous and after the battle* (London 1815), 483.

48. Napoleon II was deposed after three days by the provisional government.

49. Kempt's brigade was now commanded by Sir John Keane, who had served both in the Peninsula and in North America.

50. Convention of St Cloud, 3 July 1815.

51. The Treaty of Paris, 20 November 1815, provided for occupation for up to five years. In the event only three years was considered necessary, and the troops were removed following the Treaty of Aix-la-Chapelle in 1818.

52. James Hope, *The military memoirs of an infantry officer 1809–1816* (Edinburgh 1833), 464. The fourth battalion of the Royals must have joined Pack's brigade after Waterloo, for only the third battalion formed part of his brigade there. The third battalion of the Royals remained in France, where they formed part of the 3rd infantry division under Sir Charles Colville, based at Valenciennes.

Chapter 12: The occupation of France, 1815–18

1. On 8 January 1816 Pack was appointed colonel of the York Chasseurs, a regiment formed from condemned prisoners. The regiment was disbanded in 1819 after serving in the West Indies, where it suffered dreadfully from mortality due to fever.

2. Wellington to Bathurst, 23 October 1815: *WD*, vol. 12, 669.

3. The Second Treaty of Paris (20 November 1815) confirmed the original Treaty of Paris (30 May 1814) but with a number of modifications, including the provision for an occupying force of northern and northeastern France at France's expense. A demilitarized zone was created between the army of occupation and the French army, though France was permitted to garrison a number of towns within the area of occupation, including Calais.

4. See 'Convention concluded in conformity to the Fifth Article of the Principal Treaty, relative to the occupation of a Military Line in France by an Allied Army': *General Orders*, compiled by Lieutenant Colonel Gurwood (London 1837), 518–22. The force was spread out over the departments of Pas de Calais, Nord, Ardennes, Meuse, Moselle, Lower and Upper Rhine.

5. The inclusion of a Hanoverian contingent provided an additional five thousand men to the force under direct British control since George III was king of both the United Kingdom of Great Britain and Ireland and the newly created Kingdom of Hanover (previous to 1814 the Electorate of Hanover).

6. *General Orders*, 529–30. Two good accounts of the allied occupation of northern France are Thomas Dwight Veve, *The Duke of Wellington and the British army of occupation in France, 1815–1818* (Westport, CT 1992), and Christine Haynes, *Our Friends the Enemies. The occupation of France after Napoleon* (Cambridge, MA 2018).

7. The building of these fortresses was funded by France, Great Britain and the United Netherlands. The latter was made up of what are today the Netherlands, Belgium and Luxembourg.
8. *General Orders*, 476–8.
9. Gareth Glover (ed.), *The Correspondence of Sir Henry Clinton in the Waterloo Campaign* (Godmanchester 2015), vol. 2, 224–5.
10. *Ibid.*, 239.
11. *Ibid.*, 259.
12. See Veve, *The Duke of Wellington and the British army of occupation*, 71.
13. Reviews were held twice a year, usually in the spring and autumn. These were the subject of regimental returns. The autumn review involved a large number of units from different brigades. In 1816 and 1817 this review was held in the neighbourhood of Denain between Cambrai and Valenciennes, organized by Sir George Murray, Wellington's quartermaster-general: see BL, Add. Ms. 35060, f.453.
14. *Dutch Mail*, 9 November 1816, 2. The *Morning Post*, however, referred to hailstones and a deluge: 5 November 1816, 2.
15. 6 May 1818, NA WO 27/141 and 12 October 1818, WO 27/145.
16. Pack to Wellington, 8 and 9 January 1816: *Memoir*, 98 and 99.
17. Lieutenant Colonel Jonathan Leach, *Rough sketches of the life of an old soldier: during a service in the West Indies; at the siege of Copenhagen in 1807; in the Peninsula and the south of France in the campaigns from 1808 to 1814 with the Light Division; in the Netherlands in 1815; including the battles of Quatre Bras and Waterloo: with a slight sketch of three years passed by the army of occupation in France* (London 1831), 401.
18. *United Service Journal and Naval and Military Magazine*, 1829, pt I, 321.
19. Leach, *Rough sketches*, 401.
20. *General Orders*, 479–80.
21. The regiments of foot returned to Britain and Ireland in 1817 were the 3/1st, 21st, 27th, 40th, 81st and 88th: Veve, *The Duke of Wellington and the British army of occupation*, 116.
22. Pack was reported to have landed at Dover on 10 February 1816: *The Star*, 23 February 1816.
23. Elizabeth, Marchioness of Waterford, is buried in Clonegam churchyard at Curraghmore.
24. 2nd Marquis of Waterford to Lady Elizabeth Beresford, 14 April 1816: *Memoir*, 100.
25. William de la Poer Beresford, Archbishop of Tuam, to John Poo Beresford, 3 July 1816: North Yorkshire Archives, ZBA 21/1 f.54.
26. William de la Poer Beresford (1743–1819) was the younger brother of the 1st Marquis of Waterford. He was Bishop of Dromore (1780–82), Bishop of Ossory (1782–1794) and Archbishop of Tuam (1794–1819). He was created Lord Decies in 1812.
27. See *Memoir* for a number of these letters.
28. Pack to Lady Elizabeth, 20 May 1816: *Memoir*, 104.
29. Pack to Lady Elizabeth, 26 May 1816: *Memoir*, 104–6.
30. Pack to Lady Elizabeth, 26 May 1816: *Memoir*, 105. Pack re-employed the Parisian chef later in 1818 at three Napoleons per month. See Pack to Lady Elizabeth, 30 September 1818: *Memoir*, 118.
31. In any event Pack was senior to both Bradford and O'Callaghan.
32. Pack to Lady Elizabeth, 15 May 1816: *Memoir*, 103.

33. Lord John George Beresford (1773–1862), later (1822) Archbishop of Armagh and Primate of All Ireland.

34. Beresford to Pack, 2 November 1816: *Memoir*, 110. In fact Marshal Beresford was in Brazil at the time of the marriage. He did not return to Portugal from Brazil until September 1816.

35. www.geni.com describes Arthur as born in Kirkheaton, Yorkshire. There is no obvious connection between either the Packs or the Beresfords and Kirkheaton. Perhaps the Packs were visiting the area and the baby was born prematurely. On the other hand the *Memoir* states that Arthur was born in London: *Memoir*, 111. The Duke of Wellington agreed to stand as young Arthur's godfather. In due course Arthur followed his father into the army, becoming a career soldier.

36. Wellington to Liverpool, 20 October 1810: *WD*, vol. 4, 344. This engagement was near Sobral de Monte Agraco.

37. Reynell to Pack, 14 December 1816: *Memoir*, 111–12.

38. *Memoir*, 112–13. The new colours of 1817 were themselves retired and placed on the memorial to Sir Denis Pack in St Canice's Cathedral in Kilkenny when the 71st regiment was stationed in that city in 1837.

39. The problem of adjournments was exacerbated by the size of some courts martial where upwards of a dozen officers sat on the court.

40. *General Orders*, 513.

41. Charles James (ed.), *A Collection of the charges, opinions and sentences of General Courts Martial as published by authority from the year 1795 to the present time* (London 1820), 751–4.

42. *Evening Mail*, 17 September 1817.

43. Pack to Wellington, 18 June 1818, and Wellington to Bathurst, 26 June 1818: *Memoir*, 114–16.

44. Wellington to Bathurst, 5 October 1818: *WSD*, vol. 12, 726.

45. Pack to Bartholemew Pack, 28 July 1818: *Memoir*, 116.

46. Carew, 'A Gallant Pack', 399.

47. Pack to Lady Elizabeth, 27 and 30 September 1818: *Memoir*, 117 and 118. The King of Prussia also favoured a review. See Pack to Lady Elizabeth, 2 October 1818: *Memoir*, 119.

48. Pack to Lady Elizabeth, 2 and 10 October 1818: *Memoir*, 119 and 121.

49. James Butler, second son of the 19th Earl of Ormonde and subsequently 1st Marquess of Ormonde. See Pack to Lady Elizabeth, 10 October 1818: *Memoir*, 121.

50. The Emperor of Austria did not travel for the reviews.

51. Pack to Lady Elizabeth, 26 and 27 October 1818: *Memoir*, 128–9. The Napoleon, often referred to as a 'nap', was a gold coin produced in 20 and 40 franc denominations.

52. Pack to Wellington, 29 October 1818: *Memoir*, 130.

53. *General Orders*, 500.

54. *Ibid.*, 517.

Chapter 13: A peacetime appointment . . ., 1819–23

1. *London Gazette*, vol. 2, 1,475. General Gore Browne had served in South America in 1807 and led the force which stormed Montevideo. He resigned the post of Lieutenant

Governor of Plymouth in 1819 on being appointed lieutenant general. *Gentleman's Magazine*, January–June 1843, new series, vol. 19, 534.

2. Edward Pellew, Viscount Exmouth (1757–1833), was made even more famous as captain of the *Indefatigable* (the namesake of a vessel he actually commanded in 1795) in C.S. Forester's Horatio Hornblower novels.

3. Sir Thomas Hardy was at that time commander-in-chief of the South America Station.

4. Pack to Lady Elizabeth, 26 August 1819: *Memoir*, 133. At the time the Packs also employed a children's nurse, Elizabeth Henshaw, who died in 1861.

5. The date the Pack family moved into the governor's house is uncertain for Anne Elizabeth was reported to have been born in the citadel (*Memoir*, 134) whereas Elizabeth Catherine is stated to have been born in the governor's house. Both the governor's house and that of the lieutenant governor were in the citadel. See *Edinburgh Magazine and Literary Miscellany*, 1822, vol. 89, 137. Anne Elizabeth married the Revd George Mapletoft Paterson in 1869 and died in 1889.

6. Wellington himself visited Plymouth in September 1819, at which time he was presented with the freedom of the city, awarded to him in 1815. After Pack's death Wellington wrote to Lady Elizabeth requesting her to give up the house whenever it was convenient and stating that it had given him great pleasure to be able to contribute to their comfort. Wellington to Lady Elizabeth, 5 November 1823: *Memoir*, 164. See also Pack to Wellington, 25 October, 6 November and 24 December 1819: WP1/633/13, 634/8 and 636/28.

7. Cameron to Somerset, 10 November 1823: WP1/775/11.

8. Greenwood Cox & Hammersley to Lord Fitzroy Somerset, 5 November 1823: WP1/775/7.

9. *Galignani's Messenger*, The spirit of the English Journals: 1819/2, 3.

10. Pack to Wellington, 29 January 1820: WP1/637/14.

11. Pack to Wellington, 9 March 1820: WP1/641/8.

12. See *Memoir*, 135.

13. Louisa Hope, née Louisa Beresford, wife of Thomas Hope the noted author, furniture designer and collector. After Hope's death she married Marshal Viscount Beresford, her first cousin. Archbishop John George Beresford, Primate of All Ireland from 1822 to 1862 (1773–1862), was a brother of Lady Elizabeth Pack. Lord George Thomas Beresford, not to be confused with the Primate, was a general and comptroller of the royal household from 1812 until 1830. His London residence was at 106 Gloucester Place. Poo Beresford, like the marshal, was a natural child of the 1st Marquis of Waterford before his marriage. His London residence was 48 Harley Street. Harley Street was then very much part of a fashionable residential area but also favoured by painters, perhaps because of the commissions available. William Beechey is variously described as living at 13 and 18 Harley Street, J.M.W. Turner at 47 Queen Anne Street, Henry Fuseli at 72 Queen Anne Street and Allan Ramsay with Lady Nelson at 62 Queen Anne Street. Mr and Mrs Thomas Hope had a house in Duchess Street, while Marshal Beresford resided in Wimpole Street, which runs parallel to Harley Street, and later the marshal lived in Cavendish Square.

14. Lieutenant Pack of the 13th dragoons was injured at Waterloo and Major Robert (Roy) Packe of the Horse Guards was killed there. See Charles Dalton, *The Waterloo Roll Call with biographical notes and anecdotes* (London 1904) and John Booth, *The Battle*

of Waterloo (London 1816), 160. George H. Pack was listed as in the Netherlands; The Waterloo Roll Call with biographical notes and anecdotes, 75.

15. See *Edinburgh Gazette*, 25 December 1821. Later in life, as a captain in the 84th regiment, Anthony Pack served in the West Indies, where he became colonel of the Jamaica militia. According to the *Freeman's Journal*, Anthony Pack was an eccentric and died in penury in Kilkenny on 25 November 1857, notwithstanding possessing £4,000–£5,000 in ready money: *Freeman's Journal*, 30 November 1857.

16. *The Globe*, 25 April 1820; *The Sun* 30 April 1821. The marking of the king's official birthday was a custom that had begun in 1748, so as to avoid having to mark celebrations outdoors in bad weather on the actual birthday of George II, 9 November.

17. *The Globe*, 21 November 1820; *Morning Post*, 21 August 1822; *The Sun*, 28 October 1822.

18. *The Star*, 7 May 1821, 3.

19. Pack to Lady Elizabeth, 10 May 1820: *Memoir*, 134–5.

20. Pack to Lady Elizabeth, 8 May 1820: *Memoir*, 134.

21. Elizabeth Conyngham, later Marchioness Conyngham. She was born Elizabeth Denison, the daughter of a wealthy banker. When the king abandoned his attempt to secure a divorce, Queen Caroline ultimately accepted a financial settlement.

22. The nature of the illness in 1820 is unclear, although Peter Carew suggested it was caused by severe pain in the head due to his old wound: Carew, 'A Gallant Pack', 400. *The Sun*, 26 October 1820, 4, referred to Pack recovering from 'his late severe indisposition'. Pack was reported to have attended the public examination of officers at the Royal Military College during the Christmas vacation in 1820: *Morning Post*, 16 February 1821, 4.

23. Exmouth to Pack, 22 October 1820: *Memoir*, 136–7. Pack had of course served with both Hill and Combermere (Stapleton Cotton) in the Peninsula.

24. Pack to Lady Elizabeth, 21 May 1820: *Memoir*, 136.

25. Marshal Beresford to Elizabeth Pack, 10 April 1823: Beresford family papers. A figary is a term not much used in the twenty-first century but means a 'whim'.

26. Quoted in Harold Livermore, 'Life of Beresford', unpublished: NAM 2007-03-83. The marshal did in fact marry his first cousin, Louisa Hope (née Beresford) in 1832, following the death of Thomas Hope.

27. Pack to Lady Elizabeth, 9 July 1821: *Memoir*, 138–9. Napoleon had died on 5 May 1821 and Crokat delivered the news in England on 4 July. The autopsy had diagnosed stomach cancer, though contemporary reports also suggested arsenic poisoning.

28. Arthur's was a non-political club established in 1811. It closed its doors in 1940 but the clubhouse, at 69 St James's Street, finished in 1827, now houses the Carlton Club.

29. *Memoir*, 139–41.

30. The cost has been put at £238,000 including £138,000 out of the indemnity money received from France: See brightonmuseums.org.uk.

31. Pack to Lady Elizabeth, 13 and 16 July 1821: *Memoir*, 141 and 142.

32. Pack to Lady Elizabeth, 20 July 1821: *Memoir*, 143–4. Prince Esterhazy was a Hungarian prince in the service of the Hapsburg Empire, who was appointed ambassador to the United Kingdom in 1815.

33. Pack to Lady Elizabeth, 16 July 1821: *Memoir*, 142.

34. Pack to Lady Elizabeth, 23 July 1821: *Memoir*, 146.

35. Pack to Lady Elizabeth, 23 and 25 July 1821: *Memoir*, 146 and 148.

36. *Lightning* was subsequently renamed *Royal Sovereign King George the Fourth*.
37. The port was still under construction in 1821, building works having started four years previously. Kingstown again became Dun Laoghaire in 1920.
38. *Dublin Evening Post*, 4 September 1821, 1. An obelisk in granite was erected in Dun Laoghaire in 1823 to commemorate the visit. Several major donors, including the Archbishop of Armagh and the Lord Lieutenant, donated £113 15*s* each. Marshal Beresford donated £50, Daniel O'Connell £22 15*s*, while junior officers gave between £1 and £5. Other subscribers gave the same as Pack or double this sum at £11 7*s* 6*d*. These unusual amounts may have arisen because of the difference in value between the English pound and the Irish pound. At times £13 in Irish money was worth £12 in English money. In 1821 the discount was 7.5 per cent.
39. Elizabeth Catherine married Sir John William Hamilton Anson in July 1842 at St Marylebone Church, where her parents had been married in 1816. They had eleven children and she died in 1903.
40. *British Press*, 28 May 1822. Reportedly they stayed at Marshall Thompson's Hotel, Cavendish Square: *The Sun*, 27 May 1822. En route they stayed at the New London Inn, Exeter: *Saunders's News-Letter*, 31 May 1822, 1.
41. *Morning Post*, 29 May 1822, 2.
42. Both hotels were under the ownership of John Williams at the time. See leamingtonhistory.co.uk/the-bedford-hotel.
43. The attraction at Leamington Spa was the saline springs. In 1814 the royal pump rooms and baths were opened to cope with increasing numbers of visitors.
44. Pack to Lady Elizabeth, 8 June 1822: *Memoir*, 152.
45. Pack to Lady Elizabeth, 10 June 1822: *Memoir*, 153.
46. See http://booty.org.uk/booty.weather/climate/histclimat.htm by Martin Rowley.
47. Pack to Lady Elizabeth, 10 June 1822: *Memoir*, 154.
48. Celebrations of the victory at Waterloo seem to have kicked off following the return of the army of occupation to Great Britain in 1818. In 1820 the Prince Regent reviewed a military parade in St James's Park: *The Times*, 19 June 1820. Balls and dinners were held throughout the British Isles for many years, in some cases including re-enactments of the battle. From 1816 onwards Waterloo had been celebrated in France by the occupying forces, much to the chagrin of the French. See Haynes, *Our Friends the Enemies*, 74–5 and 80.
49. It is not known whether Pack received an invitation to the dinner in 1822. No reference has been found to Pack attending the 1823 dinner, though he could have done so shortly before his death. Marshal Beresford would not have received an invite as, much to his chagrin, he was not at Waterloo but back in Portugal with the Portuguese army. However, the Marshal was invited and attended the dinner in 1841.
50. Brydges was married to Lady Isabella Anne Beresford, while Lord John Beresford was her brother.
51. Pack to Lady Elizabeth, 15 June 1822: *Memoir*, 156. The 84th regiment (York & Lancaster) was raised in 1793.
52. Marshal Beresford to Lady Elizabeth Pack, 13 July 1822: *Memoir*, 160.
53. This would seem to have been the Royal 1st Devon Yeomanry or possibly the North Devon Yeomanry, otherwise known as the Royal North Devon Hussars.
54. Plymouth Archives, Reference 1/576.

55. The departure from Dublin of Sir Denis and Lady Pack was noted in *Saunders's News-Letter*, 13 February 1823.
56. Marshal Beresford to Elizabeth Pack, 10 April 1823: Beresford family papers.
57. *Annual Biography and Obituary*, vol. 8, 367. The *Memoir* suggests at p. 160 that he died at Marshal Beresford's house in Cavendish Square, but at that time 16 Cavendish Square belonged to George Watson Taylor. Marshal Beresford only purchased no. 16 in 1824. See *Survey of London*, Bartlett School of Architecture, University College London.
58. Beresford sailed eventually on HMS *Partheon*, disembarking in Lisbon on 10 October 1823.
59. Beresford to Wellington, 29 July 1823: WP1/767/17. That letter refers to Lady Pack's appreciation for the note sent by Wellington, but Wellington's communication itself has not been found. However, Peter Carew in his article on Pack provides the words quoted here: Carew, 'A Gallant Pack', 401.
60. Pack's remains were taken to Dublin by sea from Bristol: *Morning Post*, 12 August 1823.
61. *Saunders's News-Letter*, 12 August 1823 (taken from the *Carlow Paper*), courtesy of the British Newspaper Archive. The general's nephew and ADC Captain Anthony Pack was with the mourners. The cortège stopped at Lennon's Inn in Carlow.
62. The marshal was in Portugal between October 1823 and May 1824.
63. Marshal Beresford to Elizabeth Pack, 21 August 1823: Beresford family papers In addition to property in England, Pack also held some French funds.
64. Marshal Beresford to Elizabeth Pack, 20 September 1823: Beresford family papers
65. On 5 July 1825. Henry Parnell, *On Financial Reform* (1830), 384.
66. Marshal Beresford to Elizabeth Pack, 16 June 1825 Beresford family papers.
67. Marshal Beresford to Elizabeth Pack, 27 May 1825: Beresford family papers.
68. *Parliamentary Papers, Estimates of Army Services for the year 1831*, vol. 13, 13. *Aberdeen Press and Journal*, 8 May 1844. Pack's old friend and fellow Kilkenny man, James Butler, Marquess of Ormonde, supported the application of Anna Catherine Pack. She died aged seventy-six in April 1844: *Dublin Evening Mail*, 24 April 1844, 2.
69. Sir Francis Chantrey (1781–1841). His works included a statue of George IV, placed in Trafalgar Square. He also executed monuments of two of Denis Pack's comrades who had died in the Peninsula, Major General Daniel Hoghton, who fell at the battle of Albuera, and Colonel Henry Cadogan, commander of Pack's old regiment, the 71st, who died at the battle of Vitoria. Both these monuments are in St Paul's Cathedral, London.
70. *Enniskillen Chronicle and Erne Packet*, 2 July 1829; *Dublin Morning Register*, 26 June 1829.
71. See Appendix I.
72. The Lord Lieutenant was Lord Mulgrave. His speech is reported in *United Service Journal and Naval and Military Magazine*, 1837, pt 2, 419 et seq.
73. The colours were placed over the memorial on 16 June 1837. At the time the 71st regiment was stationed in Kilkenny. *Memoir*, 164.
74. Sir Thomas Reynell succeeded his brother Richard as baronet in 1829. Sir Thomas died in 1848. Their father, another Thomas, had been killed while serving in the army at the battle of Saratoga. Thomas ultimately became colonel of the 71st regiment in

1841, the regiment commanded both by Denis Pack and by Reynell himself during the Napoleonic wars.

75. Pack to Lady Elizabeth, 13 July 1821: *Memoir*, 140–1.

76. Marshal Beresford to Elizabeth Pack, 31 December 1830: Beresford family papers.

77. Last will and testament of William Carr, Viscount Beresford; probate granted 21 February 1854: NA, PROB/11/2185/399.

78. Lieutenant Colonel Arthur John Reynell-Pack CB (1817–1860), 7th regiment of foot.

79. Denis William Pack was a captain in the Royal Artillery. The royal warrant permitting him to assume the name and bear the arms of Beresford is dated 23 March 1854: *Edinburgh Gazette*, 28 March 1854, 254. The lands in question were at Fenagh, County Carlow.

80. Henry Hardinge to Elizabeth Reynell (she had remarried in 1831), 26 April 1834: Pack-Beresford private papers.

81. Ron McGuigan & Robert Burnham, *Wellington's Brigade Commanders, Peninsula & Waterloo* (Barnsley 2017), 225.

82. *British Army, facts*, 259.

83. Pack was awarded the freedom of Kilkenny in 1811, of Cork in 1814 and of Waterford in 1817 (3 October). Kilkenny and Waterford presented Pack with gold freedom boxes, while that from Cork was of silver. Additionally the citizens of Kilkenny subscribed the sum of £355 14*s* 6*d* which was used to acquire a splendid candelabra on which were inscribed the reasons for the gift in 1814.

84. Granted 13 December 1814. See Sir Bernard Burke, *The general armory of England, Scotland, Ireland and Wales* (London, 1884), 769. These records are now digitalized by NLI.

85. Wellington to Bathurst, 12 April 1814: *WD*, vol. 8, 425–37 at 428.

86. *Dublin Morning Register*, 26 May 1840. This article in fact dealt with the debut/coming out of Anne Elizabeth Pack in London, a highly fashionable event. It is noticeable that Pack does not appear in J.P. Knight's painting 'Heroes of Waterloo'. This may well be because the painting was undertaken some years after Pack's death and not engraved until the 1840s.

87. *Naval and Military Gazette and Weekly Chronicle of the United Service*, 31 October 1835, 22.

88. Pack's rapport with the Highlands and its people is evidenced by the fact that he was one of the initial members of the Highland Society incorporated in 1816 (56 Geo. III). A charity devoted to maintaining the traditions and culture of the Highlands, its activities range from supporting the war widows of Scottish regiments to the collection of Gaelic manuscripts and the preservation of the kilt.

89. Anton, *Retrospect on a military life*, 96. Anton suggests, however, that by the time this alternative route had been negotiated, it fell to another regiment, the 92nd, to face the designated French force.

90. Anton, *Retrospect on a military life*, 224.

91. *Highland Light Infantry Chronicle*, January 1906, vol. 6 (3), 102. Fraser joined as a private aged sixteen. For his bravery he was commissioned an ensign and became adjutant of the battalion. He died in 1824.

92. Anton, *Retrospect on a military life*, 288.

Bibliography

Manuscripts

United Kingdom
University of Southampton:
   Ms 61 (Wellington Papers). WP1/633, WP1/634, WP1/636, WP1/637, WP1/641, WP1/767, WP1/775, WP1/682
   Ms 296. Papers of Denis Pack and Thomas Reynell
British Library:
   Add Ms 35060
   Add Ms 49507
National Archives (Kew):
   PROB/11/2185/399
   WO 1/904
   WO 28
   WO 211/5
National Army Museum:
   NAM 1971-02-33-533-12
National Library of Scotland:
   Murray Papers
Public Record Office of Northern Ireland:
   D664/A/21
   D3030/4464

Ireland
National Archives:
   CSO/RP/1825/1426
National Library of Ireland:
   Ms 106
Waterford City Registers and Records

Privately held papers
Beresford family papers
Synge papers; the papers of Captain Charles Synge (private collection)

Portugal
Arquivo Historico Militar:
   DIV/1/14/CX 162
   DIV/1/14/CX 243
   DIV/1/15/057
   DIV/1/243/m0056-060

DIV/1/14/002/59
DIV/1/14/057/06-m0001-2
DIV/1/14/243-m0029
DIV/1/14/256-m0082
DIV/3/12/09-4, 5, 12 and 36
Torre de Tombo:
 MNE CX 206
 MNE CX 207

Books and articles

Aitchison, John, *An Ensign in the Peninsular War: Letters of John Aitchison*, ed. W.F.K. Thompson (London 1981).

Allen, Douglas, 'Compatible incentives and the purchase of military commissions', *Journal for Legal Studies*, January 1998, vol. 27 (1), 45–66.

Alzaga, Henrique Williams, *Martin de Alzaga en la Reconquista y en la Defensa de Buenos Aires (1806–1807)* (Buenos Aires 1971).

Annual Biography and Obituary for the Year 1824 (London 1824).

Annual Register of World Events.

Anon., (by an Irish officer), *An authentic narrative of the Proceedings of the Expedition against Buenos Ayres under the command of Lieut. Gen. Whitelocke* (Dublin 1808).

Anon., *Journal of a soldier of the Seventy-First or Glasgow Regiment Highland Light Infantry from 1806–1815* (Edinburgh 1819).

Anon., *Memorandums of a Residence in France, in the winter of 1815–1816, Including Remarks on French Manners and Society, with a Description of the Catacombs, and Notices of Some Other Objects of Curiosity and Works of Art, not Hitherto Described* (London 1816).

Anon., *The personal narrative of a private soldier who served in the 42nd Highlanders for twelve years during the late war* (London 1821).

Anon., *Vicissitudes in the life of a Scottish soldier written by himself* (London 1827).

Anton, James, *Retrospect on a military life during the most eventful periods of the last war* (Edinburgh 1841).

Army List (for May 1815).

Aspinall, A. (ed.), *Later Correspondence of George III* (Cambridge University Press 1968).

Bamford, Andrew (ed.), *With Wellington's Outposts, The Peninsula and Waterloo Letters of John Vandeleur* (Barnsley 2015).

Barrés, Maurice (ed.), *Memoirs of a Napoleonic Officer. Jean-Baptiste Barrés* (London 1925).

Bartlett, Thomas & Jeffery, Keith, *A Military History of Ireland* (Cambridge 1996).

Beatson, F.C., *Wellington, the crossing of the Gaves and the battle of Orthez* (London 1925).

Beresford, Marcus de la Poer, *Marshal William Carr Beresford 'the ablest man I have yet seen in the army'* (Newbridge 2019).

Blakeney, Robert, *A boy in the Peninsular War. The Services, Adventures and Experiences of Robert Blakeney, subaltern in the 28th regiment* (London 1899).

Booth, John, *The Battle of Waterloo* (London 1816).

Brito, Antonio Pedro da Costa Mesquita, 'As Memorias de Militares Ingleses na Guerra Peninsular, como Fontes da Historia de Portugal Coetanea-Orientacao Bibliografica', *Revista Militar* 2009, 2489/2490.

Bromley, David & Janet, *Wellington's Men Remembered*, 2 vols (Barnsley 2015).

Brown, Steve, 'British losses in the Corunna campaign', *Napoleon Series*, October 2015.

Browne, John, *Transactions of the Kilkenny Archaeological Society*, vol. 1 (1850).

Bunbury, Charles J.F. (ed.), *Memoir and literary remains of Lieutenant-General Sir Henry Edward Bunbury, bart.* (London 1868).

Burke, Sir Bernard, *The General Armory of England, Scotland, Ireland and Wales* (London 1884).

Burnham, Robert & McGuigan, Ron, *The British Army against Napoleon, facts, lists and trivia 1805–1815* (Barnsley 2017).

Butler, Lewis, *Annals of the King's Royal Rifle Corps* (London 1923).

Cannon, Richard, *Historical Record of The Fourth, or Royal Irish Regiment of Dragoon Guards: containing an account of the formation of the Regiment in 1865, and of its subsequent services to 1838* (London 1839).

Cannon, Richard, *Historical Record of the Fifth or Princess Charlotte of Wales's Regiment of dragoon guards* (London 1839).

Cannon, Richard, *Historical Record of the 42nd or the Royal Highland Regiment of Foot* (London 1845).

Carew, Peter, 'A Gallant Pack', *Blackwood's Magazine*, 1946.

Challis, Lionel, 'Roll of British officers serving in the Portuguese army', *Journal of the Society for Army Historical Research*, Summer 1949, vol. 27 (110), 50–60.

Cobbett, William, *Cobbett's Weekly Political Register*, vol. XVIII, 1810.

Cole, John William, *Memoirs of British Generals during the Peninsular War* (London 1856).

Cole, Maud Lowry (ed.), *Memoirs of Sir Lowry Cole* (Uckfield 2014).

Colman, Oscar Tavani Perez, *Martinez de Fontes y la Fuga del General Beresford* (Buenos Aires 2005).

Colville, John, *The Portrait of a General* (Salisbury 1980).

Costa, Ernestina, *English Invasion of the River Plate* (Buenos Aires 1937).

Court Magazine & Monthly Critic, vol. 11, 1816.

Cowan, Paul, *With Wellington in the Peninsula: the adventures of a Highland soldier 1808–1814* (Barnsley 2015).

Craufurd, Alexander Henry, *General Craufurd and his light division, with many anecdotes, a paper and letters by Sir John Moore, and also letters from the Right Hon. W. Windham, the Duke of Wellington, Lord Londonderry and others* (London 1891).

Dalton, Charles, *The Waterloo Roll Call with biographical notes and anecdotes* (London 1904).

De Brito, Pedro, 'British Officers in the Portuguese service 1809–1820', available at: www.academia.edu.

De Brito, Pedro, 'Os Anglo-Irlandeses e o fiasco de Denis Pack em Salamanca (1812)', *XX Coloquio de Historia Militar – A Guerra Peninsular em Portugal (1810–1812) – Derrota e Perseguicao. A Invasao de Masséna e a Transferencia das Operacoes pra Espanha* (Lisbon 2011), vol. II.

D'Espinchal, Hippolyte, *Souvenirs Militaires 1792–1814* (Paris 1901).

Divry, Arnauld, *Les noms graves sur L'Arc de Triomphe* (Paris 2003).

Downman, Thomas, 'Diary of Major Thomas Downman R.H.A. in the Peninsula from 30 April 1811 to 17 August 1812', *Journal of the Society for Army Historical Research*, October–December 1926, vol. 5 (22), 178–86.

Doyle, Arthur, *A Hundred Years of Conflict being Some Records of the Services of Six Generals of the Doyle Family, 1756–1856* (London 1911).

Dublin Evening Post.

D'Urban, Benjamin, *The Peninsular Journal 1808–1817* (reprint London 1990).

Eaton, C.A., *Waterloo Days, the narrative of an Englishwoman resident in Brussels, June 1815* (London 1888).

Edwards, Peter, *Salamanca 1812. Wellington's year of victories* (Barnsley 2013).

Esdaile, Charles, *Peninsular Eyewitnesses, the experience of war in Spain and Portugal 1808–1813* (Barnsley 2008).

Fortescue, J.W., *The British Army and the Peninsular War* (reprint Uckfield 2004), vols V–X.

General Orders Spain & Portugal.

Gillespie, Alexander, *Gleanings and remarks collected during many months of residence in Buenos Ayres, and within the upper country* (Leeds 1818).

Girod de L'Ain, Maurice, *Vie Militaire du General Foy* (Paris 1900).

Glover, Gareth (ed.), *The Diary of William Gavin, Ensign and Quartermaster of the 71st Highland Regiment 1806–1815; being his daily notes of his campaigns in South Africa, South America, Portugal, Spain, southern France and Flanders, under Sir David Baird, Sir William Carr Beresford, Sir John Moore and the Duke of Wellington* (Huntingdon 2013).

Goff, G.L., *Historical Records of the 91st Argyllshire Highlanders* (London 1891).

Grattan, William, *Adventures with the Connaught Rangers, 1809–1814* (London 1902).

Graves, Donald E., *Dragon Rampant, The Welch Fusiliers at War, 1793–1815* (Barnsley 2010).

Graves, Revd James & Prim, Augustus John, *History of the Cathedral Church of St. Canice* (Dublin 1857).

Grehan, John, *The Lines of Torres Vedras, the cornerstone of Wellington's strategy in the Peninsular War 1809–12* (Barnsley 2015).

Halliday, Andrew, *Observations on the Present State of the Portuguese Army as Organised by Lieutenant-General Sir William Carr Beresford K.B.* (London 1811).

Hamilton, Anthony, *Hamilton's campaigns with Moore and Wellington during the Peninsular War* (New York 1847).

Haynes, Christine, *Our Friends the Enemies, the occupation of France after Napoleon* (London 2018).

Haythornthwaite, Philip, *The Iron Duke* (Washington 2007).

Haythornthwaite, Philip, *Picton's Division at Waterloo* (Barnsley 2016).

Highland Light Infantry Chronicle, 1905, 1914.

Hildyard, Henry J.T., *Historical record of the 71st regiment Highland light infantry, from its formation in 1777, under the title of the 73rd, or McLeod's Highlanders, up to the year 1876* (London 1876).

Historical Record of the Fifth or Princess Charlotte of Wales's Regiment of dragoon guards (London 1839).

Hope, James Archibald, *Campaigns with Hill and Wellington; The Reminiscences of an Officer of the 92nd – The Gordon Highlanders – in the Peninsula and at Waterloo, 1809–1816* (Leonaur 2010).

Hope, James, *Letters from Portugal, Spain and France during the memorable campaigns of 1811, 1812 and 1813 and from Belgium and France in the year 1815* (Edinburgh 1819).

Hope, James, *The military memoirs of an infantry officer 1809–1816* (Edinburgh 1833).

Hughes, Ben, *The British Invasion of the River Plate 1806–1807* (Barnsley 2013).

Instruccoes para a formatura, exercicio e movimentos dos regimentos de infanteria Por Ordem de Guilherme Carr Beresford, Marechal e Commandante em Chefe dos exercitos de Sua Alteza Real o Principe Regent de Portugal (Lisbon 1809).

James, Charles (ed.), *A collection of the charges, opinions and sentences of General Courts Martial as published by authority from the year 1795 to the present time* (London 1828).

Kermack, Balfour, 'A short sketch of the campaigns of Balfour Kermack, 71st regiment Highlanders (Light Infantry) from 1806 to 1814', *Highland Light Infantry Chronicle*, 1914, vol. XIV, 128ff.

Larpent, George (ed.), *The Private Journal of F.S. Larpent, Judge Advocate General of the British Forces in the Peninsula* (London 1853).

Leach, Lieutenant Colonel Jonathan, *Rough sketches of the life of an old soldier: during a service in the West Indies; at the siege of Copenhagen in 1807; in the Peninsula and the south of France in the campaigns from 1808 to 1814 with the Light Division; in the Netherlands in 1815; including the battles of Quatre Bras and Waterloo: with a slight sketch of three years passed by the army of occupation in France* (London 1831).

L'Estrange, George B., *Recollections of Sir George B. L'Estrange* (London 1874).

McGuigan, Ron & Burnham, Robert, *Wellington's Brigade Commanders, Peninsula & Waterloo* (Barnsley 2017).

McKenzie, Thomas Arthur et al. (eds)., *Historical records of the 79th Queen's own Cameron Highlanders* (London 1877).

Maclean, Donald (ed.), 'A Highland Soldier's Manuscript', *Celtic Review*, June 1916, vol. 10 (40), 289–311.

Malcolm, John, 'Reminiscences of a campaign in the Pyrénées and South of France in 1814', *Constable's Miscellany, Memorials of the late war*, 2 vols (Edinburgh 1827).

Malcolm, John, *Scenes of War and other poems* (Edinburgh 1828).

Malcolm, John, *Tales of Field and Flood; with sketches of life at home* (Edinburgh 1829).

Marbot, J.-B. Antoine Marcelin, *Mémoires du général baron de Marbot*, 3 vols (Paris 1891–2).

Marmont, Auguste Frederic, *Mémoires du Maréchal Marmont, Duc de Raguse de 1792 a 1841* (Paris 1857).

Mendo Castro Henriques, Antonio, *Salamanca, Companheiros de Honra* (Lisbon 2004).

Moody, T.W., McDowell, R.B. & Woods, C.J. (eds), *The Writings of Theobald Wolfe Tone, 1763–98* (Oxford 2007).

Muir, Rory, *Salamanca 1812* (Yale 2001).

Muir, Rory, *At Wellington's Right Hand, The letters of Lieutenant-Colonel Sir Alexander Gordon, 1808–1815* (Stroud 2003).

Muir, Rory, *Wellington, the path to victory* (Yale 2013).

Napier, William F.P., *History of the War in the Peninsula and the South of France from the year 1807 to the year 1814* (London 1828–40).

Napoleon Bonaparte, *Correspondence Générale*, vol. III Pacifications 1800–1802 (Paris 2006).

Napoleonica, La Revue (2014).

Naval & Military Gazette and Weekly Chronicle of the United Service.

Oatts, L.B., *Proud Heritage, the story of the Highland Light Infantry* (London 1952).

Oman, Charles, *A History of the Peninsular War*, 7 vols (Oxford 1902–30).

Oman, Charles, 'Courts Martial of the Peninsular War 1809–14', *Royal United Services Institution Journal*, 1912, 56 (418), 1699–1716.

Ordens do Dia do Illustrissimo e Excellentissimo Guilherme Carr Beresford (Lisbon 1809–14).

Pack-Beresford, Denis R., *A Memoir of Major-General Sir Denis Pack* (Dublin 1908).

Parnell, Henry, *On Financial Reform* (London 1830).

Proceedings of a General Court Martial held at Chelsea Hospital on Thursday January 28, 1808 and continued by adjournment, till Tuesday March 15, for the trial of Lieutenant-General Whitelocke, late Commander-in-Chief of the forces in South America, 2 vols (London 1808).

Reid, Stuart (ed.), [Joseph Sinclair], *Journal of a soldier of the Seventy-First or Glasgow Regiment of Highland Light Infantry from 1806–1815* (Barnsley 2010).

Reynolds, Luke, 'There John Bull might be seen in all his glory: cross-Channel tourism and the British Army of Occupation in France, 1815–1818', *Journal of Tourism History*, vol. 12, 2020.

Robson, Eric, 'Peninsula Private', *Journal of the Society for Army Historical Research*, 1954, vol. 32 (129), 4–14.

Roy, R.H., 'The memoirs of Private James Gunn', *Journal of the Society for Army Historical Research*, 1971, vol. 49, 90–120.

Saunders's News-Letter, 1822, 1823.

Siborne, H.T., *Waterloo letters, A collection of accounts from survivors of the campaign of 1815* (London 1844).

Siborne, William, *History of the war in France and Belgium in 1815* (London 1844).

Stanhope, James, *Eyewitness to the Peninsular War and the Battle of Waterloo, The letters and Journals of Lieutenant-Colonel James Stanhope* (Barnsley 2011).

Survey of London, Bartlett School of Architecture, University College, London (1913–2017).

Systema de Instruccao e Disciplina para os movimentos e deveres dos Caçadores por ordem do Illustrissimo e Excellentissimo Senhor G.C. Beresford, Marechal, Commandante en Chefe dos Exercitos de S.A.R. O Principe Regente nosso senhor (Lisbon 1810).

Thompson, Mark S. (ed.), *The Services of General Sir George Allen Madden* (Sunderland 2014).

Tomkinson, James, *Diary of a cavalry officer in the Peninsular and Waterloo campaigns 1809–15* (London 1840).

Verner, Willoughby, *History and Campaigns of the Rifle Brigade 1800–1813* (London 1919).

Veve, Thomas Dwight, *The Duke of Wellington and the British army of occupation in France, 1815–1818* (Westport, CT 1992).

Ward, S.G.P., 'Brenier's escape from Almeida, 1811', *Journal of the Society for Army Historical Research*, March 1957, vol. 35 (141), 23–35.

Ward, S.G.P., 'The Portuguese Infantry Brigades 1809–1814', *Journal of the Society for Army Historical Research*, 1975, vol. 53, 103–12.

Warre, William, *Letters from the Peninsula 1808–12* (London 1909).

Welch, Howard Terence, *A History of Kilkenny College, 1538–1903* (Trinity College Dublin, PhD thesis 2002).

Wellington, Field Marshal the Duke of, *The Dispatches of Field Marshal the Duke of Wellington during his various campaigns in India, Denmark, Portugal, Spain, the Low Countries and France*, compiled by John Gurwood, 8 vols and Index (London 1844–7). Cambridge University Press 2010 version (Cambridge Library Edition) used for references.

Wellington, Field Marshal the Duke of, *Supplementary Despatches Correspondence and Memoranda of Field Marshal Arthur, Duke of Wellington*, edited by his son, the Duke of Wellington (London 1857–80).

Wellington, Field Marshal the Duke of, *The General Orders of Field Marshal the Duke of Wellington in Portugal, Spain, and France from 1809 to 1814; in the Low Countries and France 1815; and in France, army of occupation 1816 to 1818* (2nd edition London 1837).

Whelan, Kevin & Bartlett, Thomas (eds), *Memoirs of Miles Byrne – 1798 in County Wexford* (Dublin 1998).

Government Publications.

Accounts and Papers of the House of Commons, vol. 13
A List of all the officers of the army and royal marines on full and half pay with an Index and a succession of colonels 1814 and 1816
Bulletins and Other State Intelligence (1800–1823)
Journal of the House of Lords
London Gazette
Parliamentary Papers, Estimates of Army Services for the year 1831
Royal Military Calendar or army service and commission book

Newspapers

Dutch Mail (1816)
Saunders's News-letter (1822)
Bath Chronicle and Weekly Gazette (1821)
Caledonian Mercury (1817)
Dickson Manuscripts
Dublin Evening Mail (1844)
Dublin Evening Post (1821)
Edinburgh Gazette (1821)
Edinburgh Magazine and Literary Miscellany (1822)
European Magazine and London Review, vol. 67
Evening Mail
Freeman's Journal (1837)
Gentleman's Magazine
The Globe
London Magazine
Morning Post
National Magazine and Dublin Literary Gazette, vol.2 (1831)
The Nineteenth Century (July 1912)
Royal Cornwall Gazette (September 1822)
The Sun (1821)
The Times (1820)
United Service Magazine, vol.28 (1838)
Waterford Chronicle (1838)

Internet sites

http://booty.org.uk/booty.weather/climate/histclimat.htm
www.findmypast.com
www.geni.com
www.revisionistas.com.ar
www.napoleon-series.org
https://www.wikipedia.com
https://www.oxforddnb.com

Index